Take Good Care of Yourself

Growing Older in Ireland

Geraldine Kenny

GILL & MACMILLAN

Gill & Macmillan Ltd
Goldenbridge
Dublin 8
with associated companies throughout the world
© Geraldine Kenny 1995
0 7171 2044 9
Index compiled by Helen Litton

Design and print origination by
O'K Graphic Design, Dublin

Printed by ColourBooks Ltd, Dublin

A catalogue record is available for this book from the British Library.

1 3 5 4 2

To my mother and in memory of my father, who died during the writing of this book

CONTENTS

SECTION III DIRECTORY

ACKNOWLEDGMENTS

I am appreciative of the support given by the Eastern Health Board during the writing of this book.

I am grateful to my partner, John, for his support and the time and freedom to produce the work. I thank my sons, Eoghan and Fergal, for their encouragement to 'hurry up, finish'.

SECTION I
NORMAL AGEING

──────────── CHAPTER 1 ────────────

ATTITUDES TO AGEING

While society is now aware of racism and sexism, it has yet to realise that ageism exists and is a powerful force. Ageism is people's mainly negative attitudes towards older people and growing old. It is underlaid by certain beliefs which lead to all older people being seen as the same rather than individuals in their own right. These negative myths can be used to draw a stereotyped picture of older people.

— Older people are sick and dependent and many are in need of care. They have no interest in sex and even if interested, which is frowned upon, are physically unable for it.

— Older people think more slowly and lose their ability to problem-solve and be creative. They cannot learn well or quickly, and in any case lack the interest.

— Older people are conservative and do not welcome new ideas. They become irritable and withdraw from life, awaiting death.

— Older people either detach themselves from family and friends or are a burden, in need of psychological and physical care.

Positive stereotyping occurs less often but is equally untrue. This portrays older people as attaching importance to close friendships, valuing companionship and exuding serenity. Old age is seen as a time of peace and tranquillity after the hard life of earlier years. Not all older people have had a hard life, and old age for some may mean illness, loss of loved ones, and poverty.

It is unclear when a person is 'old'. The term is traditionally taken to mean someone over sixty-five; old age can therefore refer to thirty-five years of a person's life. While it would be more sensible to divide this into three stages — say, those aged sixty-five to seventy-four, seventy-five to eighty-four, and eighty-five and over

1

— current research considers anyone over sixty-five as one group, and so 'older people' in this book will refer to anyone over this age.

Who holds these stereotypes of older people?
These positive and negative stereotypes are held in many cultures and by people of all ages.

In Eastern cultures, respect for old age is not universal but is based upon personal achievements, power or the skills that the person can offer. This respect is decreasing with industrialisation and urbanisation.

Studies in the USA among young people have found that negative attitudes towards older people exceed positive. An Irish study concentrating on fifteen- to nineteen-year-olds also discovered mostly negative images of older people, with 'cranky' and 'difficult to please' top of the list. Approximately one-third held positive views, 'interesting' and 'cheerful' being the most common descriptions.

Some older people who are coping successfully with ageing see it as a positive time in their lives. An older person's perception of her age is determined by her health and her involvement in productive activity. A sick person of sixty retired from work may see herself as old, while an eighty-year-old who is well and active either in work or recreations may see herself as middle-aged.

Stereotyping leads to older people being marginalised. Some of them accept the stereotype and change to conform to it by not doing things they could (taking exercise, studying, falling in love). Others distance themselves from ageing and other older people. They believe the stereotypes do not apply to themselves and their friends who are well, but are true of older people in general and those who are ill. They will say, 'I don't want to be with that group of old dodderers' of people who are the same age as themselves.

Professionals such as doctors, nurses and physiotherapists have all been found to give credence to the myths about older people. This can have significant consequences for their medical treatment. If pains or complaints are dismissed as due to age, they will not be fully investigated and remedied. If a professional with an ageist attitude is involved in the rehabilitation of someone who needs to become physically as fit as possible or to regain speech after a stroke, she may set lower goals or push the patient less hard than a younger person. Also, professionals involved in the health care of older people are dealing with the minority and on this basis form beliefs about all older people.

Did ageism exist in earlier times?

The popular view is that in earlier periods of history older people were treated more favourably by society. However, prejudice against age is not new. In ancient Greek and Roman times older people inspired ambivalence; while playing important roles in society, they were subject to literary satire. The respect once accorded to older people for their knowledge and experience was lost with the development of writing and the use of the printing press, and the resultant wide availability of books. This was especially true for those of higher status. Among the poor, when older people grew physically unable to look after themselves, they became a burden and ended their lives uncared-for and in poverty.

Throughout history physical attributes have been highly regarded. In the past, strength was highly prized; today, the great emphasis is on looking young.

Some recent historical changes have produced a social situation more unfavourable to older people. The first change was the agricultural and industrial revolution. The workplace and home were segregated. It was work or starve. Fixed retirement from work was introduced, and age rather than ability became the criterion for working. Also, the introduction of workhouses for old people led to age rather than capacity to work being the criterion for support from government.

The second change was the huge rise world-wide in the number of people surviving into old age. This is due to better nutrition throughout life, proper sewerage systems, inoculation programmes and the introduction of antibiotics. Older people are more numerous and therefore less special. In some countries people see the increasing numbers as threatening an increasing burden, with a smaller working population being required to support a growing body of retired people.

How is ageism passed from generation to generation?

There are several ways in which ageism is shaped by our day-to-day lives.

LANGUAGE

Language is a powerful method of constructing ageist attitudes. Common words and phrases referring to older people as 'old dears', 'old folk', 'pensioners', 'grannies', 'old biddies', 'dirty old men', all present very negative images of old age.

In a recent survey the term 'the elderly' was rejected by older people to describe themselves. The term favoured in Ireland was 'senior citizen'. In Australia, 'older people' was preferred when people of all ages were consulted.

LITERATURE

The stereotype of older people in books is important as throughout our lives we are influenced by the books we read. In schoolbooks and children's books older people are often portrayed as sick and needing help. Shakespeare, studied by many second-level students, presents a very negative view of old age.

In twentieth-century literature old age is dealt with rarely, and then in a pessimistic way, as in Kingsley Amis's novel *The Old Devils*.

EDUCATION

Adults should have statutory rights to education. Educational programmes for older people in day centres and residential facilities should offer not just bingo, crafts and a little keep-fit but a broader range.

There is also a need for education regarding ageing itself, e.g. health promotion, nutrition, courses for carers, stroke victims, etc.

Pre-retirement courses are not readily available and often come too late, just prior to retirement itself. The syllabuses for these courses should not perpetuate prejudice by presenting a view of increasing disabilities with age.

HUMOUR

Jokes about older people reflect the image of ageing as negative, with ageist jokes being especially derogatory to females. Birthday-card humour contains examples of ageism, often combined with sexism. Those designed to be sent to younger people of thirty-plus contain crude jokes about ageing and all its negative aspects — loss of hair, becoming fat, inability to perform sexually, while those for older people are sentimental and reassuring about not looking your age. Some examples are:

'The four ages of man: infancy, youth, adolescence and obsolescence.'

'Doctors say forty-year-olds can do it several times a month . . . or maybe it was several forty-year-olds can still do it once a month.'

'You're forty. Don't worry about getting old. You are old.'

'Sixty. Welcome to your new decade and all that goes with that decayed feeling.'

TELEVISION

Older people are largely absent from television. In Ireland, 11 per cent of the population is over sixty-five but people from this age-group do not appear in anything near this proportion on television. Research conducted on American and British television found that older people appeared more frequently in programmes concerned with the news, current affairs and documentaries, which is to be expected as many prominent world figures are in the older section of the population. In contrast, they were noticeably absent from plays, soap operas, action/adventure programmes, comedies, films, and educational and children's programmes. Although women are in a significant majority among the older population, they appeared less often than older men.

MAGAZINES AND NEWSPAPERS

Ageing tends to have a high profile in women's magazines. Topics include post-menopausal life, and the use of products to remain young-looking. In Britain, some magazines have been developed for older people — *Choice*, *The 50-Forward Club* and *Trust*. Because of the growth of the group, it is seen as having economic power. This can be both positive and negative. Business interests can contribute to a better old age by providing goods and services that make older people part of the economic community. However, this could lead to the impression that all older people are prosperous when there is great diversity in their income.

Older people appear in the newspapers. Leaving aside the obvious death announcements, they appear in news items, stories and features. In surveys of both the Irish and British papers, few of the news items were found to be about ageing directly; rather the age of the person was highlighted, often for novelty value. There was little published offering a more positive representation of older age. The issues addressed were mainly welfare and financial in nature.

Also, labels like 'pensioner', 'granny', 'widow' are frequently used for sympathy value. It would be best if age were mentioned only when it is necessary for an understanding of what is written. This applies to people of all ages, not just older people.

Can these stereotypes be changed?

The stereotypes must be challenged. We need to be aware of the existence of ageism and have strategies to combat it. Legislation is required to protect the right to employment of older people by eliminating discriminatory practices in the advertising and filling of jobs. Mandatory retirement should be abolished. Legislation is also needed to safeguard the property, money and physical safety of older people. A picture of ageing that is based on facts rather than myths is a starting-point. The facts of the physical, psychological and social aspects of ageing are presented in this book, where the picture that emerges is one of older people as healthy and active. On average, two out of three older Europeans are either very busy or leading full lives.

All the ways in which ageism is perpetuated need to be tackled, such as our use of language, the portrayal of older people in literature and in the media. One recent initiative in this regard is the National Council for the Elderly's publications for use in the classroom at primary and secondary level.

Two factors are essential in changing the stereotypes of old age. Firstly, a recognition that older people are a group of people in the age-band sixty-five to one hundred-plus, very varied health-wise, economically and socially. Secondly, the involvement of older people in the process of change. This must happen at an individual level as well as at a group level. In Ireland, some organisations have been formed to meet the needs of older people. The Active Retirement Association is for cultural and recreational activities. Age Alliance Ireland advances the economic and social interests of retired, older people. The specific needs of women are addressed by WOW (Wonderful Older Women).

Greater contact between generations helps to eliminate ageism. An Irish example is the older people (members of the Dún Laoghaire Active Retirement Association) who run a student canteen and oversee the library in return for educational facilities. In America, many older people provide educational and/or social support to children of all ages, promoting intergenerational contact and a more positive image of older people.

This age-group is as diverse as any other. While physical illness increases with age, many older people are fit and well. Ninety-five per cent live in the community, many independently in their own homes. Older people remain mentally alert and interested, capable of learning new things. Some may become angry or depressed at the changes that come with ageing, while others adapt and overcome losses and changes.

If you have had friends and/or close family relationships throughout life, this will continue in old age. If you have been independent, so you will remain.

This is the picture of ageing you can look forward to or may now be experiencing.

CHAPTER 2

FACTS ON AGEING

How many older people are there in Ireland?

In 1991, there were 402,924 people aged sixty-five years or older living in Ireland: 11.4 per cent of the population. This percentage is low compared to other European countries, due to our high rates of birth and emigration. However, those over sixty-five in the year 2020 are expected to reach 16 per cent. This is part of a world-wide trend of those over sixty being the fastest-growing section of the population. In Ireland between 1991 and 2021 the population of those over seventy-five is expected to rise by 30.5 per cent. The number of people over a hundred is also increasing — from thirty-one in 1984 to seventy-five in 1991. In 1993 one hundred people celebrated their hundredth birthday.

The ageing of a nation is a consequence of the higher standards of living, better nutrition and improved health care, particularly the control of infectious diseases in children. There are more older people in developed countries than in the least developed countries, where mortality and fertility are still high.

In Ireland, life expectancy at birth for women is seventy-seven years and for men seventy-two. This is the lowest in the European Community. For men here there has been no change in life expectancy for the last sixty years, while women have experienced real increases. At age sixty, an Irish man can expect to live to be seventy-seven and an Irish woman to be eighty-one. This means that there are more older women than men, with almost two women for every man in those over eighty.

The greatest concentration of older people is in the east of Ireland (Dublin, Kildare, Meath and Wicklow), with 32 per cent of those over sixty-five living there. This will increase while the numbers in the west will decline at least until the year 2006, a result of migration to the east in the last fifty years.

How many older people are married, single or separated?

In Ireland in 1991, 42 per cent of people over sixty-five were married and 35 per cent widowed. In the over-85 age-group 61 per cent were widowed, 70 per cent of these women. Twenty-two per cent of those over sixty-five were single, including almost a quarter of the men. Less than 1 per cent of older people were separated. Older people who never married, are separated or are widowed are more likely to live alone, which is more costly and may lead to isolation and/or loneliness.

What is the real financial situation of older people?

One of the myths about older people is that they are poor with a low standard of living. There is a newer view that older people are quite well off, go on holidays aimed at their age-group and can afford purpose-built private housing.

The term Woopie (Well-Off Older People) is used to describe this group. Just as Yuppies (Young Upwardly Mobile Professionals) do exist in the younger population, so do Woopies in the older. However, they are a small segment of people in a much larger group. A Woopie is likely to be a younger person, be male, have worked in a non-manual job and have an occupational pension; those who are well off in earlier life tend to bring these benefits with them into old age.

In Ireland, the population of people aged sixty-five and over living in poverty declined from 32 per cent in 1980 to 19 per cent in 1987, older people faring relatively well due to pension increases. In recent years, the real change in the Old Age Contributory Pension, although positive (1.5 per cent for one adult, 1.3 per cent for a couple), has been below the increase for other welfare payments. In 1990, the Old Age Contributory Pension was only 30 per cent higher than Unemployment Benefit, and there is little difference between the Old Age Non-contributory Pension and Long-term Unemployment Benefit. One-third of all people over sixty-five receive the non-contributory pension.

Are these payments adequate for people to live on?

Currently, the non-contributory pension is 90 per cent and the contributory 98 per cent of the adequacy rate set by the Commission on Social Welfare in 1986. One-third to a half of older people are on private pensions and so may be above this rate. In a recent survey, older Irish people were divided on the adequacy of their pension. Fourteen per cent saw it as completely adequate and 40 per cent as just about adequate, while 25 per cent saw it as somewhat inadequate and 20 per cent as very inadequate.

So some groups within the older population, such as the very old, a person living alone and those who depend exclusively on social welfare, may be poor. Many of these are women. Rural workers and the self-employed are also at risk because of low incomes in old age. Those who retire early spend more years in retirement on a low income. What is needed is a flexible approach to direct extra finance to those who need it. This may mean increased means-tested assistance for older people in need rather than pension increases for everyone. However, continued efforts should be made to bring all pensions at least up to the 'adequacy rate'.

Although there has been a reduction in the risk of poverty, the proportion of old people living in households in the bottom quarter of income is high relative to other age-groups: 30 per cent compared to 4 per cent of those aged forty-five to sixty-five and 7 per cent of those aged twenty-one to forty-four. In addition to their income, older people get non-cash state benefits (free travel on bus and train for all over sixty-six, and a free TV licence, Telephone Rental and Electricity Allowances subject to eligibility criteria), which represent 19 per cent of the money value of the non-contributory pension. Price concessions are available to older people for commercial reasons. Aer Lingus gives a discount on some flights to people over sixty. CIE Aran Ferry Services allows unrestricted free transport to all holders of a free travel pass. Irish Ferries offers some reduction but not in the high season. Bord Fáilte publishes a booklet on reduced-rate holidays for people over fifty-five.

Museums and heritage sites offer either free entry or a reduced admission rate. Many theatres have concessions for older people, as do some cinemas. Some reductions are available for greyhound-racing and horse-racing and at League of Ireland football clubs. The GAA admits people over sixty-six free of charge to their grounds, with the exception of reserved seats and All-Ireland finals. However, concessions based on age could be seen as ageist. Older people themselves would prefer to have the money paid to them (Eurobarometer 1993). Also, the fact that retired people are paying less tax can mean that, taking their pensions and cash benefits, their income compares favourably with other households.

According to a recent EC survey, people of all ages support making adequate provision for a decent standard of living for older people. The services are considered the responsibility of public authorities, to be financed by contributions in taxes.

Where do older people live?

Housing is a vital component of the living conditions of older people. Substandard housing may create or worsen health problems and thereby make continued living in the community more difficult. Lack of heat and insulation can be life-threatening. For some older people with disabilities, specially adapted housing may be needed for independent living.

The vast majority (92 per cent) of older people live in houses, flats or caravans in the community. Five per cent live in institutional facilities. Twenty-six per cent of people over sixty-five live alone in private households; this rises to 29 per cent for those over seventy. Of those living in the community, a small number are in sheltered housing (3,504 units) with a warden and/or alarm. The rest live in a variety of different types, ages and conditions of housing. There is a high level (80 per cent) of home-ownership among old people in Ireland; however, some live in poor-quality housing. A substantial number have inadequate heating, kitchen facilities and bathrooms, with lack of indoor water, flush toilet or bath/shower. Dampness has also been found to be a problem.

What are the housing options for older people?

Most older people want to remain living in the community and many want to remain in their own homes. What is needed is not separate housing but a range of environments that will support and maintain independence. This may mean small dwellings in good condition and well equipped. Whatever option is taken, the older person must be involved in the decision-making.

Staying put may involve repairs or modifications to the house. It may also mean getting a telephone or personal security alarm installed. Certain services might be required (meals-on-wheels, home-help/care attendant), and the cost of these can be a problem. Some help may be available through the Task Force on Special

Housing Aid, the Essential Repairs Grant Scheme and the Home Improvement Grant for Disabled Persons. Equity release schemes can provide additional income while reserving to the owner the right to use the house for the remainder of her life. However, none of the Irish building societies or banks currently offers such an option.

A possibility for some people unable to remain in their own homes is to seek places in sheltered housing. This includes the schemes built by voluntary housing associations, some of which are rented to relatively active older people, others of which provide on-site care supports (preparation of meals, assistance with cleaning, bathing). Sheltered housing is also supplied by Local Authorities and private developers. At a minimum, all schemes have built-in alarms or a communication facility. The number of older people living in sheltered housing is very small and the number of places provided is inadequate.

What are the housing needs of older people?

Older people are different ages with different needs for autonomy and different economic levels, and this needs to be reflected in a wide variety of housing choices. For some people this will mean the upkeep, improvement and/or adaptation of their own homes. Others will choose to move to a single-storey small building. Some will opt for housing where only other older people live, while others prefer an environment with a mix of ages.

Given sufficient information and finances, older people should be able to make a choice about their housing.

CHAPTER 3

PHYSICAL ASPECTS OF NORMAL AGEING

A. SENSORY CHANGES WITH AGEING

HEARING

Because hearing difficulty is not obvious, it can be mistaken for stupidity, lack of concentration, bad manners, stubbornness or even dementia.

The person with hearing problems may feel upset and excluded by people's reactions. Remarks like 'It doesn't matter, it's not worth repeating' can be frustrating and hurtful. Mishearing words can cause misunderstanding which may be puzzling or funny to other people; this can erode confidence. Complete deafness may lead to isolation unless family and friends and the deaf person make efforts to communicate.

Hearing loss increases as we age, due to changes in the brain. The exact location and type of changes, along with disease or damage to the ears, will determine the particular hearing level of a person as she ages. These changes begin at the age of thirty but we adapt to them gradually and they may become noticeable only in old age.

Hearing impairment can result in an individual becoming detached from people and her surroundings. Shopping and social outings are difficult and may eventually be avoided. It can also affect a person's emotional functioning and lead to depression. Even a mild impairment may interfere with a person's ability to recognise and remember words. It can be difficult for someone living with the hearing-impaired person: the radio or television may be too loud for comfort; clarifying misunderstandings and repeating conversations require a lot of patience.

What is tinnitus?

Tinnitus is a hearing problem in which there is a sensation of noise (humming, ringing or buzzing) in the head or ears lasting for more than a few minutes. It can happen occasionally or frequently or be continuous. It may cause no annoyance or be very disturbing. Tinnitus can interfere with concentration, communication and sleep, and cause anxiety. It affects people of all ages, those with normal hearing as well as those who are deaf and hard of hearing.

Tinnitus is a symptom of sensory or neural disease of the ear, disease of the brain, and other diseases including thyroid gland disease, anaemia or hypertension. As these all increase as we age, approximately 30 per cent of the elderly will report tinnitus. Tinnitus can occur as a side-effect of some drugs, such as tranquillisers, quinine or large amounts of painkillers.

What help is available for tinnitus?

Many people become used to tinnitus, especially if they are reassured that it does not indicate a brain tumour or that they are going mad. If you find tinnitus is interfering with your life see your GP, who will check for wax, drug side-effects and any other diseases. She may refer you to an ear, nose and throat (ENT) specialist for further investigation. If no curable cause is found, aids may help.

A masking device is effective. Worn like a hearing-aid, it produces a quiet gentle sound which helps mask the tinnitus. A hearing-aid may be necessary if there is also hearing loss. Relaxation therapy can be beneficial if stress or anxiety are making the problem worse.

What do the age changes mean for everyday life?

After the age of thirty it becomes more difficult to localise where sound is coming from.

There is a gradual decline in sensitivity to sound, which is most pronounced for high-pitched sounds (presbycusis). This affects our ability to understand what is said. Consonants are more difficult to hear; the lower pitch of vowel sounds makes them easier to identify. However, it is consonants which are needed in order to distinguish words. This difficulty increases in noisy circumstances so it will be harder to hear someone speak if the TV or music is playing or in a pub situation. If the pace of a conversation is quick it will also affect the ability to understand. Traffic and footsteps can be heard quite well but sounds such as a flute or a kitten's miaow may not be heard. A man's voice will be heard more clearly than a woman's.

Another change in hearing with age is that loud sounds may be painfully loud and moderately loud sounds heard at a higher level. Quiet sounds may not be heard at all or may be heard at a level of normal loudness; the latter problem can be aggravated by a hearing-aid because it amplifies the sound.

Hearing may be variable, better on some days than others. This can lead to relatives believing that the person 'can hear when she wants to'.

If you have difficulty in understanding speech in situations in which other people have no difficulty, see your GP and have it investigated. You may only need wax removed from your ears or you may need other forms of help.

Do many older people have hearing loss?

Thirty per cent of people aged sixty-five to seventy-four and 50 per cent of those between seventy-five and seventy-nine have hearing problems. In all, approximately one-third of people over sixty-five have difficulty in hearing what is said to them.

Ways to help

The amount of hearing loss that constitutes a handicap to the individual depends not only on the loss itself but on the environment and how the message is conveyed.

If, speaking to someone with a hearing impairment, you mumble or talk too quickly, you may be difficult to understand, and shouting causes distortion. Speak slowly and clearly and not too loudly. It also helps if you sit at the same level and face to face so that lip-reading can be used. Distance, the clarity and volume of your voice, other distractions (noise) and the acoustics of the room all affect the person's ability to hear you.

A room in which sound reverberates is disadvantageous for a person with a hearing-aid. Hard wall and floor surfaces reflect the sound; thick carpet and curtains will improve the ability to hear in that room. Some people find that background noise makes speech more difficult to hear while others hear better with background noise.

A hearing-aid is not usually considered for an older person as gradual hearing loss is often thought of as 'normal' in her. Even when a hearing-aid is available it may not be used. There are several reasons for this: for instance, hearing-aids are still unable to discriminate successfully between speech and background noise, and the ear-piece may be difficult to insert.

If you yourself experience a hearing loss, you have to be assessed to ascertain the type of hearing-aid best suited to your needs. If you are a medical-card holder you will be supplied with one free through one of the centres run by the National Rehabilitation Board. If you do not have a medical card you can obtain an aid through one of the hearing-aid suppliers listed in the Golden Pages. You can claim back 50 per cent of the cost, up to a maximum of £200, through the Department of Social Welfare. Hearing-aids cost from £300 upwards. Most aids are worn over the ear. A mould is taken for the ear-piece and you return for the fitting.

It is preferable to have any impairment investigated as early as possible, so that if you do benefit from a hearing-aid, you can adapt to the new types of sound and keep your social contact with family and friends. You will also get used to handling the ear mould and the batteries. Getting accustomed to a hearing-aid takes time; it is also important that it is maintained properly.

Many people with hearing loss will complain of difficulty hearing the television, radio, doorbell or telephone. There are technical appliances to help with these problems. The National Association for the Deaf (see Directory) provides information and demonstrations, and can order any equipment you require.

Alarms and alert appliances are available for domestic use — for the doorbell and telephone, baby and smoke alarms — and either flash lights or vibrate. Another category of technical appliances is for television and hi-fi equipment. There are different systems for amplifying the TV: some using a headphone, others cordless, some which can be linked to a hearing-aid and/or to a sound system. You can buy a TV with Teletext on it, pages of written information and subtitles on programmes. Check that your video can record teletext subtitles. There is an adapter which will allow you to watch videos with subtitles. Many videos for hire are available with subtitles.

There are devices available to amplify the telephone, some with a hearing-aid and others without. There is also a text telephone, with a keyboard and display screen. These are available from your local Telecom Éireann office. A list of phones and attachments for deaf and hard-of-hearing people appears in the telephone directory.

Deaf people are entitled to reclaim the VAT on aids purchased.

The National Association for the Deaf sells the item without VAT, then reclaims the tax.

VISION

Vision is a very important factor in our ability to cope effectively with our environment. Our work, performance of everyday tasks (washing, cooking), social life and mental well-being depend largely on vision.

Do changes occur in the eye and vision with age?

Fortunately, most older people will not experience severe visual problems. Normally, the effects of ageing on sight are gradual and can be compensated for to some degree.

Clarity and detail in our vision (acuity) decreases with age, at least after sixty. With frequent changes of prescription for glasses and good light this is not a problem for most older people. The ability to focus on something near also declines (presbyopia), making it difficult to read. This becomes noticeable between the ages of forty and fifty. Bifocal glasses take care of the problem.

The amount of light needed to see increases with age, so it is necessary to increase the level of light in your work and home environment. Glare results from light that is too bright or pointing in the wrong direction; from the age of forty-five you will probably become more sensitive to it and take longer to recover, especially if you have cataracts on your eyes.

The total area over which you can see is important (to the side and up and down, as well as straight ahead), especially for routine activities such as driving a car. This area decreases, most noticeably in the lower portion of your vision, after the age of sixty.

Adapting to seeing in the dark is harder for older people, particularly those over sixty. This has practical significance for driving at night.

Changes in the ability to perceive colour are part of the ageing process and begin around twenty years of age. The most obvious deterioration is in the ability to discriminate between blues and greens. This could, for example, create confusion if you were taking medication with one kind of tablet blue and the other green.

The quantity of tear secretion decreases with age, reducing the lubrication and thus increasing the tendency towards infection and dryness of the eyes. A replacement solution is available from your pharmacy. The eye loses some of its brightness as it ages. A greyish-yellow ring may appear gradually around the coloured part (iris). Our ability to see is also influenced by changes in the nerves from the eye to the centres of perception in the brain.

Although not due directly to the ageing process, some medical problems affecting vision are more prevalent among older people. The most common are glaucoma, cataract, retinal disease (internal back of the eye) and corneal disease (covering at the front of the eye).

Glaucoma is an excess of fluid causing increased pressure within the eye. This condition often goes unnoticed until the person has 'tunnel vision' — seeing only out of the centre of the eye with loss of vision at the sides. With glaucoma that begins gradually you may feel your eyes are watering, have difficulty reading, suffer occasional headaches or clumsiness. If the glaucoma comes on suddenly you will have clouded vision and pain in your eye. It can be treated by laser, eye-drops and medication. Tell any doctor you attend that you have glaucoma, as some drugs can cause damage. Any impairment arising from glaucoma will be permanent but the progression of the condition can be halted. Screening can be carried out before the vision is affected, and if you have a relative with glaucoma you should have your eyes checked at least yearly.

Cataract is due to pathological changes in the lens of the eye. It will result in blurred vision, difficulty reading and/or night driving, and eventual blindness. The pupil of the eye will in time look grey-white. It can be corrected by surgically removing the lens. The person will then need to wear glasses or preferably contact lenses, or have a lens implanted in the eye. Cataracts affect up to 80 per cent of people aged sixty-five and over.

Disease of the retina and a part of it called the macula can lead to difficulties in reading or watching television but the person can generally see well enough to walk around her environment. A diabetic may also develop retinal problems. These can be helped by laser treatment. A person with high blood pressure should have her eyes checked regularly.

Disease of the cornea causes obscuring or loss of vision due to clouding or scarring of the cornea. It is treated with medication; in cases of severe damage a transplant of the cornea of a dead person can be performed. There is a good chance of vision being restored.

What are the consequences of visual problems?

Visual disability can reduce quality of life and personal independence. Early signs of an impairment include difficulties in reading, writing, watching television. The person may find she is less able to walk about, and fear of falling may increase. It will be harder to recognise faces. The person may not be able to shop, which can lead to poor eating habits and a deterioration in health. She may be less inclined to go out and meet friends, and so can become isolated.

What help is available?

For most people experiencing loss of vision an improvement can be achieved.

If you find reading has become difficult, glasses and increased light will usually enable you to read comfortably. Have the prescription reviewed regularly and then wear the glasses!

In general, the level of light needs to be increased as you age. However, you must avoid glare by placing lights carefully and ensuring they are the correct level of brightness.

If you have any of the problems associated with the eye diseases discussed above, see your GP immediately.

If, following assessment and treatment, you have a significant visual impairment, the National Council for the Blind (see Directory) can offer various types of help.

— A team of social workers, mobility and technical staff can respond with counselling, advice and training. This team is supported by local volunteers.
— Training can be given in daily living skills of mobility — 'how to get around' — and home and personal management.
— For those with poor sight, a Low Vision Aids Clinic provides and trains a person in the use of a magnifying aid.
— An Equipment Centre caters for both visually impaired and blind people with a wide range of equipment, including a talking watch, clock or calculator. An easy-to-see watch is also available. There are many games (draughts, chess), and large-print playing cards.
— Large-print books can be obtained at your local public library. The National Council for the Blind has a lending collection of Talking Books on tape, which can be sent by post. If you are blind you can be taught Braille (a raised-dot system of reading and writing); there is also a Braille library.

— A volunteer reader of second- and third-level books is available.

TASTE, TOUCH AND SMELL

Much less is known about taste and smell. The number of taste-buds decreases with age. Our sensitivity to taste may decline, especially for sweet foods, though this appears to be less severe than the decline in hearing and vision. There is no clear evidence on changes in smell. There is some evidence that sensitivity to touch declines after middle age.

B. PHYSICAL CHANGES WITH AGEING

One of the myths about older people is that they are dependent, in need of care and die from diseases that occur in old age. Each of these is untrue, as the statistics demonstrate (see Tables 1–3).

First we look at the physical aspects of ageing. Why we age is unknown but there are two schools of thought. One holds that human cells become damaged with age, causing the cells to function less efficiently. The other theory is that our genetic code programmes are ageing.

The pumping capacity of the heart decreases. Coronary atherosclerosis (narrowing and loss of elasticity of the arteries) is common as we age but can be prevented by controlling diet, weight and blood pressure, and taking regular exercise.

The amount of air the lungs breathe in declines with age. There are changes in the rib-cage and loss of muscle. The result is a greater susceptibility to chest infections.

As we age, our kidneys decrease in size and efficiency. This is important in cases of dehydration and also affects tolerance of drugs or combinations of drugs.

The liver also reduces in size, and liver function may be impaired. This has implications for the prescribing of certain drugs.

The digestive system shows little change with age. Food takes longer to go through the system, and when combined with inadequate fluid intake this can cause constipation.

With ageing, bones become weaker and less dense, due in part to loss of calcium. You are therefore more vulnerable to fractures. Some older people, particularly women after the menopause, are likely to develop osteoporosis, which can lead to loss of height and a round back or 'dowager's hump'. Osteoporosis is more of a risk if you have taken certain types of drugs. It is made worse by lack of movement, smoking and excessive alcohol consumption. A diet rich in protein and calcium helps to prevent osteoporosis. Hormone replacement therapy may also be prescribed.

Over time, your skin loses its ability to retain water. It also loses its strength and elasticity and fat from beneath the skin, as well as becoming less oily. It will appear to sag and wrinkle. The skin is now more susceptible to pressure and can develop ulcers. It is more prone to crack and to be infected. Skin heals more slowly as we grow older.

The amount and strength of muscle declines with age, but less so in someone who is physically active. As a consequence of the degeneration of stronger muscle fibres after the age of sixty, the strength of people over seventy is at least 20 per cent less than that of younger adults. If regular physical activity is maintained, loss of strength and power is minimised.

Regular exercise is crucial to physical fitness at any age, yet exercise in old age is often regarded as unnecessary. As people get older, the gap between what exercise they can do and what they actually undertake widens — what is known as 'the fitness gap'. Some of this is culturally determined, with exercise in old age seen as inappropriate. While biological ageing is responsible for small reductions in physical functioning, most people's functioning deteriorates much faster because they are not staying fit. It has been shown that even people who begin to exercise in old age can benefit, with increased muscle strength, power, stamina and joint suppleness. If you are worried about your ability to undertake regular exercise, see your GP or physiotherapist, who can advise you on the safety of exercise and any steps you can take to reduce risk.

Aim to walk for an hour a day, in various activities including walking and climbing stairs. Stamina can be built up by two or three weekly sessions of brisk walking or swimming for twenty to thirty minutes. Playing bowls or golf, ballroom dancing or gardening will keep you as fit as walking, swimming or cycling, and are sufficient to maintain strength in the legs of an older person. Suppleness can be improved by simple stretching exercises. Exercise only to a degree of pleasant tiredness. While these guidelines are appropriate for a healthy older person, if you are very unfit or in ill health you will need more specialist advice. A major survey in Britain found that 45 per cent of men and 79 per cent of women aged between sixty-five and seventy-four were not fit enough to sustain continuous normal-paced walking. They judged their level of fitness to be higher than it was in reality.

Some older people do not show these declines in physical functioning. While we do not know what causes ageing, our genes play a role, so if you want to live a long healthy life pick your grandparents and parents. After that, watch your diet, exercise regularly, live in a healthy environment, and be well off.

Are older people dependent and in need of care?

The vast majority of older people live independent lives, with 80 per cent of them not in need of any care except short-term, when ill. Most pursue healthy independent lives in the community. Of the remaining 20 per cent, half are dependent at a medium-to-high level in the physical (dressing, washing, eating food) and/or psychological (intellectual and emotional functioning) areas, and most need help with activities of daily living (shopping, preparing meals, housekeeping, use of telephone and public transport). According to figures from Europe, getting up or going to bed, feeding and washing oneself is in general impossible for less than 10 per cent, even among the very old.

Table 1 Activities with which older people experience no difficulty

	Men aged			Women aged		
	65–69	70–79 %	80+	65–69	70–79 %	80+
Getting on or off a bus	63	59	33	60	39	18
Climbing a flight of stairs	72	64	35	70	52	24
Walking half a mile	77	74	40	74	55	26
Taking a bath without help	80	75	45	83	62	28
Dressing without help	92	88	73	92	82	60
Hearing easily	86	81	58	90	83	62
Seeing, reading a newspaper	87	84	64	87	78	56

(Whelan & Vaughan 1982)

Table 1 shows that many older people continue day-to-day activities without difficulty. If someone cannot perform a particular activity she should not be viewed as disabled and requiring total care; rather she should be considered in need of a certain degree of specific help.

As these figures make clear, the majority of older Irish people are able to carry out the day-to-day tasks. Where difficulties arise they are specific; dependency in one activity does not necessarily mean dependency in another. A person could be able to dress herself but unable to go to the shops and buy food. In fact, what are seen as 'problems of the elderly' and attributed to all those over sixty-five are more prevalent in the older age-groups, especially in people over eighty-five.

Table 2 Household tasks which older people (65+) can do with no trouble

Task	%
Washing and tidying up	81
Washing floors or cleaning windows	44
Making a cup of tea	90
Preparing a hot meal	67
Doing own laundry	50
Shopping for groceries	63

(Whelan & Vaughan 1982)

A substantial majority of older Irish people can do light household work (see Table 2). A little more than half had some difficulty in doing heavier jobs — washing a floor, cleaning windows or doing laundry.

Dependency that arises with ageing and ill health must be viewed not just on an individual level but in terms of:
— social and economic policy: the type of residential care offered and the money to buy care
— professional and institutional practices: the type and range of options offered to people who are dependent in one way or another.

The needs for care of older dependent people are examined in Chapter 10.

What diseases do older people have and eventually die from?
Sixty-seven per cent of older Irish people rate their health as good or very good.

The most common illnesses are those affecting the muscular

skeletal system (arthritis), the respiratory system (chest, breathing problems) and the cardio-vascular system (heart and related problems). In old age, people are more likely to have more than one illness. These diseases are not confined to old age; they can occur at any age and often begin in earlier life.

Older Irish people die of chronic diseases, some related to personal habits (smoking, drinking, being overweight). A significant number die from accidents or injuries which could be prevented.

Table 3 Causes of death in Ireland 1991

	Age		% of people over 65
	65–74	75+	
Heart disease	3,707	8,589	50
Cancer	2,276	2,860	21
Pneumonia	261	1,681	8
Accident/Injury/Poisoning	243	544	2

(Census 1991)

Older people account for the majority (94 per cent) of deaths from pneumonia, which can be treated by antibiotics if diagnosed early. See your GP promptly if you have a chest problem, as pneumonia can develop quickly in an older person.

C. SLEEP

As people get older, general satisfaction with sleep tends to decline. Many complain about difficulty falling asleep, frequent or lengthy awakening at night and early-morning waking. Approximately 30 per cent of older people have sleep difficulties or insomnia, in that they feel they do not get enough sleep and are distressed by the lack of it. The next day they feel fatigued, moody, unable to concentrate.

Are there changes in sleep due to ageing?
As you age, sleep becomes
— more broken, with more awakenings, approximately five, of longer duration than in younger people
— lighter, in that it will take less noise to waken you

— shorter, with 5.75 hours at ninety years being average.

Older people nap more during the day, though not necessarily those who sleep less at night. Taking this into account, older people in general sleep less. While staying asleep is more difficult, getting to sleep is less frequently a problem, although it may take longer. Older people tend to spend longer in bed in the morning, perhaps trying to make up for the sleep lost during the night.

What influences sleep?
There are two groups of influences on sleep, those inside the body and those in the environment.

INFLUENCES INSIDE THE BODY
These are not common and may affect only a very small number of older people.

One of the awakenings may be to pass urine, as the need to do so at night increases with age.

Some people suffer from short periods of sleep apnoea — absence of breathing. Such periods are normal but if you have them too frequently you won't find sleep refreshing.

Movements of the limbs can cause problems. Night-time muscle spasms or twitches may disturb sleep. 'Restless leg syndrome' is where you have an uncomfortable sensation like pins and needles or bugs crawling deep inside your calf muscles. This is relieved by vigorous movements of the legs and you may feel you have to stand up and walk around. You should be checked for anaemia since the syndrome is sometimes associated with iron deficiency. Cramps are particularly common in older people and may interfere with sleep.

Any condition that causes pain (arthritis, chest or back pain) can disturb sleep.

A person who is severely depressed will have a sleep problem, tending especially to waken early in the morning. If you have anxious thoughts you may lie awake at night and have difficulty in switching off.

A person who has dementia sleeps less deeply, is more likely to awaken at night and much more likely to nap during the day. The night-time awakening may be associated with wandering. The sleep problems correspond in severity to the degree of general impairment, and are particularly difficult for carers.

Some medicines may contribute to sleep problems. Diuretics ('water tablets') are among the most common of all medicines prescribed for older people. If this drug is not taken at the correct time it will lead to the need to urinate during the night and thus disturb sleep. Some of the medicines used to treat high blood pressure (hypertension) can cause disturbed sleep. If you are withdrawing from sleeping-tablets, your sleep may be disturbed.

INFLUENCES OUTSIDE THE BODY
These include your level of activity and the environment you live in. Regular moderate exercise has been shown to help sleep. A lack of physical or mental activity may lead to insomnia.

If you feel insecure in your surroundings — perhaps following a bereavement or a burglary — this can cause sleep problems.

If you are too hot or too cold it will interrupt your sleep. A comfortable bed is also important. Noise may contribute to interrupted sleep.

If you are out of your familiar environment your sleep pattern may worsen, e.g. in hospital, where a high level of noise can compound difficulties.

What help is available?

Firstly, any of the influences on sleep within the body or in the environment need to be examined and remedied. You must understand the changes in sleep that happen with ageing — the amount of sleep required decreases and sleep becomes lighter and more broken.

Remember that you cannot force sleep.

In general, it is preferable to manage sleep disturbances without medication, especially for an older person. The use of sleeping-tablets rises with age; surveys show that they are taken regularly by at least 10 per cent of the older population. This rate is even higher for older people in institutional care.

Sleeping-tablets do increase the amount of time a person sleeps and decrease awakening. However, the effects of the most usual type of sleeping-tablet (benzodiazepines) are short-lived, as after some time (two to three weeks) of continuous use they may lose their ability to help you sleep. Long-term use of sleeping-tablets may produce unwanted side-effects, particularly as an older person is more prone to the toxic effects of medications. Some of the sleeping-tablets can cause daytime drowsiness, confusion at night and lowered mental functioning. Do not suddenly stop taking sleeping-tablets; you must reduce intake gradually under medical supervision.

There are certain good habits that can improve or maintain sleep quality. They can be used alone or along with some of the relaxation methods outlined below.

The older you are the more important it is to have a regular time for going to bed and getting up. If you have a nap, take it at a regular time too; don't nap out of boredom.

Check your bed and bedroom. Is the bed comfortable? A sagging mattress can lead to aches and pains in your joints during the day. The bedclothes should be as light as possible while still giving warmth; a duvet may be more suitable. The room needs to be neither too hot nor too cold. If it is noisy — directly over the TV room or where there is a lot of street disturbance — you may need to change it. If this is not possible — e.g. for someone in a nursing home — the background noise from a fan can mask the disturbing sound. If all else fails, try ear-plugs. Light can be a problem in a shared room; changing lights from the centre to spot- or table-lamps can overcome this.

While there is controversy regarding the best bedtime drink, it is better not to take stimulants such as tea and coffee near to bedtime. A snack is permissible, but not of spicy and high-protein food (e.g. meat). While alcohol does help you get to sleep, it leads to lighter and interrupted sleep.

It is best to avoid physically and/or mentally exacting activities in the late evening. A 'wind-down' routine is helpful — for instance, preparing for bed, locking up the house, putting the dog out, preparing for breakfast.

There are particular psychological approaches to managing sleep problems.

The first involves strengthening the relationship between your bed/bedroom and sleep, and weakening any association between your bed/bedroom and non-sleeping (reading, listening to music). While this may not have caused the insomnia, it can lead to it continuing. In practice, this means going to bed only when sleepy. If you have not fallen asleep within fifteen minutes leave the bedroom, returning only when sleepy. Do not use the bedroom for anything other than sleep (reading, eating, worrying). Get up at a regular time regardless of the amount of sleep you have had. Avoid daytime naps, and if one has to be taken, take it in the morning. Follow a pre-bedtime routine. You will need to do this for at least two weeks to see any results.

The second approach involves learning a method of relaxation.

There are several ways to relax, including:

(1) **Breathing:** Deep rhythmic breathing is the simplest relaxation technique, and is often part of other techniques.

(2) **Progressive muscular relaxation:** A very common technique, this requires you to tense specific muscle groups, then release the tension to become deeply relaxed.

(3) **Yoga:** The goal of yoga is to enable you to control the body and mind and deal with the tension/stress in this way.

(4) **Visualisation:** This is used to focus the mind on positive images. You could imagine a peaceful scene or tension flowing out of muscle groups. This is often used in conjunction with progressive muscular relaxation.

Some people successfully combine a relaxation method with the first approach of strengthening the association between bed/bedroom and sleep.

While these approaches concentrate on helping a person get to sleep, they can also improve the quality of sleep.

The third psychological approach is to help a person deal with anxious, depressing or worrying thoughts. She needs to identify them and then problem-solve during the day rather than doing it in bed at night. If the worry is about not sleeping itself, it is helpful to relax and not to force sleep, concentrating on calming thoughts.

Overcoming sleep problems in older people may be a matter of education for some, while others need medical problems treated or changes in their environment. Some will benefit from a short course of sleeping-tablets, while more could benefit from one or more of the psychological approaches.

If a sleep problem is leaving you fatigued and unable to function in your everyday life, there is a lot that may help, so do not accept that nothing can be done.

D. SEXUALITY

Are older people interested in and able to have sex?
Two generations ago, sexuality was not a problem for older people,

as they did not live much past child-bearing age. As people began living longer, the myths of older people being uninterested and incapable of sexual activity developed in society. Adolescents think their parents are no longer sexually active and these middle-aged parents think the same of their older parents. This view is often held until a person faces her own ageing. If you, as an older person, experience sexual interest and arousal, you may either deny these feelings or be concerned that they are not normal or moral. Older people vary in their views of how appropriate sexual fulfilment is to them.

Society's attitude to sex for younger people has been changing with the use of contraceptives, as it became possible to separate sex from child-bearing. Women now know more about their bodies and what they enjoy, while men have become more interested in satisfying their partners. The latest change in attitude towards sexuality stems from awareness of the HIV virus and AIDS. Yet society's attitude to sex in older people remains negative, in part because they are considered physically unattractive and therefore sexually undesirable. It is also seen as inappropriate since they are supposedly physically fragile. Older people who claim to be sexually active are regarded as 'dirty' or 'boastful'. The association of sex with youth and beauty, especially for women, has given the impression that sex is not for the disabled or the older person. This can lead to sexual satisfaction being linked with beauty and physical capability. Comparisons with traditional societies reveal Western culture to have the most negative view of sexuality in older people.

Sex, at any age, is not essential, but it can contribute to the quality of life. Sexuality has many facets. It can mean the ability to see oneself as a sexual being, who is still attractive to the opposite sex. For most people it is part of a relationship within which the intimacy of touching and being held is a special aspect. Sexual activity, and particularly genital sexuality, may or may not be an element in the intimacy. The attitudes and experiences you have had of intimacy and sex will colour how you approach sex in old age. Also important is correct information about the normal changes ageing brings, and the effects on sexual functioning. These should not be seen as failure or deterioration but as physical changes to which you can adapt.

Research has shown that older people remain interested and active sexually into their nineties. If you have enjoyed a long and fairly frequent sex life, without extensive breaks, you are more likely to remain interested and active than people of the same age who have not had a similar experience. Having a partner, and one in reasonable health to have sex, is clearly a significant factor — particularly for women, as they live longer and tend to marry men two to three years older. A woman can be without a male partner for eight or nine years at the end of her life. It is also more socially acceptable for men to have younger partners. One major study (Starr & Weiner 1981) found that 30 per cent of women were not in a sexual relationship, while only 7 per cent of men were not sexually active. The average frequency of sexual relations in the older American population was 1.40 per week (women 1.39 and men 1.44). Other American research (Brecher 1984) found that 65 per cent of women and 79 per cent of men over the age of seventy were sexually active.

Intercourse is not the only form of sexual activity, and masturbation is practised by older people, more by those who are without a partner. Women continue to masturbate throughout their lives, while men report a decline. This was true for women whether they were married, widowed, divorced or single. Older people may define and express their sexuality in more varied ways.

What sexual changes take place in men?

The physical changes begin for men in mid-life, and the timing and extent of change will vary from one to another. In general, it will take older men longer to get an erection (e.g. five to six minutes in a 75-year-old). The erection is less firm. Often, an older man will require more touching of the penis before an erection is achieved. He takes longer to reach ejaculation, orgasm may be shorter and a second orgasm may not be possible for an increasingly long period. Men also report that they no longer want an orgasm every time they have sex. The amount of semen reduces with age, as does the number of sperm. A man is capable of fathering children whatever his age. Because arousal is slower, the older man is likely to spend more time in foreplay or 'pleasuring' and can have intercourse for longer without having orgasm.

Being mentally or physically tired, being sick, eating or drinking too much, taking certain medicines and being anxious or bored will have a greater effect on the older man's sexual response than on a younger man's.

If a man or his partner does not know of or understand these normal changes, it may cause anxiety about sex. Anxiety at any age will lead to more difficulty in getting and maintaining an erection, in turn creating anxiety that this may happen again. Some people may avoid sex as a result. Some men seek new sexual partners to 'prove' themselves or for the excitement. However, the novelty is short-lived and their sexual response will become as before.

If a man in his mid to late fifties or older does not have sex for a year or more, he is likely to experience difficulty in getting and keeping an erection. Again, this can generate a lot of anxiety and sometimes avoidance of further attempts. He needs an understanding partner and several unhurried and undemanding sexual experiences. Some men may benefit from hormone replacement therapy.

While erectile problems sometimes have a physical basis, most older men will continue to enjoy sex if they have a positive attitude to it, remain sexually active, understand the physical changes and make adjustments.

Case 1

Joe (sixty years old) noticed a year ago that he had some difficulty in keeping his erection long enough to have intercourse. His wife, Ann, was aware of this but said nothing for fear of upsetting Joe. She knew he was under a lot of pressure at work as the company was making some of the workers redundant. Joe began to worry about losing his erection, and then developed difficulty getting an erection. He thought it would help if Ann touched his penis, but their pattern of foreplay did not include this. Joe began to avoid any sexual relationship, and Ann felt hurt and rejected. She read of a similar situation in a women's magazine and decided to follow the advice given. She talked to Joe and they came to understand that the changes that take place with age, along with the anxiety in work, had led to the problem. Ann also learned that she needed to touch Joe's penis directly and that they should not try to have intercourse until Joe's erections were happening easily for him. Having overcome some embarrassment they now feel they are solving the problem together.

What sexual changes take place in women?

A woman needs to understand the physical changes that take place so as to reject the myth that she is unable to have and enjoy sex.

The menopause brings to an end a woman's capacity to have children naturally but not her ability to enjoy sex. The age range for menopause is thirty to sixty years old, with most women experiencing it at fifty.

There is a great variation in the effect of the menopause on women. Eighty per cent have few or no symptoms. The two main symptoms are hot flushes, and a decrease in the lubrication and elasticity of the vagina. Others include night sweats, difficulty sleeping, mood swings, poorer memory and concentration and weight gain. If you have severe symptoms they can be treated by hormone replacement therapy. The kind and number of physical changes vary from woman to woman. After the menopause most women maintain the capacity to have multiple orgasms, particularly if they are in good health and have sex regularly.

As it takes longer for the vagina to become lubricated (approximately five minutes) and the amount of fluid may be less, more time in foreplay is necessary. It can also help to use a water-soluble lubricant, which can be bought in the pharmacist without a prescription (e.g. K-Y Jelly). The walls of the vagina become thinner and less elastic and intercourse may be painful; this can be helped by hormone replacement therapy. Your GP or local Family Planning Clinic or Well Woman Centre can advise you.

Many older women find that it takes longer to reach orgasm and the orgasm itself may be less intense. A woman may find the contractions of her uterus (womb) during intercourse painful, and if this happens often may start to avoid orgasm. The problem can be overcome by hormone replacement therapy. Older women who have intercourse may be more susceptible to urinary tract infection.

Despite these changes in the body, most women continue to have and to enjoy sex, but not as frequently or with the same intense arousal as in middle age. However, women say that they are interested in sex to a late age and their interest is greater than their level of activity.

As with a man, a woman of fifty-five or older who has a year or more of a break from intercourse may have physical changes in her vagina which can make intercourse difficult and/or painful. With an understanding partner and gradual sexual activity, these changes can be reversed in six to twelve weeks. If the problem remains unresolved seek professional help.

How do people adjust to the physical changes?

For both men and women to maintain a mutually satisfying sexual relationship into their seventies and beyond, it is essential that they understand the physical changes, communicate with each other and adjust sexual behaviour. As at all ages, a harmonious relationship is necessary for a happy sexual relationship.

There will be a need to slow down the pace of sex, something most women see as very positive. Intercourse may not be possible every time a couple has sex. Different positions and techniques for intercourse may be required, to help a man keep his erection, or to accommodate a painful, stiff or paralysed limb or other health problems. Oral or manual stimulation may be used. Sex aids (vibrators and dildos, artificial vaginas) can give pleasure to both men and women. They can be helpful for older couples and for a person alone. Varying in cost from £10 to £70, they can be obtained from some Family Planning Clinics, Well Woman Centres, shops specialising in sex aids, and by catalogue by post (see Directory). They may not be acceptable to everyone and their use must first be discussed with a partner.

Do health problems mean an end to sex?

Illness can complicate an older person's sexuality. Some people believe that illness means the end of their sex life. This is not true in most cases. However, if you are severely ill, your body's energy is taken up by recovery. A chronic illness with pain and weakness can have the same result.

If you are recovering, or your chronic illness has stabilised, sexual activity can be resumed if you so desire. Ask your doctor for information on how and when this is safe.

ARTHRITIS

Arthritis causes stiffness and pain in your joints. Fear of pain will prevent you becoming aroused and so can interfere with sex. Arthritis of the hip is extremely common and can cause particular difficulty for women. One of its earliest symptoms is pain when opening your legs or rotating your hip. This affects intercourse, and the woman will find lying on her back very painful or even impossible. Similarly, painful back, knees or shoulders will necessitate a change in position. A position for intercourse that does not put pressure on either person is both lying on their sides with the man behind the woman.

Discuss with your doctor taking some medication that would allow pain-free sexual activity. Sex may benefit people with arthritis because of the possible effect of cortisone, which is produced in the body during physical exertion.

HEART ATTACK

If you have heart disease, you may be fearful about having a heart attack during sex; similarly if you have had a heart attack or coronary bypass surgery. Although all patients need time to recover physically and psychologically from a heart attack or surgery, the majority can then resume sex. Tests can be done to determine the exact level of physical stress that is safe, and your doctor can then advise on the level of sexual activity that is suitable for you. It is usually recommended to resume sex in a gradual and undemanding way. This may involve lying on your side or back and not taking the extra strain of your body weight. Sexual activity need not always involve orgasm. Use of vibrators or dildos is a way of making it less physically demanding.

HIGH BLOOD PRESSURE AND STROKE

It is essential to take medication to control high blood pressure; otherwise, you are more likely to have a stroke. However, the medication may cause some erectile or ejaculation problems in men. Discuss this with your doctor, as it may be possible to try another type of medication.

If you have had a stroke and have suffered some weakness or loss of movement, you may need to change position for intercourse. An added problem is that a stroke is often accompanied by severe depression. This may make it more difficult for you to become interested in attempting to have sex. It is worth trying, and an encouraging partner is very important.

Case 2

Mary (seventy years old) and her husband, Jack (seventy-three), had a fulfilling sexual relationship until Mary had a stroke. She recovered well but had a weakness on the left side of her body affecting her face, arm and leg. She was depressed after the stroke and felt she no longer looked attractive; she found day-to-day activities took much longer and there were some things she could not do, as she walked with a stick. Jack encouraged and supported

Mary in the time following the stroke. He reassured her that she was attractive to him and remained affectionate towards her. Little by little Mary began to feel more positive about her body and to enjoy the affection. Several months later she was ready to allow Jack to touch her body sexually. In this way they gradually resumed their sexual relationship. They have intercourse with Mary's leg supported by pillows. Mary finds she feels better in herself as one part of her life is normal again.

DIABETES

Diabetes mellitus, which is common in older people, can cause a man to have difficulties getting and maintaining an erection. While it may be exacerbated by tension, the erectile problem is not itself caused by anxiety. The man remains interested in sex. While intercourse may not be possible, other forms of sexual activity can be tried. The condition can leave a woman unable to have an orgasm due to nerve damage.

CANCER

Because there are many types of cancer and varying degrees of severity, there will be different effects on sexual relationships.

In general, a diagnosis of cancer is shocking and upsetting to the person and her family. Depression and anxiety often occur and interest in sex decreases. In addition, the disease or treatment for it can leave her sick and low in energy.

Although the person may feel anxious or depressed, closeness and affection, whether sexual or not, can be of benefit; she will feel loved and supported and cared for.

OPERATIONS

It takes an older person longer to recover from operations and anaesthetics. There is also the psychological upset of going into hospital and coming home again. The person and her family may be faced with the possibility of death. Any or all of these can affect sexual interest and/or activity.

Get all the information on the operation and its consequences. You have to sign a consent form beforehand; ask for clarification on anything that you do not understand or that is worrying you.

Prostate gland operation: The prostate is a gland at the base of a man's bladder and if it becomes enlarged it can interfere with bladder control (see p. 76) and with a man's enjoyment of sex.

Sometimes the enlarged prostate can lead to pain in the penis, difficulty in maintaining an erection or having an orgasm. This may cause problems for partners, who can become frustrated by an unsatisfactory sexual relationship. A sex aid may help.

See your GP and have the prostate problem investigated. An operation may be recommended. After surgery most men will remain interested in sex and have erections. They will experience a less intense feeling at the time of orgasm and may find no semen was emitted, as it was forced into the bladder.

If the prostate gland is cancerous, a more radical type of surgery is usually required which may affect a man's ability to have erections. If cancer is present, removal of the testicles may be necessary; this will result in loss of sexual feeling. You may need counselling to cope with the surgery, the changes in your life and having a life-threatening disease.

Hysterectomy: The removal of the uterus may be psychologically difficult, even for older women. After the menopause, a woman has no practical use for her womb but she can feel anxious about having it removed, as it is linked with periods, pregnancy and femininity.

The womb can be removed through the vagina, leaving no scar, or through a surgical cut in the abdomen, leaving a scar. The vagina may be a little shortened but the woman's capacity for intercourse and sexual enjoyment remains, though some women report a decrease in their level of enjoyment.

Mastectomy: The removal of a breast, usually done because of cancer, can be psychologically traumatic for a woman and her partner. A woman's breast is part of her female identity. After a mastectomy, a woman can therefore feel unfeminine and mutilated. Her partner may find it difficult to respond sexually to her. Both people are also confronted with the threat of a terminal illness.

Before surgery, a woman should discuss with her doctor all available forms of treatment for breast cancer. She should know beforehand if there is a possibility of a total mastectomy. If so, counselling is on offer and this is extended to the recovery period (Reach to Recovery; see Directory).

MEDICINES

A common cause of sexual difficulties in men is the side-effects of prescribed drugs. Some medicines for high blood pressure lead to problems. Major tranquillisers may result in difficulties with erection and ejaculation. Other drugs also affect sexuality. If you experience any changes after commencing a drug, discuss them with your doctor; it may be possible to use a different drug. Drugs can also lower the sexual response in a woman and affect her orgasm.

What can you do if your partner dies?

We have so far looked at the sexual relationship between two older people. The issues discussed apply to both heterosexual and homosexual relationships. Yet there is a problem, in that the older a person gets, the less likely she is to have a partner. This is especially true for women, as they live longer and marry older men.

What are the options? Remarriage is often difficult: male partners are scarce, and there may be personal or family concerns regarding loyalty to the deceased partner or concern about inheritance. However, an older person may meet someone whom she wishes to marry or take as a lover. Adult children may find this hard to accept because of the stereotypes about older people. This can result in the family's being critical or rejecting the new partner, putting pressure on the older person to end the relationship. Sex outside marriage may be unacceptable to many older people but some do make this choice. The partner may be younger, older or married. Sex with a person of the same sex may be undesirable or unacceptable to many older women; however, such a relationship can be as loving and as rewarding as a relationship between a man and a woman. In homosexual male relationships, when a long-term partner dies, there is less prospect of the surviving partner forming a new relationship.

Masturbation is an option for a person without a partner or whose partner is ill. The use of fantasies during sex may contribute to the enjoyment. Masturbation helps a man to maintain his ability to have erections, and a woman to maintain the elasticity and lubrication of her vagina.

What happens to sex if you live with family or in residential care?

The idea that an older person or couple should continue to have sexual feelings may be difficult for family or care staff to accept, resulting in attitudes and practices which ensure that no sexual activity can take place. Privacy is essential for a person to be sexual, alone or with someone else. Knocking on doors before entering a room or providing a key so doors can be locked are very basic ways of safeguarding privacy. In residential care, practices and policies should also consider the needs of all residents, whether they are sexual alone, with another resident (who may be of the same sex) or with a non-resident. There should be 'Do Not Disturb' signs for private time in rooms, rooms available for those who wish to be sexually active, and accommodation for guests. Yet in nursing homes or institutions, contact of an affectionate or sexual nature is restricted to the sitting-room. Married residents have been separated for sleeping purposes on the assumption that no intimate relationship exists. This is denying that at all stages of life human beings need to be cared for and shown affection and may want to have sex.

This section has examined the physical abilities, pleasure and problems associated with sex. Sexual satisfaction or happiness also includes the emotional aspects of intimacy, affection, caring and companionship. These are important aspects and especially so for older people. The slower and less intense physical aspects of sexuality can lead to greater emphasis being placed on the emotional and sensual side. If older people understand the physical changes, making adjustments for them and for any illness or disability, sexuality can be a rewarding and interesting element of later life.

What help is available?

First see your GP to rule out a physical or drug-related problem.

If you have a sexual problem there are counselling services available in the Irish Family Planning Clinics in various parts of the country (see Directory). Some men with difficulties getting an erection can be helped by an injection each time intercourse takes place. A device which is inserted during surgery (penile implant) will allow a man to achieve an erection; its effectiveness depends on the attitude of the man concerned. Your GP can refer you to a specialist.

Sex in later life can be fulfilling, although some people of all ages have well-adjusted lives without sex.

As we go through life we must ask, 'What do I need sex for?' Many people of all ages enjoy sex for the intimacy, physical stimulation and sexual pleasuring it provides. Over time each of these aspects, even for a long-term couple, will change. Sexual pleasuring is somewhat altered by physical ageing but is also influenced by the knowledge you have, your attitudes and experiences of sex both now and in earlier years. The knowledge that sexuality and its expression will change with physical ageing and certain diseases and medicines need not be feared and can be positive.

E. ACCIDENTS AND SAFETY

Older adults have the highest death rates and the highest disability rates from accidents. In Ireland in 1991, 31 per cent of all fatal accidents, injuries and poisonings happened to people of sixty-five and older, yet this age-group represented only 11 per cent of the population. Accidents, injuries and poisonings are the fourth leading cause of death in the over-65 age-group. This high death rate makes essential the prevention of accidents of all types. Also, many more older people sustain injuries which lead to pain and, for some, disability.

Accidents are a consequence of doing everyday things (walking, cooking, driving a car) fundamental to a good quality of life. Where is the balance between your right to take risks, which may lead to an accident, and your right to quality of life? If risks are identified, you can make personal choices about the types and levels of risk which are appropriate for you in the different situations in your life (e.g. in the house or garden, shopping, on the road).

Falls, road traffic accidents and burns are common accidents for older people. There are two major groups of contributory factors:
— factors within the person: the physical changes that occur with ageing and any illness
— factors in the environment: how familiar it is, furniture, flooring, cooking appliances, hot water, electricity and vehicles.

FALLS

In any given year, approximately one-third of people over the age of sixty-five living at home have a fall, but only one or two require medical attention.

Even if you are not injured, you may be left with a fear of falling, which can lead to anxiety and loss of confidence, restricting your daily activities and social life. Families may be anxious and become over-protective, wanting you to stop doing certain things or move to residential care.

Falls occur among more older women than men, and the older you are, up until your eighties, the more you are at risk. Women over seventy-five are also more likely to suffer serious physical injury (fracture of hip, wrist, upper arm or pelvis) from a fall. This is due to osteoporosis being more common in women than men, although it is found in men.

While few older people are seriously injured by a fall, 82 per cent of those who died from accidental falls were over sixty-five. Accidental falls outnumber any other accidental cause of death.

What are the reasons older people fall?

Falls are not attributable to old age itself. Physical changes that occur with ageing in some but not all people may predispose an older person to fall.

The causes of falls differ according to age, level of health and level of mobility. Also, the same person may fall at different times for different reasons. Falls may be caused by any one or the interaction of four factors:
(1) health
(2) effects of medications and alcohol
(3) environmental factors
(4) social and psychological factors.

(1) HEALTH

Falls are more likely if you have poor health and mobility problems. Impairments in balance and gait (pattern of walking) create problems.

Balance difficulties can have several causes. As you age, you become more dependent on vision to maintain balance; visual changes (e.g. reduced acuity, glare) and eye diseases (e.g. cataract, glaucoma) can produce a greater likelihood of falling. Any diseases that affect the information to the brain about the position of your head in space can place you at risk, e.g. diseases in your legs or feet. As your ears contribute to your ability to balance, any disease affecting them may cause falls.

Other diseases, such as low blood pressure (hypotension), transient ischaemic attacks (see p. 92) and some cardiac conditions, can contribute to a tendency to fall.

If you do fall, have a physical examination by your doctor to rule out any physical cause.

(2) EFFECTS OF MEDICATIONS AND ALCOHOL

An older person who is sick is more likely to fall. Medicines being taken for an illness may increase this risk, particularly if several medications are combined. Alcohol can contribute to falls and you need to be more careful of the amount you drink as you age.

(3) ENVIRONMENTAL FACTORS

Dangers outside the home appear to be more prevalent causes of falls by active older people, and dangers inside the home for the very old and ill — loose rugs, poor lighting, coffee tables and stairs can all become hazards.

Poorly fitting shoes on icy or uneven ground can lead to falls. Some would recommend that older people do not wear slippers unless a foot condition requires it. If they are necessary they must fasten securely with a zipper or velcro.

(4) SOCIAL AND PSYCHOLOGICAL FACTORS

If you adapt your environment and activities to suit any health changes, it will help prevent falls. If you are stressed or hurried you may not pay attention to your environment, fail to see a hazard and fall. Being depressed can make you less attentive and contribute to a fall.

Can falls be prevented?

There are many steps that planners, architects, older people and their carers can take to reduce the risk of falls. A leaflet on *Safety in the Home* (1992), available from the Eastern Health Board, offers helpful advice on this topic. The following precautions are recommended by the Kellogg International Work Group (1987):

— Be aware that certain diseases and medicines may increase your risk of falling.
— Obtain and wear your glasses.
— Wear shoes that are a secure fit, with enclosed heel if possible, a low broad heel, a slip-resistant sole.
— Do not wear long nightwear or dressing-gowns.
— Take regular physical exercise and eat a balanced diet.
— Take time to regain your balance when getting up from a chair or bed.

The following simple changes reduce hazards in the home without requiring structural alteration.

Floors: Carpets should be short-pile with the edges well tacked down. Replace worn carpet because it can cause you to slide and trip. Use non-slip polish on hard-surfaced floors. Keep all floors clear of dust, crumbs and liquids.

Lighting: There should be even and high levels of light throughout your house. This is particularly important on stairs and between the bedroom and bathroom. Light-switches should be near every doorway.

Bathroom: Grab-rails are recommended for the shower and bath, in conjunction with a non-slip mat. The height of the toilet seat can be raised and you can use a seat in the bath or shower.

Furniture: It should not have casters or wheels or sharp edges. Couches, chairs and bed should not be too high, low or soft.

Stairs: They should be well lit. Tack the carpet down securely. Make sure the carpet is not a repeating pattern, and is not worn. Securely mounted handrails should extend the full length on both sides, and be designed to signal the bottom of the stairs; alternatively, the last step can be marked with bright tape.

Climbing: Always consider whether it is safe for you to climb, and always use a step-ladder rather than a chair.

What to do if a fall occurs

There is a useful Eastern Health Board leaflet on *Coping with Falls* (1992).

If you fall, even if you are not injured, it may be a sign of illness and you should report it to your doctor.

If you fall and cannot get up, several methods have been suggested. One is to roll onto your side, get onto your hands and knees and crawl to a nearby sturdy bed or chair. Bend the knee nearest it, place your hands on the surface and push yourself to a sitting or standing position. If you are physically unable to crawl, shuffle on your bottom to a nearby piece of furniture. Further advice can be obtained from a physiotherapist.

If you are unable to get up, and you live alone, you need to be able to summon help. Leaving a bell under a chair may be useful. There is also a wide range of personal alarms available which are worn around the neck.

ROAD TRAFFIC ACCIDENTS

In Ireland in 1991, 20 per cent of all deaths from road traffic accidents were among people of sixty-five and over. While casualties on Irish roads are higher for those between the ages of fifteen and sixty-four, younger and older people had the highest rates of pedestrian injuries.

Are there changes with age that predispose you to a road traffic accident?

As an older driver or pedestrian, there are factors you must consider for safety on the roads. These include the need for adequate light to see sufficiently clearly (night-time driving is more difficult), the reduction of peripheral (sideways) vision, sensitivity to glare, diminished hearing and slowed reflex responses, decreased ability to process a lot of information quickly.

Many older drivers have always had good driving skills and continue to perform well. The ability to drive can be important for independence at any age but perhaps particularly as you become older, as it may be possible to shop and visit family and friends by car but not by walking or using public transport. Older people may have declining capacities but can compensate by driving more cautiously, at slower speeds, for fewer miles, on less demanding routes or only in good weather. Older drivers are more likely to have accidents at intersections when they are turning or yielding right of way. Accidents involving lack of attention (at traffic signals) also tend to increase with age. Following and skidding accidents decrease with age due to the decrease in driving at high speed. Healthy older drivers have been found to have superior driving skills and to make fewer errors.

The problem is that there is no special test to find out who is safe to continue driving. The traditional test to obtain a licence does not supply such information. A more extensive test for older people might work, provided that the test assessed the skills known to be necessary for driving. Remember that it is not age itself which leads to accidents, but problems in physical and psychological functioning. Older people, like younger people, are a mixed group and no sweeping generalisations can be made about their driving abilities.

How can you avoid being involved, injured or killed in a road traffic accident?
As a pedestrian and driver you can take the following steps:
— Have regular eyesight checks.
— Wear glasses.
— Wear a hearing-aid if needed.
— Use pedestrian crossings and only when the light has just turned green, to allow time to cross.
— Be extra-aware of reversing vehicles.

As a driver you need to be conscious of any limitations in your physical or mental capacity. Do not drive if you are affected by the medicines you are taking — check with your doctor or pharmacist. As you get older it takes less alcohol to affect your driving.

Your choice of car design may assist you to drive more safely. A car with automatic gear-change is easier to drive. A two-door car gives a marginally bigger opening, which is helpful if your joints have lost mobility; however, you have to get out to let rear-seat passengers in or out. Check that the seats, pedals and steering-wheel are adjustable for height and distance. Pedal layout is crucial; markedly offset pedals may aggravate painful knees or hips. Pedals which are heavy can cause problems with weak ankles or legs. Power steering is now provided on many new cars and this is useful for any shoulder problems. Lightly tinted windows can help to cope with glare sensitivity, but must not be too dark. Tinted glasses should not be worn at night.

Inside adjustments of external mirrors, press-button controls for windows and central locking make driving a car easier.

Check that you can climb into and out of the car easily. Inspect the boot; a low-loading boot opening at bumper level is beneficial with lessened agility and strength.

Improved technology is providing cars with anti-locking braking, side-impact protection and automatic inflatable air-bags.

Safety and ease of access to public transport needs to be improved by the use of handrails on buses and the lowering of step height.

BURNS
Many burns in older people are sustained during cooking or bathing. Loss of sensation in the skin can lead to reduced awareness of a burn. Another source of burns is tap-water, due to decreased sensitivity and a slower reaction time. The temperature of

44

domestic hot water in the bathroom should be limited to 115 °F (46.1 °C) in order to prevent accidental scalding.

In cooking accidents grease and food are the main sources of fire, along with leaving food unattended. Unattended cigarettes are another cause of fires; they can set chairs, sofas, mattresses or bedclothing alight.

In Ireland in 1991, 67 per cent of burns fatalities were people aged sixty-five and over. The death rate from the effects of a burn is higher in older people. The extent and degree of burn needed to cause death is much less than in a younger person.

Can accidents that cause burns be prevented?

As with other accidents, prevention is possible. You can help prevent a fire in your home as follows:

— Never leave a cooker in use unattended — especially if frying something.
— Don't hang tea-towels over the cooker.
— Check the temperature of the water carefully before you get into the bath or use the shower.
— Avoid trailing flexes as you can trip over them or knock something (e.g. the kettle) down on yourself.
— If you have difficulty holding your teapot or pouring, get a teapot-stand.
— If you have an open fire use a fire-guard and have your chimney swept regularly. If you have a boiler have it serviced regularly.
— If you feel like sleeping in your chair, keep it away from the fire.
— Do not smoke in bed. Use an ashtray and make sure your cigarette is extinguished.
— If you use an electric blanket, an over-blanket is safer than an under-blanket. Electric under-blankets should always be unplugged before you get into bed (unless the directions specifically say otherwise).
— Always use a cover on a hot-water bottle to avoid possible burns.
— Oil heaters should be avoided if possible. If you use one, make sure it cannot be knocked over. Good ventilation is also important with oil or gas fires.
— Electric radiator or convection heaters are safe.
— Do not use any electric appliance (TV, fan heater, kettle) with frayed wire or a broken or loose plug, and unplug all appliances at night.

— Install a smoke alarm and if possible a fire blanket in the kitchen.

The above advice is based on *Safety in the Home* leaflets available from the Eastern Health Board and the Fire Prevention Council.

F. MEDICINES AND YOU

Although more than 60 per cent of those over sixty-five reported their health to be excellent or good, people in this age-group are the major users of medicines. Not only do they take more medicines than younger people but they often are on a number of different medicines because of varying health problems. Older people are also more likely to be particularly sensitive and vulnerable to side-effects. Due to changes in liver and kidney functioning, more of a medication is retained in the body. It is therefore essential to take only the prescribed amount at the correct time. Sometimes a doctor will prescribe a smaller dose of medication for an older person.

Reactions to medicines can lead to confusion or to a medical emergency and the need for hospitalisation. Some of these adverse reactions could be avoided if medicines were managed sensibly in the following ways.

Take only medicines that are prescribed for you. It is not advisable to share medicines which have been prescribed for a friend or relative. In particular, you may need a different dosage to people who are either younger or older. You must finish the course; do not stop taking the medication because you feel better.

Do not mix medicines bought over the counter with medicines prescribed by the doctor, as if these are of the same type you may actually accidentally overdose, or one medicine may 'interfere' with another one. Ask your pharmacist, as she will have a record of your prescribed drugs.

Tell your doctor if you drink alcohol, as many medicines cannot be taken if you drink. Also tell your doctor if you drive, as some medicines cause drowsiness, making it unsafe to continue.

You need to be aware of and recognise any side-effects of your medication. The most commonly reported are dry mouth, drowsiness, passing water frequently, constipation, feeling or being sick and faintness or dizziness. Other side-effects are diarrhoea, developing a rash, erectile problems in men, the feeling your heart is thumping. If you have side-effects tell your doctor, who can then check whether you are taking the correct dose at the right time.

Sometimes other medication can be tried, or the possibility can be considered that two types of medication are interacting. Tell your doctor all the medicines you are taking, including ones bought without prescription. Some side-effects can not be eliminated and may have to be tolerated for the sake of your overall health.

Medicine containers must be clearly labelled. Containers which are child-proof can be very difficult to open — especially for someone with arthritis — so easy-to-open containers or aids to open some packs, e.g. 'blister packs', are required. Keep medicines out of the reach of children. The storage of medicines is important. Do not use them past the expiry date, which should be printed on the label or box. Many medicines need to be stored in a cool dry place while others have to be kept away from light.

Ask the doctor

It is useful to have written information about your medicines from your doctor. Information given in the doctor's surgery can easily be forgotten or not absorbed at the time because of other concerns. Written information can be kept and referred to later by you or your relatives.

It is a good idea to ask questions about the medicines prescribed for you (Herxheimer 1976, Cartwright & Smith 1988), such as:
— the name of the medicine
— what it is for
— whether there are any side-effects
— how long you should take it for
— whether you can drive safely or operate machinery
— whether you should avoid alcoholic drink, food or other medicines.

If you are given a repeat prescription, ask whether you should still be taking the medication. When a new medicine is prescribed, list for the doctor the medicines you are already taking and ask:
— whether this is instead of or as well as your other medications
— whether you should take the new one at the same time
— whether there is any danger the medicines will interact and cause problems.

In this way you can remind your doctor to review the medication you are taking. When you bring the prescription to the pharmacist she will write the details of how much of the medication to take and when. The pharmacist can also inform you of side-effects, and whether you should avoid certain food, drinks or activities.

Taking your medicine

As you grow older your memory may not be as good and this needs to be taken into account when organising medicine-taking. For a person of any age taking several medicines, a clear system is required to ensure that the right medicine is taken at the right time. Also, when taking medicines long-term it can be difficult to remember whether the medicine was taken that day or the day before. So older people who generally take more than one medicine over a long time must be particularly careful. However, they have been found to be just as scrupulous as younger people in this regard. Age was not a factor but knowing what medicines to take and when to take them was. Other significant factors were believing it important to take the medicines exactly as prescribed, and not fearing the illness.

There are two systems which can help you to take medicines in the correct amounts and at the correct times.

One system is to keep a chart listing the medicines and the time each one is to be taken, e.g. 8 a.m., 8 p.m. You can draw one up for each week and tick off each medicine as it is taken.

Another system is to buy a daily or weekly container for medicines. It can be organised — by you or by someone else for you — for the number of times a day you take tablets, with each section containing the medicines for that day and time. You need to be able to remember to take the medicine for this system to work. Some people use a digital watch with an alarm to remind them to take their medicines. In the future, more sophisticated equipment will be readily available that will emit a bleep or tell you it is time to take your medicine.

CHAPTER 4

PSYCHOLOGICAL ASPECTS
OF NORMAL AGEING

A. MYTH OF INTELLECTUAL DETERIORATION

Do intellectual abilities decline with age?
There is a common assumption that decline in intellectual abilities, senility and old age go together. Intelligence is generally viewed as the capacity of a person to act purposefully, to think rationally and to deal effectively with her environment. Scientific study has shown that the popular myth of an inevitable decline in intelligence in old age vastly overstates the case. People of average health can expect to maintain or even increase their level of intellectual functioning into old age. Again, we have to remember that individuals differ in many ways, physical health and intelligence being no exception.

Mental functioning in later life is complex. The studies of older people use intelligence tests and laboratory investigations that often do not relate to real life. Some of them show slight decline in certain activities but an unimpaired ability to function in day-to-day life. Indeed in the performance of well-learned activities, e.g. a typist working at speed or an engineer designing bridges, no decline has been found. Being involved in a familiar, complex and stimulating environment can help preserve intellectual function in old age. There are differences associated with the level of education, with more educated people showing less decline as they age, this possibly being related to their better health.

Older people have been found to be fractionally slower than younger people. The reason is not known but it has to do with the central nervous system rather than muscular functioning. This slowness, although slight, may be seen in everyday behaviour, e.g.

zipping clothing, dialling a telephone, cutting with a knife, or writing. However, if very healthy old adults are compared to less healthy younger adults, or older adults who take part in exercise regularly are compared to people the same age who do not, the healthy, fit older adults are faster overall. Also, older people value accuracy over speed and this may affect their response when speed is being measured. All this evidence refutes the negative stereotype of inevitable intellectual decline in old age.

Does memory decline with age?

Older people themselves believe that their memory for events and activities 'isn't what it used to be'. They complain of decreased ability to remember recent and distant events, names, dates, appointments, threads of thoughts in conversation, and where they put something. While a degree of forgetfulness occurs for some older people, it does not lead to a severe memory problem. Some older adults have better memories than some younger ones. There is individual variability in memory throughout life. Older people who remain healthy and who are mentally active may find less decline in their memories than sick and/or inactive people of the same age. It should also be borne in mind that memory difficulties are often made worse by hearing loss and poor vision. It is conceivable that some normally ageing people simply forget how imperfect their memory was even in youth. Such a perception of one's memory may be fuelled by the knowledge that abnormal ageing — senile dementia (see Chapter 7) — is accompanied by severe memory problems. If the memory difficulties interfere with daily life, this is not normal and help should be sought, initially from your GP.

What do we know about older people's memories?

Some research has been carried out on memory for everyday events and activities. While younger adults did not recall exactly conversations they had, older people recalled slightly less. Television is a major source of information and entertainment for adults of all ages. Some research found that older people of lower verbal abilities remembered less of the television programme, possibly due to the more verbal group being more mentally active. As regards reading books, the evidence for poorer memory in older people is conflicting. Similarly, it is unclear whether an older person will remember where a shop is located if she has recently moved to a new area.

In conclusion, while there is some evidence of slight decline in memory as people age, it appears to be variable. Older people compensate by making lists, writing down appointments in a diary, calendar or reminder-board, getting a key-stand for the hall, or routinely leaving objects (e.g. glasses) in the same place.

Can older people learn?

Older people may not learn as quickly or efficiently as younger people but they can and do learn. What may be much more important than the ageing process are the person's attitudes and situation, and the policies and practices of educational providers and employers.

A person's attitude to learning may be based on her school experience. She may see education as formal, examination-oriented. Some older people have ageist attitudes regarding their own ability to learn. Some do not have time for such activities as they care for someone in their families. Also, older people are reluctant to go out at night due to the cold and their fear for safety. Transport cost may also be a barrier. Lack of awareness of what is available and suitable is another obstacle to later-life learning.

The providers of education/training must promote courses and establish appropriate locations and times. However, some of them are under financial pressure to run courses that bring in revenue, while people who cannot afford courses often do not apply. Another option is distance learning, e.g. the courses offered by the Open University, where few major differences are found between older students and other adults, the overall pass rate showing no difference between people under and over sixty. The reasons people do these courses are varied — to keep active, because of missed opportunities, to get a degree, to continue to develop as a person, to get a better education.

It is important that employers encourage learning. Rather than updating the skills of middle-aged and older workers, they sometimes prefer to retire them early, in the mistaken belief that older people cannot learn and their productivity is lower. Training is often designed for the learning style of younger people and may need slight modification; if this is carried out, older workers can absorb and apply new material just as effectively.

While the Irish Congress of Trade Unions in its Charter of Rights for Older People supports the right of older people to participate in formal and informal adult education, their needs in this area are recognised only to a limited extent.

The Vocational Education Committees throughout the country have adult education organisers who try to meet the requirements of lifelong learning with daytime courses. There is no specific educational programme for people over sixty-five in Ireland. Participation of old people is low but rising. Pearse College in Crumlin is the only daytime adult education college in the country. The many Active Retirement Associations provide some educational activities for members. The need for learning opportunities in old age should be more widely recognised, as well as the differing requirements of people living in rural Ireland and those in cities and towns.

The University of the Third Age (U3A) was started in France (1973) for older people. Defining first and second age as childhood and work, it sees the third age as one of post-work activity, a time for expanding one's mind and experience. The University of the Third Age is not a building but a group of people, of activities, though some older students do organise a course with the help of a university. In some countries it carries out research (legislation, social, economic, etc.) and fosters preventive health and social initiatives. Today there are 300 Third Age Universities in Europe and North America.

In 1994 the organisation Age Action Ireland (see Directory) received a grant to promote the University of the Third Age in Ireland and has established an advisory group.

A successful example of a U3A programme, 'Learning in Later Life', has been run in Scotland since 1987. Tuition is offered from beginners up to undergraduate level. Over half of the students left school with no educational qualification, and find starting to study with their own age-group less threatening. The outline of the programme is planned by the teacher but students contribute to individual lessons. Weekly homework is requested by the students as informal assessment of how effectively they are learning. Older adults prove effective and efficient learners, although for some the pace of learning may initially be slower. The social aspect of the courses is important, with clubs, exchange trips and events in the community part of the overall programme.

Learning/education can and does take place in old age. There are many aims for these endeavours: providing personal fulfilment, keeping older workers in the workforce, promoting self-confidence or mental and physical health. Some of the 47 per cent of older Irish people who said they often had time on their hands might find it useful and enjoyable to undertake a form of learning.

B. MYTH OF PERSONALITY CHANGE

Do older people have the same personality?

One of the biggest myths is that older people are all alike in having an 'elderly' personality. The stereotype is a very negative one, the older person being seen as rigid, selfish, intolerant, conservative. Another element of the myth is the view that old age is a period of serenity, spent in a rocking-chair, mellow, sweet, with the world passing you by. The reality is, of course, that people over sixty-five years of age are as varied in their personalities as any other group.

What is personality?

There are several different definitions of personality but three essential aspects. The first is the attitudes, values and motives that contribute to the way a person thinks and interprets the things in her world. The second is the way a person behaves — how she does things, how active she is, her sense of humour and methods of coping. The third is the roles or patterns of behaving associated with society's expectation of that person — woman/man, daughter/son, employee/employer, and so on. People in their roles reflect some of their individual typical responses as well as part of their core attitudes, values, motives, expectations. Each of us lives with other people in the immediate social environment but also in a broader cultural and historical context which moulds and influences our personalities. An example is the effect of a war or a cultural change (World War II, the Swinging Sixties) on people alive then. All these aspects interact to give each person her unique yet changing personality over the course of life.

Personality is used to mean that the person is herself and different from everybody else. She is consistent and predictable in her thinking, feeling and behaviour. If we say someone has a good sense of humour or is happy or contented, we mean this is the way she is most of the time — this is her personality. This consistency or sameness, however, does not imply that a person's personality never changes. On the contrary, people change and adapt throughout life. They learn from life experiences and respond to different social and biological factors, and this may lead to a change in attitudes, behaviour, ways of thinking and feeling.

Does personality change in old age?

Just as there is stability in intellectual functioning in older people, so there is general stability in personality. There may be some personality differences between age-groups, e.g. those who are forty and those who are sixty, but within an age-group people maintain their own characteristics throughout life and each person maintains her individual personality.

What changes in old age, particularly in response to the losses and the physical and environmental differences, are attitudes, behaviour, and underlying beliefs, assumptions and feelings. Also, older adults may look less to the future for hopes and dreams and feel happier with their present lives and selves. In 1993, 74 per cent of Irish people over sixty-five said they were generally as happy as they had ever been.

Does personality affect successful adjustment to old age?

High self-esteem is essential to successful adjustment throughout life and older people have generally high levels of self-esteem, even in stressful situations such as going into residential care. Also, people who age successfully are likely to show acceptance of things that cannot change and more inclined to attach meaning and purpose to undesirable events in their lives. High self-esteem has been found to be maintained throughout old age by having a number of hobbies, having outings from the home, being active and having people important to you outside the family. A positive attitude to old age is a significant contributory factor.

People who have adequate intellectual and physical health, high self-esteem, ability to hope in the future and to face difficult situations head-on, have the best chance of successful adaptation, provided their way of adapting is matched to the changes in their lives. A study that followed older people over many years in Germany (Rott & Thomae 1991) showed that they did adapt to the changes in their lives. Their coping strategies were varied but did not alter notably as they aged. There was no evidence of everyone adjusting to life in old age in the same way, as each retained her personality and her own style of adjusting.

CHAPTER 5

SOCIAL ASPECTS OF NORMAL AGEING

(i) RELATIONSHIPS

A. LONELINESS AND ISOLATION

One of the myths about ageing is that older people are isolated and lonely. Both of these are, in general, untrue for the majority of older people. Isolation and loneliness are in fact two distinct experiences.

Isolation is lack of social contact with other people. People who live alone are more likely to be isolated and 26 per cent of people over sixty-five live alone in Ireland. Bereavement is more likely to be associated with feelings of isolation; people who have had a very long and self-contained relationship with their partners seem to be left particularly isolated. Retirement from work is also associated with feelings of isolation.

People who are isolated find pastimes which they can enjoy — reading, watching television, gardening, knitting, listening to the radio. Some of them would recommend getting to know neighbours well enough to drop in on them, keeping in touch with friends by telephone and encouraging people to call to the house. They also suggest becoming involved in the community.

What is loneliness?
Not all people who are socially isolated are lonely. Some people with few social contacts are happy with their lives and do not feel lonely. In contrast, some people who know and meet many people are lonely.

There is no agreed definition of loneliness. One is 'an unwelcome and unpleasant feeling caused by lack of companionship or feelings people have about too few social contacts or contacts which are not close enough' (Power 1984).

Are older people lonely?

Older people are often believed to be the only lonely group in society. Loneliness exists in all age-groups — college students, divorced/separated people, those who have just moved are all more vulnerable to loneliness than others. While the one in four of Irish people over sixty-five who live alone have an increased chance of being isolated and/or lonely, many people who live alone are neither.

Younger people are more likely to think of loneliness as a problem of ageing than old people themselves, who see poor health as a much more critical problem.

The exact percentage of older people who are lonely is difficult to know. There may be a reluctance for people of all ages to admit to loneliness as it can carry a stigma. Different studies ask different questions and loneliness will vary in degrees. A recent survey (1993) in Europe found that a significant minority of older people were lonely. There were wide variations between countries, with 5 to 9 per cent of older people in Britain who often felt lonely as against 36 per cent in Greece. Between 10 and 14 per cent of older Irish people reported that they often felt lonely.

You have a greater chance of being lonely if you live alone, are widowed, female, unmarried or in poor health. As older people are more likely to encounter these situations they are more likely to be lonely, but it is not ageing itself that causes loneliness. More women than men are lonely at all ages. Loneliness can lead to depression and add to the existing problems.

Loneliness may affect older people in particular situations. Very old people, especially those living in an adult child's home, were often lonely, primarily because they saw less of their friends. Women who have raised large families may be prone to loneliness in old age, as often they were too busy to make many friends. The same may be true for people who worked in very demanding occupations or needed to work a lot of overtime.

Women caring for ill husbands and widows who did so for long periods prior to a partner's death are also prone to loneliness. Childless couples whose marriages were especially close and exclusive are more likely to be lonely, particularly if they move after retirement.

It becomes clear that friendship is more important than family in avoiding loneliness. While we expect people's emotional needs to be met by family, principally spouses, the evidence points to the significance of close confiding relationships outside the family. Many studies have shown that a lifelong outward-looking approach leads to a healthier adjustment in old age. Older people who partake in activities and attend various clubs and day centres are more likely to meet new friends, making loneliness less of a problem for them.

B. SOCIAL SUPPORT AS WE AGE

Each of us lives in some relationship to other people. Within our various relationships we give and receive support, which can be divided into practical help and emotional support. Help can take the form of personal care (bathing, dressing, preparing meals), shopping, home maintenance, giving presents. Emotional support entails providing closeness and understanding, listening, giving advice. Such support helps us to maintain our social identity and may be a source of new social contacts.

Support enhances our ability to cope with physical and psychological stresses, and has been shown to hasten recovery from illness. It is also significant in terms of our self-esteem and happiness.

Each of us has direct and indirect ties linking us to a number of other people, who may be family, friends or neighbours, often known as a network. Factors affecting the type of support network you have include the size of the family you were born into, your place in the family, whether you married, whether your partner is alive, the number of children you had, the sex of the children, whether you or your family and friends have moved area, county, country, and where you live (how accessible you are). In later life, your network of support may change if you become more dependent.

The increase in life expectancy and the higher numbers of older people have many implications for social support networks. The average age of marriage has dropped so people have long marriages, many of forty years, with most women outliving their husbands and being widows in old age. The birth rate has dropped, which may mean that family resources are scarcer in old age. Most later-life families, i.e. those where the older generation are at least fifty, are multi-generational.

What relationships do older people have and what support do they get within the relationships?

COUPLES

The marriages which have survived into old age are either good ones or have lasted because of duty, resignation or the lack of an alternative. The quality of the marriage may affect the supports given and received within it.

In 1991, 42 per cent of those over sixty-five were married. The supports given and received by couples are companionship, affection and help in carrying out daily tasks of living. The relationship between spouses is the most interdependent of all, with reciprocal caring and general responsiveness to needs.

Belonging to a couple brings material supports, as the financial resources are greater on which to live and run a home. Also, if your partner is alive you are more likely to have your own home and therefore more privacy.

For both women and men the companionship of a spouse is a crucial support. This can apply even if the relationship is distant or if there is conflict. Most married older people receive emotional support from their partners. Giving affection and having a sexual relationship are also important.

As a couple age there is an increased chance that, due to declining health, one of the partners will need help in carrying out everyday tasks (dressing, washing, cooking). Spouses give greater levels of care than other relatives. Wives more often than husbands provide help or care as they are younger and may be healthier. However, men do care for their wives if necessary. The giving of care in a marriage changes the long-standing nature of the interdependence in the relationship. This can be a difficult time of adjustment for both people.

WIDOWS/WIDOWERS

The end of marriage for many older people, mainly women, is due to the death of their partners. In Ireland in 1991, 49 per cent of women aged sixty-five and over were widows, while 69 per cent of those over eighty-five were widowed. Widows outnumber widowers by more than three to one in the over-65 age-group. Immediately after the death of a spouse, family, friends and neighbours rally round to provide emotional and practical support. For the widowed person the first few months after the death of a spouse is spent adapting to the loss of the various supports within the relationship. The social support network is changed in that the death of a husband is also the death of a father and a grandfather and a brother. The family and its support network is altered by the death.

The widow's stage of grief affects how she perceives the social support being offered to her. Emotional support has been shown to have the most positive impact on the newly bereaved widow's well-being. Later on, her well-being is influenced by contact and intimacy along with emotional support. The loss of companionship and living alone are often the most deeply felt changes. However, those who have been widowed for one or two years have established new supports, including relatives — especially children, brothers, sisters — friends new and old, and neighbours. Widows are more likely than widowers to make new friends, while the men are more likely to marry again.

SINGLE/SEPARATED OLDER PEOPLE

In Ireland, in 1991, 22 per cent of those over sixty-five had never married. Less than 1 per cent were divorced or separated.

Older people who never married may have developed a close relationship with their parents over the years. Especially if female, they may be caring for their parents. In other families, the older parents may have fewer health problems than the younger unmarried person and be the carers.

Unmarried people have small family networks with less frequent contact than married people, due to the absence of a spouse and children. Their family life revolves around brothers, sisters and their families. They may be asked to celebrations, such as Christmas and birthdays. Unmarried older people also find companionship and support with people who are treated as family due to the close relationship that has developed.

Although the number of separated/divorced older people in Ireland is small, it is likely to increase for future groups of older people. The age at which people separate and whether they remarry has implications for their support network in later life.

Divorced older people can belong to one of three groups, based on their age and the number of times they separated/divorced. The first group separated in their early or middle years and never remarried. There are more women in this group as men tend to remarry. Many of the women will have raised their children and have their support as they enter old age.

The second group is the older newly separated/divorced who split up after many years of marriage, often when the children left home. While they have children and grandchildren, it is a difficult adjustment period for all the family, and adult children may take sides and support one or other parent. Older people who are newly divorced do not have partners to rely on for help if they are ill and will need to develop alternative sources of assistance.

The third group is those who have had several relationships that ended in separation/divorce. They may have complex family relationships, possibly with children from more than one marriage. There may be many people potentially within their support network, but willingness to help may vary. It is likely that the children of the most recent relationship will help the older person.

C. CHILDREN

There are two main myths about older people and their families. The first is that in previous generations the extended families, grandparents and children lived together and the older person was respected and supported. The second is the belief that today older people do not live with and are not cared for by their families.

Examined historically, the reality is quite different. Until the recent past people did not live into old age in any great numbers, and so many families were not multi-generational. Daily life was much more of a struggle. People had to work physically very hard. Few had a pension or financial security. If you were able to work you had money, and if not poverty followed. If you owned land, you retained it, and younger people had no alternative but to remain unmarried or for a son to marry and move into the parental home. Living together is not at all the most significant factor in the relationship between old people and their adult children and may not be a harmonious arrangement. A large number of older people live in their own homes, initially as part of a couple and then as a widow or widower. Most prefer to live independently, unless they are sick and/or poor.

Older people do have regular face-to-face contact with their families, as shown by the results of a 1993 European study, given below.

Table 4 Older people's contacts with family

	% **Ireland**	% **UK**	% **EC 12**
Every day	50.1	21.9	44.4
Two or more times a week	19.3	28.3	18.3
Once a week	14.1	19.0	15.5
Once a fortnight	2.5	6.8	6.1
Once a month	3.8	5.6	4.6
Less often	6.8	14.5	7.6
Never/No family or friends	3.4	4.0	3.4

(Commission of EC, Eurobarometer Survey, 1993)

As can be seen from Table 4, half of older Irish people see a family member daily. Only 11 per cent of people with family see them monthly or less. These rates of contact compare well to the European average.

How far older people live from a relative is the major variable in how often they have contact. Families often live near one another. However, in Ireland, as in other countries, having a telephone and/or a car has made distance a less significant factor.

The quality of contact is as important as the quantity. Are the visits brief or lengthy, friendly or hostile, based on affection or obligation? Feelings of affection, responsibility and mutual respect are critical in making the ties between parents and children viable and durable. Many adult children feel that they should help their elderly parents. For some the fact that there is give-and-take on both sides keeps the bonds strong.

What types of social support do parents and children give each other?

These are varied and differ between families and within families at different times. Older people and their adult children visit, have family celebrations, share leisure activities, care when a member is ill, give social and psychological support, may give business/career advice and in some families give financial assistance. The amount of help and care exchanged between parents and adult children is greater than between any other relatives. The amount and direction of help and care depends on the relative resources and needs of each. Excluding the small number of frail and sick older people, parents provide their children with more assistance (help when someone is ill, care for grandchildren, shopping), especially money.

Sick or frail older people are cared for by their families, mainly by the women — daughters and daughters-in-law. This is not a reversal of the child–parent relationship but a relationship based on emotional maturity and independence. It is not based on guilt or a desire to rectify earlier conflicts. This can be a difficult situation for adult children as they are caught between responsibility towards their parents and their personal hopes and wishes.

The expectation that adult children will care for their parents is neither unlimited nor unconditional. There is not common agreement in society regarding what exactly children should do. People consider what other responsibilities adult children have, particularly care of their own children. However, women adult children are seen to have more obligation to care than men.

Another myth about older people and their children is that increased contact with children and grandchildren will raise older people's morale. Family history can be positive or negative, but even if positive, the morale of older people has been found not to be raised due to contact with their adult children, unlike contact with friends. A possible reason is that friendship is a voluntary and mutual choice, thus contributing to the self-esteem of both people. Also, if increased contact is a result of the older person's being in need due to illness or disability, she would associate this with undesirable dependency and loss of confidence.

Older people may feel that they annoy or irritate their children and are unwelcome in their lives. Some older mothers feel that they are emotionally dependent on their children, that they need their children more than the children need them. As a result these women give presents and help at a cost to themselves and do not get the emotional and social rewards. This can lead to low self-esteem and low morale because they are not valued and have no power in the relationship.

GRANDCHILDREN/GRANDPARENTHOOD
Grandparenthood is a part of family life for many people. Between 60 and 70 per cent of middle-aged and older people are

grandparents. In Western societies the average age of becoming a grandparent is approximately fifty for women and a little later for men, so you could be a grandparent for twenty-five years. There is a wide variation in when people become grandparents — from their forties to their sixties. The age at which you become a grandparent may influence your role. Sometimes grandparents are unsure what their role should be.

Grandparents report seeing their grandchildren regularly and being satisfied with the level of contact. The research has found that the maternal grandmother is most involved and emotionally close, and has the most frequent contact.

Grandparents continue to provide emotional and financial support to their adult children, and so indirectly influence their grandchildren's quality of life. They can care for the younger child where the parent is single or where both parents work outside the home, or for short periods, such as holidays. They can be involved in playful leisure activities. Another aspect of grandparenthood is passing on information and values to their grandchildren, as well as cultural and family history. Some grandparents are rather distant from their grandchildren, however, and seldom see them except on holidays.

Grandparents can have an important role when parents divorce. A grandparent can be a continuous and supporting person for both grandchildren and their parents. It can be a difficult time for the grandparents themselves if they feel a failure because their child's marriage has not been successful. Another difficulty is in getting access to their grandchildren. In America, grandparents can now petition for legally enforceable visitation rights to their grandchildren even if the parents object.

Grandchildren generally view their relationship with their grandparents favourably. The age of the grandchildren may colour the reasons for this. Young children of four or five value their grandparents because they spoil them. Eight- to nine-year-olds share fun or enjoyable activities. The older age-group of eleven to twelve are more distant. Grandchildren over eighteen give emotional and practical support to their grandparents. This is partly in return for what they received earlier in their lives, although the grandparents continue to give as well as receive and play an active role in their grandchildren's lives.

D. BROTHERS AND SISTERS

In the area of family relationships, brothers and sisters are important to older people, providing psychological, social and recreational support. An older person can count on a sibling's help, especially as siblings often feel an obligation to one another. If the person does not have a spouse or children to support her, she may rely on such assistance.

Sibling relationships differ from other family relationships in that they are lifelong, have a common background with shared experiences and environment, and are generally equal. Childhood experiences may lead to close relationships, or in some cases to distance.

As a person moves into adulthood, contact with siblings becomes less frequent. Brothers and sisters marry and are focusing on themselves and their careers, a pattern which may continue for the rest of their lives. Although there may not be regular contact, siblings often feel very close to one another, particularly sisters. A small number share intimate details of their lives and fewer still consult siblings about major decisions.

OTHER RELATIVES

Other relationships may provide emotional and practical support to older family members. Nieces and nephews, for example, can be a considerable support to those who do not have children of their own. It has been found that an older person expects relatives to keep in contact if she has no immediate family.

E. FRIENDS AND NEIGHBOURS

Older people remain in touch with their friends and neighbours and receive support from them. They have a small number of intimate friends and a larger number of people with whom they have friendly contacts.

A friend is someone whom you can trust and talk openly to about anything; someone to whom you can turn for help and whose company you enjoy.

Friends are made and lost throughout adult life. Women tend to have closer friends than men, who may have a wide range of social acquaintances. Older people will have frequent contact with their friends. Friendships are freely chosen and their contribution over the years is based on commitment, rather than the obligation or proximity on which family relationships can be based.

It has been found that for healthy older people contact with friends is more fundamental to a high morale, happiness and satisfaction with life than contact with family members. Friends do not substitute or compare with family but give different types of support and with different expectations. Friends and neighbours expect that help will be returned in some form while relatives do not. However, in long-term friendships where failing health requires changes in the relationship due to dependency and need for help, some friendships do not expect the usual return. This is especially true of a friend who is dying, who will receive help and support and cannot return it.

Neighbours may be friends but not necessarily so. More usually, they develop the characteristics of acquaintances, with less closeness than is typical of friends. While family give long-term and practical support, neighbours give help in practical ways on a more short-term basis, particularly if there is an emergency where someone near at hand can be very useful. Neighbours can be of all ages while friends are usually nearer in age to each other.

Neighbours have been found to be important for socialising and day-to-day companionship. In rural Ireland of the 1980s they were the most significant source of contact for more than half of those over sixty-five. 'Level of contact with neighbours varied according to location of house, health, number of immediate family contacts and the person's general attitude' (NCA 1984). Many of these neighbours were themselves old and in turn dependent on another neighbour for support. This can be a very fragile support system, especially as people grow very old.

The friends of older people are usually long-term ones at around the same age and stage of life; this makes older people more vulnerable to losing friends through illness or death. Other friends become inaccessible through frailty and restricted mobility, a problem often compounded by inadequate transport facilities or lack of money (for bus, rail, taxi fares). In addition, it may be more difficult to make new friends as the older person does not have as many of the sources which lead to friendships in earlier life — the workplace, school and after-school activities where one meets other parents, a range of leisure activities, and so on.

In order to retain existing friends and make new ones, an older person is probably best to continue living where she has always lived, or at least in the same area. If leaving her home, the best move may be to housing where her own age-group is living — e.g. a retirement community. There are associations and clubs (Active Retirement Associations, University of the Third Age, Irish Association of Older People; see Directory) for older people which provide them with opportunities to pursue interests and activities together and to make new friends. However, older people should feel free to join clubs based on interest, not only those specifically for older people (e.g. bridge or golf clubs, Irish Countrywomen's Association).

In terms of older people supporting themselves other than by family and/or friends, a system of mutual aid/service exchange can be useful. This is a system to which people contribute one service and receive a different one. People of all ages can join. Examples of this form of exchange — baking, preparing/sharing meals, home decorating, shopping — are as varied as the people who take part. This provides a reliable and inexpensive service as well as the chance to socialise.

One area of support in which older people do not like to turn to families or friends is that of money or financial help. They prefer to seek advice and assistance from formal organisations — e.g. bank, state bodies.

F. FAMILY SUPPORT FOR THOSE IN RESIDENTIAL FACILITIES

In the majority of cases, families have been supporting older people before their admission to residential care. The admission to care can alleviate strain on a family, resulting in their improved mental and physical health. This can allow concentration on the emotional and social support needs of the older person, and/or give her an extra social outlet as she now has somewhere to visit. Generally, families stay in contact with their older members in residential care. Similarly, their own health permitting, friends keep in touch. The more support the person has from relatives and friends, the better the adjustment she makes to residential care.

(ii) WORK AND RETIREMENT

A century ago work was part of life until illness or death ended it. Subsequently, compulsory retirement of people aged sixty-five became the norm. In the 1980s a new generation of people retiring was aged fifty-five and upwards. Redundancy, voluntary early retirement and disability are increasingly determining the work status of older people. These, in turn, are affected by the performance of the Irish and world economies. During the early eighties there was slow economic growth and high unemployment; this was followed by an upturn in the economy. The beginning of the 1990s brought a further recession.

In Europe from the early 1980s the participation of older people (over sixty) in the labour market decreased. In Ireland, while it has declined, it remains relatively high but, as one would expect, decreases with age. In 1991, 15 per cent of men and 3 per cent of women over sixty-five were working. The difference between men and women reflects a lifelong pattern of less participation in work by women for this generation. This is changing with increasing participation rates for younger women.

The unemployment rates for men and women between sixty and sixty-four were 83 per cent in 1990. Older workers experience longer spells of unemployment than younger ones, and many who are made redundant are unemployed for a long time prior to retiring.

Unemployment has made retirement at an earlier age more common. An unemployed older worker finds it very difficult to get another job. (The removal of age limits in recruitment advertisements has been recommended.) Older unemployed people also get low priority for retraining. Early retirement schemes are an encouragement to leave the labour force and could be seen as discriminating. While such a scheme may be adopted in the belief that it will vacate jobs for younger people, often this does not happen. Reclassifying older unemployed people who receive the Pre-retirement Allowance as early retirees is a way of changing their work status and is another form of discrimination.

What are the reasons for retirement?
Retirement no longer occurs only when a person reaches sixty-five; just one-quarter of people now retire at this age. Those doing manual work are more likely to retire earlier than professional and

managerial workers. The reasons people give for retiring are health, age and redundancy. Manual workers retire more often on health grounds than other groups; this may be due to the classification of the older person as disabled and not necessarily because older people are in bad working conditions. For people in professional and managerial work, age was the most common reason for retirement. Redundancy accounted for 13 per cent of older workers retiring, with the rate being three times higher in the private than the public sector.

Is there an ideal age at which to retire?

There is not a fixed age at which all people will want to retire, whether it is sixty, sixty-five or seventy. The phenomenon of early retirement (before sixty-five) can be 'voluntary' in name but pressure may be brought and the older worker is expected to leave. As mentioned, this can sometimes be a means of combating unemployment among younger workers, or it can provide a way for firms to restructure and/or introduce new technology or work practices. It is also based on the belief that older people cannot adjust and learn.

There are consequences of early retirement for the employers, workers and society. The effect on employers may be positive in terms of reorganising and becoming more competitive. However, they may have underrated the strengths that older workers bring to the job, such as loyalty, reliability and conscientiousness. Also, businesses have not looked at the issues of job redesign and training for older workers. One example of such successful training is Bayer, the German chemical company, which trains and updates all its employees. It found that older workers can perform as well as or even better than younger workers, and that they tend to be more stable because of their experience. Older workers took longer to learn the new technologies but their performance was not significantly different. Bayer found that older workers were best suited to certain jobs requiring experience and some specialisation. Training will become a necessity in countries with a high proportion of older people. In Ireland we have an excess of people in all age-groups who are seeking work.

The impact of early retirement can vary. While many people welcome the opportunity, it is generally not introduced for older workers' well-being but for economic reasons. Early retirees do not consider themselves unemployed, employed or retired and do not identify with older pensioners. They are concerned with the level of income in years to come. Often no preparation is given to early retirees, and due to loss of income, missing the people and the work itself, some may regret the move. There can be a knock-on effect for middle-aged workers as their short remaining work-life may mean they are not promoted or given training.

For society, the primary consideration is the financial cost of paying benefits in one form or another — whether it is a pension or a disability benefit, but unhappy people are another cost to society.

As regards the timing of retirement, two options are favoured: flexible and phased retirement. The European Commission has recommended phased retirement, with increased scope for combining earnings with income from pensions. Flexible retirement allows the person some choice regarding age; this is available and encouraged in some EC countries. The USA prohibits mandatory retirement in the Federal Civil Service at any age, and mandatory retirement before the age of seventy in industrial and commercial firms. Pensions are adjusted accordingly, with early drawings at a reduced rate, or deferment and a possible increased rate of pension when it is finally drawn.

Phased retirement makes the transition from work to non-work gradual, providing time to develop interests and activities. Phasing involves steadily reducing the time spent at work while still being a full-time employee. This can vary from extra week(s) off in the years before retirement to a gradual reduction in the number of hours worked each week for the year or two prior to leaving.

These options give people choice and perhaps a greater level of adjustment to retirement. The financial implications for the state and the retired person need to be examined. The desired freedom of choice for older workers is only notional if the pension available at a given age is inadequate.

Where and how do you prepare for retirement?

It is believed that formal preparation for retirement is important and helps people to adjust. Only a small proportion of those retiring in Ireland get the opportunity to attend a pre-retirement course or counselling, and an even smaller proportion (3 per cent in Ireland and 5–10 per cent in the EC) actually attend a programme. Its importance is being recognised and initiatives such as the recent Irish Congress of Trade Unions publications stress the need for pre-retirement education. Similarly, the Retirement Planning Council has issued guidelines for employers to provide comprehensive pre- and post-retirement programmes.

But at what stage should planning happen? There are several points in a person's working life at which pre-retirement education/planning should take place. There are some variations in expert opinion, but putting several of the programmes together the following overall one emerges.

(1) **Mid-life planning:** The course is offered to all employees aged fifty. It is seen as a time to take stock, an opportunity for personal reappraisal in terms of work, financial planning, health, family and leisure.

(2) **Planning for retirement:** This is the more usual course available, at present offered a short while before or on the point of retirement. It is recommended that this take place about ten years before normal retirement. The length of the course can vary from one to three days and it is common for a person's partner to attend too. Some companies offer a short course and individual counselling. The style of the course should encourage participation and allow time for self-reflection. Content can include:
— ageing and adjustment to a new way of life
— health, diet, first-aid
— financial matters: pension, social welfare entitlements, investments, taxation
— housing and living arrangements
— legal matters: making a will and probate
— work and leisure options
— security, safety in the home.
   Following the course, ongoing sessions and access to professional advice and assistance are recommended by the Irish Congress of Trade Unions. A shortened version might be offered midway between the full course and the next stage.

(3) **Pre-retirement course:** Very similar to the above, this is given shortly before retirement and is specifically geared to the retired person — financial, health and leisure needs.

(4) **Retirement function:** A retirement function should be arranged for the employee and her spouse/family. However, her

wishes should be taken into account as regards the type of function and gift — not everybody wants the same thing.

(5) **Post-retirement support:** Some form of contact can be offered to the employee, and a few years after retirement a course can review her adjustment.

There are several ways an employer can support a retired employee.

— Provide counselling. This could be for adjustment to retirement, bereavement, or other problems.

— Encourage an active retirement association.

— Continue to offer membership of group VHI schemes, business, sports or social clubs.

— Continue to send any regular company newsletter.

— At a time of illness or bereavement make contact and offer support as appropriate.

The above programme is a long-term comprehensive and integrated package. Remember that people who retire suddenly, perhaps through redundancy or voluntary retirement, may miss out on one or more of these stages. Their needs for planning or education should also be met.

Do people adjust to retirement?

Retirement is not just a matter of giving up work: you need to adjust to a number of other changes. There will be a decrease in your income and you will have more free time. In the more distant future, your health may decline, resulting in reduced activity. Changes occur in your relationships, and society regards you differently. So while you continue to be the same person, many aspects of your life will change.

Only one-third of retired people have a serious problem adjusting; a person with a low level of tolerance for change may find it especially difficult. About ten years beforehand you recognise that retirement is part of your life but it seems a long way off. The obvious time of change is as you are about to retire, with the prospect of the lessening of income, loss of colleagues, spending more time with your spouse, more time for leisure activities. Immediately afterwards, you may be excited, with a sense of freedom. A few months later, you may feel disenchanted, missing your colleagues, finding you have too much time on hand and not enough money to maintain your customary lifestyle. Most people learn to adjust and establish a new organised and happy life. The amount of change you have to make will also depend on how important your job was to you.

Why do some people adjust to retirement more successfully than others?

There is much debate about why some people adjust better than others. Certain variables contribute to adjustment.

It is often believed that if your work is either a small or big part of your life, and gives you a little or a lot of satisfaction, you will adapt well to retirement, though it is unclear why this should be so. What is known is that if you can voluntarily retire from work you will adjust better.

Financial and personal resources are critical in adjustment to retirement. Your income is one of the most central aspects; how secure you perceive it to be may be more important than the level of income or standard of living. Low income is associated with dissatisfaction in retirement. Greater satisfaction in retirement is linked to good health. Poor health may mean a person experiences pain, disability, the need for care or the need to move house, and more difficulty in dealing with retirement. There is no decline in health due to retirement, so people who die soon after this point die because of an existing medical problem.

Personal resources, in terms of family and friends to offer support, smooth the transition from work to retirement and make it easier to adjust. For a married couple, the retirement of one requires changes for the partner. There will be a lot more time to spend together — which may be good or bad. A woman whose husband retires may find he is around the house competing for the jobs she has always done, or sitting in the chair waiting for her to include him in her social life. If the person retiring has relatives, neighbours or friends who are also retired, this provides other people who have gone through the same process and may be available for companionship.

A key element in your adjustment to retirement is the type of person you are. If you have been adaptable to change in your life, retirement will be approached in the same way. If you are flexible and do not resist change, you will adjust more easily. A problem-solving approach to life will help you see retirement in a positive light.

Being actively involved in a hobby or leisure pursuit is

considered helpful in adjusting to ageing and retirement. This can mean continuing with existing activities, renewing old or taking on new ones. Hobbies can vary from the sporting (golf, tennis) to the social (card-playing, dancing) to the solitary (reading, watching TV). Some people start, continue or resume their education by taking courses. Others work either in a voluntary capacity or in paid employment. The area of voluntary work is one of huge potential. Older people have a lifetime of knowledge and experience, and can use existing skills or learn something new. Possibilities in the local community include working with young people in play-groups or nurseries, adult literacy schemes, and services for older people. Voluntary organisations, of which 600 are listed in the Directory of National Voluntary Organisations published by the National Social Service Board, are looking for people with many kinds of abilities, from listening/counselling to skills in selling, art, sport, typing, finance, and so on. A Senior Service Programme, run by the Agency for Personal Services Overseas for people aged fifty-five to seventy, is an opportunity to share management, professional and technical experience with developing countries.

Finally, if you are positively disposed to retirement you are more likely to make a favourable adjustment and more likely to plan for retirement, i.e. make financial arrangements, organise activities for yourself, and attend some form of pre-retirement programme.

PROBLEMS AND THEIR EFFECTS

CHAPTER 6

INCONTINENCE

What is incontinence?

Continence is the ability to control the passing of the contents of the bladder (urine) and bowel (faeces), and to pass the contents only when you want to. Incontinence means the loss of that control. Incontinence of urine is more common and can occur during the day and/or night.

Incontinence is *not* a disease but an indication that some medical, psychological or environmental problem exists.

Is it a serious problem?

Incontinence can be a very distressing and embarrassing problem, leading the sufferer to hide the problem even from her doctor. It can also give rise to depression, guilt, shame and loss of self-esteem, and a reduction in activities outside the home. Due to the embarrassment it may affect the person's sex life.

Case 1

Each year, Jean went to stay with her niece at Christmas, Easter and during the summer. However, one Christmas she refused to come, saying she had a 'heavy cold'. At Easter time she was vague about her reasons for not staying. Her niece had also noted that she had stopped travelling into the city centre but would shop locally and go on short bus journeys. Her niece invited her for the usual summer holiday and Jean was again vague, saying she was expecting her daughter from abroad and felt 'low in herself'. Her niece questioned her further. She raised the possibility that Jean did not want to stay with her and implied she was hurt. Jean

---

became upset and explained that she had begun to have occasional accidents at night during the past year. Prior to that, she was 'leaking' during the day. She had not told her doctor or the Public Health Nurse who visited her regularly. She felt ashamed of her lack of control and depressed because she had to stop going on longer journeys and holidays. She had been using only sanitary towels and they became wet in a short time.

Incontinence is also a problem for carers. It involves more work in washing the person, the bed-linen, clothes and perhaps the furniture and carpets. For some, this increase in dependency and extra workload is the last straw. In this position you may be angry and resentful towards your relative, feel you can no longer cope on a full-time basis and seek residential care for her.

Is it a common problem?

Incontinence is not part of normal ageing. As we age:
— the amount the bladder holds is reduced
— a small amount of urine may not be passed
— the desire to urinate may be delayed
— the bladder may become excitable and contract.

These changes may mean that a person passes urine more often and gets less warning than she needs to. However, only 6 to 11 per cent of people over sixty-five living in the community and in institutions have been found to have urinary incontinence. An even smaller number, 3.1 per cent, have faecal incontinence. Urinary incontinence becomes more frequent with age, with 21.7 per cent of those over eighty experiencing it. The embarrassment surrounding the condition adds to difficulties in estimating the problem.

Are there different types and causes of urinary incontinence?

There are many different types and causes. The most common are:

Urge incontinence: The muscles of the bladder contract very frequently before your bladder is full. This leads to you wanting to pass water urgently. You may leak if you do not get to the toilet immediately. This is one of the commonest causes of incontinence in older people. It can occur with no obvious cause or following a stroke, dementia or Parkinson's disease.

Stress incontinence: Caused by weak muscles around the bladder opening, this is especially common in women after childbirth or after the menopause. You may leak a little when you laugh, cough or sneeze, run or lift something. It may also happen when you go upstairs or downhill or get up from a chair or bed. Exercises to strengthen the pelvic floor muscles are recommended for this type of incontinence.

Overflow incontinence: You may notice that you are dribbling urine all the time. You have to strain to pass urine. Your water is a trickle rather than a stream. It can also happen that you leak immediately after you think you have passed all your urine. This type of incontinence is more common in men, due to an enlarged prostate gland. Constipation can also cause overflow incontinence as the very full bowel may put pressure on the opening of the bladder.

Underactive bladder: You may have to strain to empty your bladder, you sometimes dribble and need to go to the toilet often. The bladder muscles are unable to contract properly. This type of incontinence is common in people with diabetes or injury to the lower part of the spinal cord.

Medicines: The bladder may be disturbed by certain medicines, e.g. diuretics (water tablets), tranquillisers, some medication used for chronic asthma or bronchitis. Also, certain medications may affect the person's mental alertness (sedatives, sleeping-tablets) and contribute to the development of incontinence. Talk to your doctor; it may be possible to change the type of medicine or dose.

Physical ability: Incontinence can be related to the physical ability to manage the act of urinating. Some diseases (arthritis, stroke, Parkinson's disease) make it difficult for the person to reach the toilet, undress and sit down on time.

Environment: The environment, by being unfamiliar, uncomfortable, unsafe and/or lacking in privacy, may contribute to incontinence.

Depression: Depression, anger or apathy can also contribute to incontinence, although this tends to be rare. However, it is important that physical causes are investigated and that the person is not blamed if the problem is emotional in origin.

Dementia: Some people who have dementia may develop incontinence in the later stages of the disease (see p. 85).

Sometimes incontinence can be the result of several problems together, e.g. arthritis, depression and a bladder problem.

What help is available?

There are many ways in which incontinence can be improved or made easier to manage. Don't suffer in silence. Talk to your GP. She may refer you to a hospital consultant or to the Public Health Nurse, a special continence nurse or a physiotherapist. Your doctor will take a history of the problem and send a sample of urine to check for an infection or undetected diabetes.

Depending on the assessment, you may be:

— referred to a specialist for further investigation
— prescribed medication
— given exercises to strengthen the muscles surrounding the bladder
— given a programme for 'retraining' the bladder, which helps extend the time between each visit to the toilet
— given surgery to repair the bladder or for the prostate gland
— taught self-catheterisation, where you or a relative drain the bladder a few times a day by putting in and taking out the catheter. This is used in the management of underactive bladder.
— referred to an occupational therapist if incontinence necessitates changes to your environment, e.g. a higher toilet seat, commode or urinal (bottle), or clothing that is easier to manage
— prescribed plenty of fluids so your urine does not become concentrated. If you are on water tablets, check with your doctor how much you should drink. Drinking fluids also prevents constipation. Between six and twelve cups per day are recommended, with water and juices being the best drinks.
— given various sizes and types of pads for day and night if your incontinence cannot be cured or improved. There are also different types of collecting-bags which can be used, some for men only. A man who is confused due to dementia may pull off these bags. Once the bag is regularly emptied, you can be dry, comfortable and odour-free.

Jean informed the Public Health Nurse of her incontinence. Following assessment she was advised to spend more time on the toilet and try to make sure her bladder was empty. She was advised not to cut down on the amount she drank, but not to have too much to drink after her tea. These suggestions helped but some leaking continued. She was supplied with a pad, and pants to hold it, for use every day, with a larger size for when she is away from home for longer and unable to change and dispose of the pad. She uses an incontinence bed-pad which keeps her skin and the bed dry.

She resumed her visits to the city centre, has stayed with her niece and no longer feels 'low in herself'.

Are there different types and causes of faecal incontinence?
Leaking may be caused by weakening of the muscles which keep the rectum closed. This can be the result of childbirth, lack of exercise or straining when constipated. Leaking can also occur due to severe constipation. This is because watery faeces begin to leak around the hard faeces in the bowel.

Injury or damage to the spine or brain (stroke or accident) may affect the nerves that send the messages between the rectum and the brain. Some medicines (painkillers) can cause or increase constipation, leading to leaking of watery faeces. Problems, such as depression, or major emotional upsets, such as bereavement, can also lead to faecal incontinence.

What help is available?
As with urinary incontinence, the condition can be improved and often cured. It is not a part of normal ageing. If you have a change in your normal bowel habits, blood in your faeces, incontinence or leaking, see your GP, who will take a history of the problem and refer you on if necessary. If the problem cannot be cured, incontinence pants can be worn and bed protection is also available. Emptying of the bowels prior to intercourse, protection of the bed if there is leakage, or exploration of alternative sexual fulfilment will ensure that your sex life continues.

Residential and nursing homes should have a policy on managing incontinence. Their routines should fit in with the needs of the person, with assessment of each individual essential. The physical environment is particularly important, with at least one toilet for every four residents, not too far away. Help needs to be given in a way that allows people to maintain their dignity.

CHAPTER 7

DISEASES WITH PSYCHOLOGICAL CONSEQUENCES

A. ALZHEIMER'S DISEASE AND OTHER DEMENTIAS

What is dementia?

Dementia is due to disease and is not part of the normal process of ageing. It is 'a condition which damages the brain leading to a slow progressive impairment of memory, personality and intellect which limits the individual's ability to cope with the needs of everyday life' (Report of the Working Party on Services for the Elderly, 1988). The person is awake and not drowsy. Dementia is a disease of long duration, it is progressive and generally irreversible. It is difficult to predict the rate of its progress: it can be steady but just as often can be erratic and uneven. Similarly, it is difficult to predict how long the person will live, but once diagnosed, people generally live for between two and ten years, longer in some cases.

Dementia occurs in 6 to 10 per cent of people over the age of sixty-five and increases to 20 per cent of those over eighty. In the over-65 age-group in Ireland, up to 40,000 people may have dementia. The majority of sufferers are cared for at home.

Dementia is used to describe different diseases that lead to decline in various abilities. Certain vitamin deficiencies, a brain tumour, meningitis, thyroid problems or severe depression can cause symptoms of dementia in older people. These diseases may be treatable, in which case the symptoms of dementia will disappear.

Alzheimer's disease is the commonest cause of irreversible and progressive dementia. The causes of the disease are not fully understood. While there is no cure, a full medical examination is necessary to make sure the symptoms of dementia are not related to another disease.

Multi-infarct dementia is the second most common cause of irreversible dementia. It is due to stroke and cardiovascular disease. A stroke happens in the brain, and causes an area of it to die. Each stroke is in itself minor but the damage accumulates and dementia results. Because of the variation in the site and number of strokes, people with multi-infarct dementia will vary in their disabilities and the rate at which the disease progresses. Because of the associated risk of strokes, it is essential to control high blood pressure; similarly heart disease and diabetes. Some people have both Alzheimer's disease and multi-infarct dementia.

How do you find out if someone has dementia?

To arrange a medical assessment for dementia see your own or your relative's GP. An assessment may be carried out by a GP, a geriatrician, or a psychiatrist who specialises in working with old people. The assessment will involve a detailed history being given by someone who knows the person well. The doctor will examine mental functioning in the areas of memory, concentration, ability to think and copy simple designs. A clinical psychologist may be needed to assess these functions in greater detail. The doctor will order various laboratory tests, and a scan of the brain may be arranged.

The results of the assessment can be helpful to the person and her family. What a person can and cannot do for herself is established, and plans for support now and in the future can be made. The person may need to make a will or be made a ward of court, if she cannot handle her own affairs.

At this stage, family and carers may be puzzled and frightened. The changes are sometimes put down to an accident or some other recent incident. A bereavement is often seen as the cause, when in fact the deceased was helping the person with dementia and so it went unnoticed by others. Sometimes the person with Alzheimer's disease is seen as awkward or difficult.

The diagnosis can be shocking, and sometimes families and carers go through emotions similar to those experienced following the death of someone close. It may be helpful to attend a relatives' support group (Carers' Association, Alzheimer Society; see Directory). A family meeting — with the sufferer involved, if possible — can examine the needs to find out what professional help is available to the carers.

What happens to the sufferers?

A person with Alzheimer's disease can live for several years after the diagnosis is made. It is hard to be sure when the disease started to develop; by the time of diagnosis it may have been present for some years. The signs of Alzheimer's disease vary from person to person. The first change the person herself may notice is in her memory, and this might be ascribed to old age, depression, anxiety, a recent bereavement or stress at work. Sometimes it is only looking back that the symptoms are recognised as early signs of Alzheimer's disease.

As the disease develops, the symptoms become noticeable to other people. Due to memory problems the person often repeats herself in conversation. It is extremely tiring for the carer to listen endlessly to the same questions and stories, and it requires endless patience to repeat the same remarks and answers. Kettles and saucepans are boiled dry or burned, or worse the gas may be left on and not lit. The person may get lost when out or want to go shopping at night. These memory losses increase the burden of care. The person becomes a less complex version of herself; this is a particular burden for carers. There are, however, exceptions, with the person undergoing a drastic personality change, doing and saying things she would never before have done. In some cases, the changes in the brain and/or the stress of the disease cause aggression. The person with Alzheimer's disease can become upset if asked about any of these difficulties; she may be angry or deny there is any problem. As the disease progresses, greater amounts of care will be required. Carers must regularly review the situation (see Chapter 10), and ask, 'Can I continue? What help do I need?'

When Alzheimer's disease has progressed for what may be several years, the person is likely to be disabled in many ways. Her memory will be very poor. She may be unsure who the family members are — daughters can be mistaken for sisters. A woman who has been married may give her single name. The relationship between the carer and the dementia sufferer is gradually changed; some carers may feel it is destroyed. There can be progressive deterioration in the person's ability to understand what is said to her and to express herself so she can be understood. She may not know the time of day or her address. She may need a spoon to feed herself or need to be fed. She may become incontinent at night, then during the day. Help will be needed with dressing and washing. The sufferer can be emotionally withdrawn. Some people in the last stage of Alzheimer's disease will be unable to walk or talk.

Each person with dementia needs to be seen as an individual. While some problems are common to all (memory loss, loss of intellectual ability, personality change), each person will have different problems and different reactions to them. The variance may be due to the type of dementia, the stage of the illness, the extent of the damage, the person's age and physical health.

Case 1

Kathleen (forty-five years old) works part-time as a nurse, and is caring for her mother (sixty-five) in the suburbs of Dublin. Kathleen has two children aged eight and ten and has been separated from her husband for three years. She moved into her mother's home following her separation. Though a bit forgetful, her mother had been coping with living alone and could mind the children if Kathleen went out for an evening. However, she grew more forgetful and got lost out on a walk while on holidays. Following this, she was assessed and Alzheimer's disease was diagnosed. She is very confused, clinging and reluctant to be left alone. She has occasional incontinence at night.

Kathleen cares for her mother during the week and gets a break when she attends a day centre, one day a week. Kathleen's sister takes her mother to her home each weekend, from Friday to Sunday evening. Kathleen's children go to their father for the same time. Kathleen works Friday and Saturday nights in a local hospital.

At present, Kathleen feels she is coping but has no social life, especially as she has moved and lost some of her friends and neighbours. She had a good relationship with her mother, who was very supportive during her marital problems. However, Kathleen resents the fact that she is left to carry the main load of caring and that her two other sisters living in Dublin give no practical help.

What are the problems of dementia?

The person with dementia should be treated as a normal adult but given the practical and social support needed to allow her to live as independently as possible. As long as enough support is available, it is best if she can remain in her own home. The majority of people with dementia are cared for in their own or relatives' homes. Dementia gives rise to many and varied problems. As a carer you need to consider your own needs. Accept all offers of help, seek professional advice and try to get some time for yourself. You are facing problems in day-to-day living as well as the behavioural difficulties of a person with dementia.

Some of the common problems are outlined below but more detailed information is available in books devoted entirely to the subject (see Bibliography) and from the Alzheimer Society of Ireland.

PROBLEMS OF DAILY LIVING

Constant watching and minding: Irish carers of people with dementia find this the most difficult aspect. Daily life is unpredictable and it can be hard to establish a routine, making caring more stressful.

Safety: While this is important for all older people (see p. 39), the deficits of dementia make it more so. The following areas need special consideration:
— fire risk due to memory problems: gas cookers, heaters, smoking
— dangerous substances: medicines, household cleaning fluids can be taken unknowingly
— cooking and boiling water: again, memory problems may mean these are not attended to
— driving: whether the person is able to drive safely and find her way.

Personal hygiene: The person may forget or lose the ability to carry out the task of washing or dressing. Initially, a tactful reminder may be all that is required, but over time direct help will be necessary.

Eating: Since people forget to shop, cook or eat, weight loss may result. As the disease progresses, help with feeding may be necessary and/or the use of aids and food that make it easier to eat by oneself.

Social life: Both the sufferer's and the carer's social life will be affected. It is essential that the carer continue her social life. Changes will gradually need to be made to the sufferer's social life, e.g. going to a different restaurant or pub that is informal or quiet.

PROBLEMS OF DIFFICULT BEHAVIOUR

Wandering: This is used to describe different behaviours, from aimless activity, to the person wanting to be somewhere else, to night-time walking. While restricting the person's access may be necessary, locking her in a room is not advisable; she may become frustrated and angry. If she tends to wander outside, a bracelet with her name, telephone number and address should be worn.

Anger and aggression: If the person with dementia is angry or feels threatened or unable to cope or communicate, she may be verbally or physically aggressive to you. This can occur as a worsening of a previously irritable or aggressive manner; it can also represent a complete change of behaviour for this person. The abuse and aggression can appear in any situation, but may be more likely when the carer is in close proximity to the person, e.g. washing, dressing or showering. It is best to avert the confrontation if you can. Try to keep calm and do not be angry. Give her more space and try again later.

If this behaviour is common, you need help. This may mean someone to listen to you, or it may mean professional help — to work out what triggers the aggressive behaviour or to prescribe medication. If, in the long term, the outbursts continue, you may have to consider seeking residential care for your relative.

Case 2

Jane (seventy years old) cares for her husband, Bill (seventy), who has dementia. Before his illness, Bill was gentle and even-tempered.

He was diagnosed as having dementia a year ago. The condition has progressed rapidly and he is very confused and forgetful. Over the past few months, he has become irritable and aggressive towards Jane. The worst incident was when he hit her when she was helping him to wash himself. At other times he pushes her away. Also, he is very moody and can be verbally aggressive and argumentative with her. Jane felt both frightened and ashamed of what happened. She was anxious that the same thing would happen again and concerned she would become angry with him. Jane told a friend of hers, who also cared for a husband with dementia, and she advised Jane to tell the GP. He referred Bill to a geriatrician who prescribed some medication. This helped, in that Bill was less irritable. The aggressive outbursts during washing have been helped by Jane's not insisting that he wash every morning. If he resists, she leaves it and tries again later in the day.

The couple lived in their own house in a town in a rural area. They have children living locally who call regularly, but because of Bill's aggression Jane does not want him to stay in any of their homes, which would give her a rest. She would like to know she could take a break a few times a year, with Bill going into a local nursing home, but is worried that he might be aggressive. She is under a lot of stress and knows she cannot continue to care alone; she is anxious and lonely and is only coming to accept the loss of the kind person Bill was for the forty years they have been together.

Incontinence (see Chapter 6): Up to a third of people with Alzheimer's disease wet themselves and have bowel motions in their clothes or in the wrong place or container. Incontinence occurs more often in older people who have dementia. This can be due to a problem with the bladder, inability to recognise the need to urinate or defecate and be able to plan to do so, or inability to find the toilet. In a small number of dementia sufferers, smearing of faeces is a problem. This can be due to constipation or the person not cleaning herself after using the toilet. Diet, exercise and sufficient fluids are important to prevent constipation. If it occurs, medication can be given to re-establish bowel movements; it is not advisable to use laxatives habitually. If incontinence happens suddenly, it may mean the person has a urine infection or is constipated, both of which can be treated by a GP. Indeed, infection and constipation can lead to apparent greater confusion and agitation in a dementia sufferer. A Public Health Nurse in your area may specialise in the management of incontinence problems and advise you on how to deal with it and on appropriate aids and incontinence wear. Do not accept that nothing can be done for the incontinence because your relative has dementia.

Case 3

Tom (seventy-six years old) lives in a remote rural area and has been caring for his wife, Rose (seventy-four), for the past six years, since Alzheimer's disease was diagnosed. Rose is now unable to talk to Tom or even to recognise him. He has to dress and wash her. She can feed herself with a spoon. By being taken to the toilet every two hours, Rose is dry in the day, but soils herself regularly. At night Tom uses incontinence sheets. For the past six months, Tom has been finding caring for Rose a strain. He feels tired, as she gets up most nights. He also cannot leave her alone in the house. He takes her for walks. He drives to the local village weekly to buy groceries, and a neighbour sits with Rose. He goes for a drink but has difficulty relaxing and does not stay long. His sister calls once a week and helps practically by doing some housework and the ironing. The only other source of support is Rose's nephew, who calls one or two evenings a week. Tom enjoys their conversation on farming and sport as he has no other conversation in the week.

Tom feels sad and depressed at losing the person Rose was. He hopes he can keep caring for her at home until her death, when he will lose the 'shell of a person she has become'.

Repeating the question and clinging: These are two very wearing and irritating behaviours for you as a carer to live with. The problems develop because of the person's poor memory and a sense of insecurity, leading to a need for constant reassurance. To cope, you need time away from the person. If you have a personal stereo, the headphones may enable you to escape into some music or radio programme. If you can reassure the person rather than answering the question it may be helpful. If the person can still read, you could write out the day's activities or the answers to the questions being asked.

Embarrassing behaviours: In the later stages of Alzheimer's disease some people take off their clothes in an inappropriate place, accuse people of stealing from them, or scream and shout for long periods. These behaviours can be hard to manage but are the result of brain damage.

What is caring like?

Caring for someone with dementia is a demanding task both physically and emotionally, which may extend over many years. You need to take care of yourself by having time off, getting help and support, and examining your legal and financial position. If you decide to place your relative in a nursing home, do not feel guilty. Accept that you did your best with a very difficult disease which often leaves a 'shell of the person' you once knew. If your relative goes into residential care you may experience a sense of relief. This may be mixed with a sense of emptiness, of wondering what to do with yourself after years of coping. It takes a long time to build up a new life (see Chapter 10).

How can dementia sufferers be helped?

While there is no cure or drug that will halt the process of dementia, major changes have been taking place in our thinking about dependency in older people and dementia sufferers. Various forms of assessment have been developed of the needs and interventions that will increase independence. This assessment should be offered to care-givers in the community. Each dementia sufferer should have an individual care plan of her needs, with interventions based on this. People who suffer from dementia can learn new information, change their behaviour, and relearn some skills, e.g. washing themselves, although they learn at a slower rate. Behavioural approaches to the management of difficult behaviours, incontinence or aggression can be taught to carers. Reminiscence therapy, which is using memories as a way to communicate and socialise, can be tried. Its progress can be steady but can just as often be erratic.

The design of environments for people with dementia attempts to deal with the problems and deficits of the disease. In residential facilities, the design aims to help the resident enjoy privacy, dignity and self-esteem, and to feel at home.

Planning of buildings should accommodate wandering and allow stimulation without stress. There should be easy orientation and identification of key facilities (e.g. toilet, sitting-room) and a clear route to them. There should also be areas of interest and activity, a bay window, alcoves with tables and chairs so a person does not continue walking when she is exhausted. An open-plan layout helps to achieve these goals and lessens the need for corridors, which are not recommended for people with dementia. Staff also have the opportunity for unobtrusive observation. If corridors are unavoidable, they need to be wide and allow space for activity. Colour-coding can counter visual confusion and disorientation.

There are guidelines available for the design of windows, e.g. not to extend down to floor level as they can be mistaken for doors. All windows should be fitted with a restrictor which allows the resident to open the window for air without either falling or being able to climb out.

Carpet in general is preferable to vinyl as it avoids the problem of reflection and glare. It should be plain, as patterns can give the impression that there are holes in the floor or that the level has changed. This can lead to confusion, anxiety and sometimes impaired balance in people with dementia.

Walls should be neutrally covered. Patterns should be avoided as bold designs can be overstimulating and small patterns can produce blurred vision.

Finally, dementia sufferers can be assisted by providing the informal and formal support services they need. This leads to less stressed and healthier carers who are not paying a high personal price and can therefore deliver high-quality physical and psychological attention.

B. ACUTE CONFUSIONAL STATE

In an acute confusional state the person has problems in her thinking, attention and behaviour. Generally beginning suddenly, it is sometimes mistaken for dementia, but unlike dementia it can be treated and is not permanent. However, some people with dementia can also develop an acute confusional state. The condition is more common in older people. Because the confusion is temporary and is associated with severe physical illness, the exact number of sufferers is difficult to measure.

How would you know if someone had an acute confusional state?

The onset is sudden, the condition generally developing over hours or days. The person may fluctuate between being alert and drifting into semi-consciousness. She has difficulty in concentrating and knowing where she is and who is with her. She may be hard to understand, and may misconstrue things around her (e.g. noise, lights). The person is frightened and may be unpredictable and aggressive. She may be agitated and have difficulty sleeping, the confusion being worse at night. There can be a wide variation in symptoms. One person can be very agitated, another quietly confused. Also, the disturbance of consciousness can vary from a person being unaware of her environment, to being very easily distracted, to focusing on looking for something that is not there. The condition can vary within the same person.

What causes acute confusional state?

Acute confusional state develops as a side-effect of an illness, medications, an environmental change or emotional problem. The causes can be grouped as follows:

Organ function disorder: A heart, kidney or liver disorder can contribute to an acute confusional state.

Infections: Often chest or urinary tract infections can produce an acute confusional state in an older person.

Metabolic disturbances: Under- or over-activity of the thyroid and the pancreas are causes of acute confusional state.

Nutritional imbalance: Dehydration and vitamin deficiencies point to the importance of an adequate diet. As vitamin deficiency may develop slowly, confusion may increase over a period of time.

Stroke: A stroke, head injury or, more rarely, tumour may lead to acute confusional state.

Medications: Older people are more vulnerable to the side-effects of medications (see p. 46), a problem compounded by the fact that they are often on several medications. As the effects may take weeks or months to build up, the acute confusional state may develop over a similar time-span. Some of the medications which can cause confusion are long-acting benzodiazepines, medicines for Parkinson's disease and certain antidepressants. Alcohol can be associated with this condition, because of a decline in toleration with age or because it is taken with medication.

Surgery: There is some evidence that older people experience confusion after an anaesthetic.

Environmental change: Acute confusion is much more common among older people than younger people admitted to hospital. In older people, the normal age change in vision and hearing and the effects of illness and medication, when combined with a lot of stimulation (bright lights, lots of activity), can produce disorientation; similarly in cases of reduced stimulation brought about by hearing and/or visual problems.

How can acute confusional state be managed?

Recovery from the condition depends on its cause and severity. If treatment can be given for an underlying medical condition recovery will be good, with little or no lasting impairment. If the treatment can be carried out at home and care can be arranged, the person may remain there. However, if she wanders, refuses to drink or eat and is very agitated or fearful, admission to hospital may be necessary.

Because acute confusional state may take several weeks to clear, it is vital to provide a consistent and supportive environment. Due to misperceptions and disorientation, the person will tend to misinterpret her environment. Extremes of noise or light should be avoided, e.g. no totally darkened rooms. The surroundings should be as familiar as possible. If a person is in hospital, the presence of familiar things is recommended, e.g. it is better if her bed is not moved within the ward or, when possible, that she remains in the same ward.

C. PARKINSON'S DISEASE

Symptoms and problems

Parkinson's disease affects the part of the brain which controls muscular movements, and it results in rigidity of muscles, slowing of movement and tremor. These symptoms may not all be present or may not appear equally in each person. Sometimes too much movement is the problem (tremor) while at other times not enough, leading to difficulty in initiating movements and stiffness. If the muscles of the throat are involved, speech is slow and slurred. Swallowing may become a problem for some people. The tremor affects the hands and possibly the legs, head and jaw. The slowness of movement is the most disabling part of Parkinson's disease. This can result in loss of expression in the face and sometimes drooling. The person looks as if she is stooping, and does not swing her arms. These changes, along with a shuffling type of walk, can lead to unsteadiness and falls. There may be constipation, urinary incontinence and erectile problems.

Some but not all people with Parkinson's disease have memory and intellectual problems, similar to those seen in Alzheimer's disease. They are found more often in the later stages of the disease, and a contributory factor may be depression, more common in those with Parkinson's disease. This may be related to the person's knowing that she has the disease and that it is progressive. Possible changes in her ability to function in her job, social life and day-to-day activities may result in an altered view of herself, which can lead to depression. It may also be due to the actual brain damage interfering with the person's mood.

Parkinson's disease usually begins between the ages of fifty and seventy. Estimates of the number of people who have the disease range from one to two in a thousand of the population. More older people may have Parkinson's disease but not be diagnosed. The severity and rate of progress of the disease varies from person to person. For some there is little interference with normal activities for several years. The disease may develop over a ten- to fifteen-year period.

What causes and helps Parkinson's disease?

The cause of Parkinson's disease is loss of brain cells in a particular area of the brain and the loss of a chemical called dopamine. What causes the loss of these brain cells is unknown.

Medications (e.g. levodopa) which help to compensate for the chemical loss are prescribed. Other medication may also be used to deal with the symptoms. This treatment can give a better quality of life and also increase life expectancy.

Research is being carried out involving a surgical operation in which a number of the same type of cells that are lost from the brain are transplanted from a foetus. These operations have not yet produced a breakthrough in the treatment of Parkinson's disease.

Physiotherapy can be beneficial to a person with Parkinson's disease. In order to help the rigid muscles remain in use, partaking in daily activities and exercise is important; also, the person needs to do as many things as possible for herself, no matter how slowly. Family members can help by giving encouragement and being patient, taking part in any exercise programmes, and being supportive if the person is depressed or angry.

D. STROKE

Stroke usually happens suddenly and is a shock to the older person and her family. She may be fearful of permanent disability and the end of her active life.

If the blood supply to the brain is disrupted, a stroke (cerebrovascular accident or CVA) may occur. Strokes happen over minutes or hours. They may be mild or severe, and a person may have several small strokes. They are more common the older you become. Five per cent of people over sixty-five have had at least one. More men than women suffer from a stroke.

What are the causes and types of strokes?

There are often many factors that put a person at risk for stroke. An inherited tendency to heart disease, smoking, high blood pressure, being overweight or having diabetes put someone more at risk of having a stroke.

There are two main types of stroke: one is due to the death of brain tissue because of insufficient blood supply to an area of the brain (infarction); the other is due to bleeding into or around the brain (haemorrhage). Because of the different types of stroke and areas of the brain affected, each stroke patient's problems will be different.

In the first type of stroke, death of brain tissue (infarction) occurs due to a clot forming within a vein or artery in the brain or travelling there from somewhere else in the body. The person may be conscious and may have a headache.

The second type of stroke is caused by bleeding in the brain itself causing a clot to form, and is primarily a consequence of high blood pressure. With this type of stroke the person frequently will have a headache, dizziness, nausea and vomiting. She gradually becomes sicker and may go into a coma. Bleeding around the brain into its very thin covering (subarachnoid space) is due to a weakness in the wall of a blood vessel blowing up like a balloon (an aneurysm). The aneurysm may rupture and cause a haemorrhage. This type of stroke usually occurs during strenuous activity or shortly afterwards. The person has a sudden severe headache and may develop a stiff neck and pain down the back over several hours. Consciousness may be lost within seconds or minutes.

Some people may experience blurring of vision, double vision, brief tingling or numbness in a hand or foot or weakness in an arm or leg, dizziness, difficulty swallowing or confusion or difficulty talking. These are temporary impairments due to an insufficient supply of blood to a part of the brain. The symptoms may last a few minutes or hours before the person recovers. Dizziness without other symptoms is not an indication of these 'mini-strokes' or transient ischaemic attacks. If you experience such an attack, see your doctor immediately. Only some people who have these symptoms will suffer a stroke in the future.

What happens after a stroke?

The disability you have following a stroke will depend on where in the brain the stroke has occurred. Following a severe stroke, you may lose consciousness and when you come around may be confused and disoriented. If the stroke occurs during sleep you may find yourself unable to get out of bed or call for help. Quite often, one side of the body is weak or paralysed. Your balance may be affected. Loss of control of bladder and bowels may occur. There may also be problems with sight and hearing. Your ability to understand what is said and to express yourself may also be impaired. You may have poor concentration and memory, and may tire easily. You may be irritable or changeable in mood. Sensation may be altered or — commonly — reduced, and there may be numbness and pins and needles. You may lose the ability to know what position your limbs are in, and feel as if your arm or leg does not exist. Care must be taken to avoid injury or burns. Exaggerated sensation causes exaggerated reactions to heat, cold and pain. Movement may be painful, which can make rehabilitation difficult.

If you have had one stroke you will not necessarily have another, but this does happen to some people. When a stroke has been associated with high blood pressure (hypertension), medication can be prescribed to reduce the pressure and lessen the risk.

Recovery after a stroke

About one-third of stroke victims make a good recovery, another third have considerable disability and the remainder die within a month of the stroke. We do not know how recovery takes place. It depends on the amount and kind of damage, and the extent to which other areas of the brain can take over from the damaged area. If you have had a severe stroke or have no one to care for you at home, you need to go into hospital. If the diagnosis is unclear, you need tests to ensure you are not suffering from another disease.

Recovery generally proceeds at a faster rate in the earliest stages and then levels off, but can continue in small steps for a variable length of time.

We look first at the psychological aspects of recovery. Following a stroke you may become depressed. This may be due to the amount of brain damage, physical disability, the psychological adjustments to the losses and changes in your life or how your family reacts. You will have difficulty motivating yourself, which may affect rehabilitation. In most cases, the depression will lift over a year, but if it is severe, counselling may be necessary. Anti-depressant medication may also be helpful.

You may find that following a stroke you are very emotional, crying (or less often laughing) more easily, more often, more vigorously or in circumstances that you previously would not have cried in. The emotionalism can range from being close to tears to sobbing, and the episodes can last from under a minute to fifteen minutes. The majority of people know when they are going to cry and have some degree of control over it. It happens in many situations, e.g. following a kind act or expression of sympathy, visitors coming or going, being unable to do something, watching something sad on television.

Some people who are very emotional are depressed, while others are not. The emotionalism develops within a month of the stroke and tends to diminish over the first year. It helps if you and your carers know that this problem is common and generally resolves itself with time. It may be important for the carers not to console you each time it occurs. A physiotherapist or occupational or speech therapist involved in rehabilitation will usually agree to pause until the emotionalism has passed and then continue therapy.

You may experience some memory problems, due to difficulties in concentrating or in recording or recalling the memories. You may be able to learn to use memory aids, such as diaries and timetables. Of course, these are of no use if you do not remember to consult them regularly.

Communication problems, both in understanding what other people say and in expressing yourself, are among the most common disabilities following stroke. This can be frustrating for you and your family. Language impairments can vary from mild (difficulty in finding a familiar word) to severe, where you can say nothing or repeat the same thing over and over again. Some people's speech consists of nonsense words. A speech therapist will assess you and devise a suitable rehabilitation programme. If the problem is very severe, a method of communication using a letter or picture board may be devised.

Loss of movement in an arm or leg can make it hard to walk, stand up, get out of bed, wash, dress or feed yourself. The physiotherapist will provide a rehabilitation programme to combat these difficulties. The earlier physiotherapy begins, the better the results produced; early treatment also prevents stiffness in the affected limb. An occupational therapist can advise on appropriate aids (e.g. bathboard/cutlery) or adaptations to the home that will enable you to function as independently as possible. She may also recommend suitable activities.

Depending on where you live, there may be a nearby branch of the Volunteer Stroke Scheme (see Directory). The scheme provides a volunteer to visit on a weekly basis to work on a programme drawn up for you by the professional (usually a speech therapist). A club is organised where stroke victims meet and are helped. Regular outings are also organised. The scheme provides a counselling service for stroke sufferers and their families. To become involved you need a referral from a speech therapist or your GP.

A stroke changes the life of the victim and her relations for the worse. This can lead to feelings of guilt and selfishness. It is important to express these feelings. The hospital social worker or the Volunteer Stroke Scheme can be of assistance.

CHAPTER 8

PSYCHOLOGICAL PROBLEMS

A. DEPRESSION

Is depression a problem for older people?

Most older people are satisfied with their lives. They have reasonable health, cope with changes, and experience only passing lowering of moods. Therefore, symptoms of depression which persist should not be ignored as a feature of getting older. Up to 3 per cent of older people have severe depression, while another 15–20 per cent have symptoms of depression. These symptoms can be as difficult to cope with as severe depression. Depression is more common in people who are physically ill, but it is unclear whether there is an increase in depression in old age. As at younger ages, women tend to report higher rates of depression. While the majority of older people are not depressed, the fact that it is sometimes considered part of old age means it may be missed or dismissed.

What is depression?

The term depression generally refers to feeling low in mood. We are not including unhappiness here but by depression mean a definite group of symptoms and problems in everyday life, which lasts over several weeks.

The symptoms of depression vary in severity and not every person has all the symptoms, which can be physical, behavioural or psychological.

Symptoms	How you are
Low moods/Sadness	Crying, having difficulty in stopping
Loss of energy and interest	Feeling fatigued, losing interest or pleasure in your usual routine
Feelings of worthlessness and guilt	Thinking your life is worthless, feeling a failure, possibly wanting to punish yourself
Preoccupation with physical complaints	Constipation, increased pains, indigestion
Sleep disturbance	This can vary from difficulty getting to sleep, to waking early in the morning, to being unable to get back to sleep.
Thoughts of death and suicide	The present and future look black. The idea of ending it all can lead to plans to commit suicide: 'Life isn't worth living.'
Concentration	You may find it harder to concentrate or make a decision.
Agitation	You feel your thoughts are 'racing'. Some people repeatedly wring their hands, walk up and down or seek reassurance: 'Will I be all right?' Some may not want to be left alone, even for short periods.
Retardation	You may be slowed in your movements and thoughts. It takes you a long time to answer a question and your walking may be slowed.
Change in eating	Poor appetite or increased appetite with weight loss or gain.

Depression in older people is much the same as in younger people but there are some differences. Older people do not always complain of being depressed but may complain of physical problems — sleep difficulties, constipation, pain or lack of energy and appetite; they are less likely to say they feel guilty or worthless. Also, in a very small number of cases, a depressed older person may appear to be confused and have memory problems. This is not dementia; she will be able to think and remember clearly when no longer depressed.

Several things may contribute to depression in old age. If a person has been under stress recently (death of a close family member, physical illness, retirement) and does not have someone to whom she can talk and feels close, she is more likely to become depressed. Long-term difficulties, such as housing, financial, marital/family, can also contribute to depression in old age. We take a closer look here at some of these problems.

Some older people suffer multiple losses, including loss of health, impaired vision and hearing, loss of income and work role with retirement, and loss of role in their families and perhaps in their wider communities.

BEREAVEMENT

This is one of the most common losses of old age. Loss of a person close to you leads to grieving, a normal part of which is sadness, crying, sleep problems, anger and anxiety. As a bereaved person, you may be depressed for periods as you work through your grieving. If you remain very depressed over several weeks, you may need help to deal with your grief.

PHYSICAL ILLNESS

Physical health problems in old age can be painful and chronic (arthritis, diabetes, stroke) and may give rise to feelings of vulnerability and helplessness. Illness can be a threat to life, to future plans, to carrying out a daily routine. Depression is more common in people who are ill. How you cope depends on your past ability to deal with stress, and the practical and emotional support available to you.

Some physical illnesses can lead to depression, as can medicines given to treat certain illnesses. Check with your doctor.

MARITAL PROBLEMS

If a couple with marital conflict spend more time together following retirement, the rows and arguments may increase. The situation may worsen if one becomes dependent due to ill health. The carer may feel angry and resentful. The person cared for may also resent the situation, be critical and unappreciative and feel hopeless. Depression may be a consequence for either person.

FAMILY PROBLEMS

This includes difficulties between parent and child and between adult sister and brother. Conflicts that could be avoided when you had little contact will emerge if you are together for longer periods. If people who dislike each other live together this will generate resentment and a strained atmosphere, which can contribute to depression.

Older people can feel a failure if their children's marriages fail. Loss of contact with grandchildren can also be an upsetting consequence.

What kinds of help are there for depression?

Older people should seek help for their depression, just like younger people. Unfortunately, depression is not always recognised in older people, and even if it is, help is not always offered. This is a serious matter as older people who are depressed have high rates of suicide. Older people in institutions also become depressed and require help.

Medication: Antidepressant medication can be prescribed by your GP or a psychiatrist. You may in addition or as an alternative seek counselling.

Another form of physical therapy for depression is ECT (electroconvulsive therapy). A small electric impulse is passed through your brain while you are under general anaesthetic. You will normally need a number of treatments. Only a small proportion of older people with depression are treated with ECT, although it is used more commonly for older than for younger people.

Counselling/Therapy: Older people may find the idea of a 'talking cure' somewhat strange but can benefit as much as younger people from therapy. It is important that the counsellor/therapist you attend is qualified and a member of her professional body. The therapist will see you by appointment either at home or in her office. Usually, you will need several visits.

If social or financial problems are at the root of or contribute to your depression, these need to be addressed. For a list of useful organisations, see Directory.

Physical health: Ill health may contribute to depression in several ways:

(1) Depression may be the first sign of an underlying physical illness; you must go to your doctor to have this checked out.

(2) Some medications prescribed for physical illness can lead to depression, as can combinations of medicines. Check with your doctor and ask for a review of your medication, especially if you become depressed after taking a new tablet.

(3) Illness or pain can change your view of yourself and your ability to enjoy yourself. When ill, you can be limited in your activities of daily living (cooking, washing, etc.). This results in greater dependence, which in turn can result in a more negative self-image and feelings of depression. Proper control of pain is essential and this should be discussed with your doctor, or with a hospice in the event of a terminal illness.

Case 1

Margaret (seventy-two years old) is a widow, living alone. She had nursed her husband for several years, prior to his death two years before. After his death she found she had few friends, due to the time and attention she had devoted to him. Her daughter, who lived three miles away, came to visit regularly and phoned her daily. However, Margaret found the days long and empty. She had had difficulty in sleeping after her husband died but within two months slept well again. Approximately eighteen months after his death, she began wakening about 4 a.m. and could not get back to sleep. She had no energy and constantly felt tired. She could not think clearly or make decisions, and thought her life was a failure. She did not want to do her daily shopping.

Margaret went to her GP because she felt so tired all the time. He organised some tests, which showed she was in good health and did not have anaemia. Two months later she went back seeking sleeping-tablets. He discussed Margaret's other problems with her and concluded that she was depressed. He suggested that

Margaret get out more; she did not think she could, given how she felt. Her GP prescribed some antidepressant medication and referred her to the local clinical psychologist.

The clinical psychologist helped Margaret to look at her life and to change the many negative thoughts she had about herself, her life and the future. With this shift in her thinking and weekly support, Margaret began to feel less hopeless. Gradually, she started to socalise more by going to a local Active Retirement Group and re-establishing contact with an old friend whom she phoned weekly and met occasionally. Six months later Margaret felt she was 'back to herself' and had built a new life.

Like younger people, many older people will overcome depression. The earlier you seek help, the better your chances of recovery and the less likely you are to become depressed again; social contact is also significant in this regard. Early recognition and help is critical to prevent long periods of depression. In addition, factors that contribute to depression, such as poverty, loneliness and poor physical health, all need to be tackled at societal and political levels.

B. SUICIDE

Do older people commit suicide and why?
We tend to think that it is younger people who will kill themselves. However, while suicide attempts are more common among the young, the rate of completed suicides is higher among older people, decreasing again among the very old. More men than women of all ages take their own lives. Since 1993, suicide is no longer a criminal act in Ireland, which may help to get the true figure for suicide, currently greatly underestimated. In Canada, although people over sixty-five form less than 10 per cent of the population, they commit between 16 and 25 per cent of all suicides.

Older people less often tell someone they are thinking of suicide. If a person does tell you she is considering it, take it seriously. Talk to her about it and seek help, initially by discussing it with her GP. Other signs include putting affairs in order, making a will and giving belongings away. Of course, these things may be done by an organised person who accepts her own death, so exercise caution.

Someone who talks about death and suicide, though not relating it to herself, may be seeing how the family would react. If someone displays a sudden change in religious interest, either a loss of faith or a resurgence, it may indicate that she is thinking of suicide. These are changes that only a close family member would notice, and you must be aware of what they may mean.

Some of the ways that people commit suicide are by drowning, shooting, hanging and overdosing on medication. Also, older people may fail to take medication that is essential or stop eating and drinking or have 'fatal accidents' which were really suicide acts.

As mentioned earlier, many people who commit suicide are depressed. If an older person suffers severe loss and is socially isolated, she may feel dejected, unwanted and unloved. Her self-esteem lowers, she can see herself as inadequate and feel hopeless. However, only a minority of older people who experience such loss kill themselves.

If a person has a tendency to find change or loss difficult to tolerate or a tendency to feel hopeless, she may be more likely to commit suicide. A person of any age who abuses alcohol to get relief from depression and other problems is more at risk of committing suicide. Drinking large quantities of alcohol increases anxiety and depression. Alcohol may reduce a person's self-control and contribute to her making a suicide attempt. A person may become more isolated through alcohol abuse, shame or fear. All of the factors associated with alcohol abuse, including guilt, may make suicide a more likely option.

It is crucial that anyone depressed seeks and gets help. Also, people who are ill and in pain commit suicide. Many people who are in pain are depressed, making control of pain essential for both physical and emotional health. See your doctor and ask if anything more can be done for pain and disability.

Case 1

John (seventy years old) lived alone following his wife's death three years earlier. He had one son, who lived in Australia. John and his wife were very close and he found it very difficult to come to terms with her death. He began to drink heavily. He had arthritis and was finding it harder to cook and to drive. John did not seek help from any service. He attended his GP for his arthritis but did not tell his doctor of his difficulties with day-to-day living.

John killed himself in his own garage by carbon monoxide poisoning from the exhaust pipe of his car. He left the following note to his son:

> Dear Pat,
> I cannot go on. I miss your mother more every day. The pains seem worse every day and I can't take any more. I do not want to be a burden on anyone. So I'm doing what seems best.
> You have been a good son and I'm proud of your success.
> Your father John.

If someone close to you commits suicide, it is harder to grieve, as you may feel guilty for not noticing how they felt. You may also feel very angry that they did this. Where a member commits suicide, many families will need to attend counselling (Bereavement Counselling, see Directory).

C. ANXIETY, PHOBIAS AND HYPOCHONDRIASIS

Anxiety could be described as excessive worrying. We all worry and become anxious at some time in our lives. It is normal to be somewhat anxious if you have to walk after a fall, are about to have an operation or have been mugged recently. However, if you worry for a long time, if it is very severe or if you start to avoid situations (going out from home) or things (dogs), you have an anxiety problem. In other words, if the anxiety is interfering with you living your everyday life and relating to your family and friends, then it is at a level where you need to seek help.

Surveys of older people have found general anxiety to be a clinically significant problem for at least 4 per cent of them. Another 5 to 10 per cent have phobias (excessive anxiety about a particular thing or situation). Another indicator of anxiety problems is the usage of minor tranquillisers (e.g. Valium), higher in older people than in any other age-group.

Some older people have anxiety symptoms associated with a physical disorder (e.g. an over-active thyroid gland, a small stroke), some medications bought over the counter, or the withdrawal symptoms of sedatives, sleeping-tablets and alcohol. This shows

103

how important — and sometimes difficult — it is accurately to pinpoint clinically significant anxiety. Anxiety can have effects wider than the feeling itself, in that it can lead to sleep disturbance or sexual problems, and can aggravate certain medical conditions (e.g. high blood pressure and heart disease). Some people suffering from anxiety may also become depressed.

What are the signs of an anxiety problem?

The different types of anxiety are:
— anxiety that is generalised
— phobia: anxiety in one or more situations, e.g. lifts or open spaces, or fear of a specific thing, e.g. insects. Avoiding these situations or feeling intense anxiety (panic) if you face them interferes with your daily life.

The symptoms of anxiety are:
— Your heart beats faster, you breathe more quickly, you may feel sick. Your mouth dries up and you start to sweat. You may feel on edge, irritable, restless, have difficulty in concentrating or in sleeping.
— A feeling of extreme fear may develop into one of panic, where things around you may seem unreal.
— You may have feelings of something terrible being about to happen, and find yourself thinking, 'I'll die,' 'This is awful,' 'I have to get out of here.' You may fear you are going crazy or are out of control.

Specific phobias can be about many things; common examples are animals, insects, heights, thunderstorms, blood/injury.

Agoraphobia is the fear of going away from home, going on public transport, going into crowds. Agoraphobic fears often occur for the first time after the age of sixty-five, and can be triggered by some episode of physical illness or trauma, such as a mugging or fall. Some older people who develop phobias have experienced previous fears or depression.

What help is available?

Anxiety problems can be treated by therapy and/or medication. The medication prescribed for anxiety may be more useful for generalised anxiety. For phobias, including agoraphobia, exposure therapy is the primary treatment, with medication used only occasionally. Exposure therapy is where the feared situation is gradually approached in a number of small steps. Each step is practised until the anxiety is very low. The person then proceeds to the next step, until she can cope with the feared situation or thing. She will also be helped to change her thinking about the nature of the anxiety and her ability to deal with it.

Even in generalised anxiety, therapy — part of which is relaxation training — can enable the person to cope better with the symptoms with less or no medication.

Therapy for anxiety problems, and for phobias in particular, is usually carried out by a clinical psychologist or behaviour nurse therapist. You can enquire about these specialists from your GP or your Health Board. They usually work in the Special Hospital Care Programme.

Some of the medicines prescribed for anxiety problems (benzodiazepines) have the side-effects of sedation and muscle relaxation. If they have been used daily for more than several weeks, it is necessary to reduce the dose gradually, as they can lead to physical dependency. If you are thinking of giving up these drugs see your GP, who can monitor you.

Taking benzodiazepines has been found to affect the storage of new information, though long-term memory is not impaired. This may be especially important for an older person, due to normal decline in memory with age. If you notice a change in your memory after taking medication for anxiety, discuss it with your doctor.

Case 1

Marie (eighty years old) was very anxious and would not go outside her house. She lives with her son, Eamon, who retired early. Having fallen and broken her hip eleven months before, she was in hospital, had an operation and then convalesced in a nursing home. Marie was three months away from her house and when she returned was very fearful she would fall again. Her eyesight had deteriorated, which made her feel more vulnerable. Due to her anxiety, she did not want to be left alone except when she was in bed, and would not go out with Eamon. She felt very low and spent a lot of time in bed. Eamon found his life very restricted.

Her GP referred her to a clinical psychologist for management of her anxiety problems, and the psychologist saw Marie at home weekly for several months. Marie learned a method of relaxation. She also drew up a list of situations in which she felt anxious and, over the months, faced the situations one at a time, starting with the easiest (sitting in a chair by the bedside). At the end of the programme, Marie was able to walk alone to the local shops and go to the church. She no longer feels anxious when she is alone in the house and Eamon can go out when he wants to.

HYPOCHONDRIASIS

Hypochondriasis is used to describe a condition where people are convinced they are physically ill, have an amount of pain out of proportion to any physical disease they might have, and look for medical care with repeatedly unsuccessful results.

An older person will have some minor aches and pains. Also, people close to her may be seriously ill. These factors can raise anxiety and lead someone to see a minor problem as a serious illness or to believe she has an illness for which no cause can be found.

If an older person experiences difficulties in relationships or has a low level of contact with her family, being sick can bring extra attention from others. As in any such situation, people express their problems in differing ways.

What help is available?

The first step in approaching hypochondriasis is to check for any medical cause by a full physical investigation. The second step is to find out if the hypochondriasis is related to depression or anxiety.

If someone is depressed, the hypochondriasis may start suddenly. The person may complain of constipation or severe bowel problems.

Head and face pain are also commonly reported by someone who is depressed. Other preoccupations may be with the heart, urinary and genital areas of the body.

Anxiety is often associated with hypochondriacal complaints. Raised anxiety usually heightens the perception of pain and the experience of pain heightens anxiety, creating a circular problem. The person must be given a medical examination, reassured and given clear information. She should not be told she is 'imagining the pain': the pain is real for her, despite the fact that no physical cause was found.

The person can also be helped by exploring her beliefs about the nature and consequences of the illness. Use of relaxation training is often useful in the management of the anxiety. Any relationship difficulties that exist — whether marital problems, dependence on an adult child or perceived lack of attention — will need to be addressed as they may be playing a role in the hypochondriacal behaviour.

Hypochondriasis can be a frustrating problem for the family, the medical profession and sometimes the ambulance service. One or all can receive 'emergency calls' several times a day. This can be an expensive misuse of medical resources.

Case 1

Joan (sixty-nine years old) had a mild heart attack two years ago. She had always been a worrier about her health and visited her GP frequently. Since her heart attack she became very anxious and began visiting her GP weekly. She soon started to phone her son in the evening, reporting that she thought she was having another attack. Initially he came to her house but could not keep this up, as his mother phoned his office every day and his home every evening. She also began ringing her GP between her weekly visits, and phoned the Public Health Nurse regularly. On two occasions at the weekends she phoned an ambulance to take her to the hospital. Joan had several complete investigations of her heart functioning and the doctors pronounced her well.

Her son, PHN and GP were feeling stressed and frustrated, and the calling of the ambulance was a waste of resources. Joan was prescribed medication for anxiety but this did not help her. She was seen by a clinical psychologist who drew up a programme whereby each person involved with Joan gave her specific reassurances. She visits her GP weekly, her son phones each evening and the PHN calls weekly. Joan has learned a relaxation technique and different ways of interpreting her body's pains. As she had a lot of time alone in which to think about her health, she now attends her local Social Centre three times a week. Here she meets other older people and takes part in activities. Joan is happier, as are the people involved with her, and she has been able to remain living at home.

D. ALCOHOL ABUSE

Older adults are more likely to use alcohol than other drugs that alter mood. Alcohol acts as a depressant on the central nervous system and essentially affects the ability to think, reason and judge effectively. As much as 10 per cent of people over sixty-five abuse alcohol to some extent. For some people this is a pattern continued from earlier life; for others the abuse begins in later life. Women are more likely to begin alcohol abuse in later life, a fact which has been linked to widowhood and loneliness.

Older people cannot tolerate alcohol as well as those at earlier stages of life, due to physical changes. At any age, alcohol abuse shows itself in several ways. A person may neglect herself, have relationship and social difficulties, have financial problems due to spending too much of her income on alcohol. She may be violent or aggressive to those around her. She may have memory difficulties or suffer from anxiety or depression. Drinking may make her more likely to fall, with the consequent greater risk of injury. Also, alcohol will interact with any drugs and can be medically dangerous. A person committing suicide often takes alcohol, which may help to overcome any reluctance.

A person who has been abusing alcohol over a long time can suffer from a form of alcohol dementia that includes impairment of memory and intellectual functioning, sometimes also suspiciousness and jealousy. Symptoms of withdrawal from alcohol can occur during total abstinence or a reduction in intake. The first and most usual withdrawal symptom is 'the shakes'. The person can be irritable, depressed, feel nauseous, and be unable to sleep. Illusions and hallucinations may occur. A type of epileptic seizure can develop in someone who has abused alcohol over a long time. She may develop a delirium and physical complications which can be life-threatening, especially in older people. For this reason an older person who has been abusing alcohol may need to go into hospital to be detoxified.

Older people can stop abusing alcohol. However, there is often a discriminatory view that due to their age it is not worth their doing do. They must first admit the problem, as denial is common among alcoholics of all ages. Many people benefit from the Alcoholics Anonymous Programme, or from attending one of the addiction counsellors employed by the Health Boards. Residential therapy is available in the Rutland Centre in Dublin and in several centres throughout the country (see Directory). Any additional problems, like an unresolved bereavement or loneliness, need to be addressed.

Case 1

Mairead (seventy-five years old) lived alone since the death of her husband two years previously. She had been a very moderate drinker, drinking only on social occasions — weddings, Christmas and if she went out to dinner. She found her husband's death very hard to cope with. A shy person throughout their marriage, she had gone out socially only with him. After he retired, they had gone everywhere together, even to do the shopping. When he died, Mairead went to stay with her daughter Imelda, as she felt she could not stay alone in her house. She returned home after three months but felt very lonely. She had taken alcohol regularly in her daughter's house, as they drank with dinner every weekend and went out regularly. Mairead discovered that when she drank she felt less shy and more relaxed.

Back at home she continued this new pattern of drinking but drank alone. She gradually began drinking more. She drank during the day before she went out to shop and every evening. Mairead knew she was abusing alcohol but thought it did not matter as she 'did not have many years left to live'. Her daughter noticed that she was drinking a lot when Mairead stayed with her over Christmas, a year after her husband's death. She commented on it to Mairead, who said it was just over Christmas that she was 'drinking a bit extra'.

The following summer, Mairead attended her GP and he noticed she looked thin and had neglected her appearance. He suspected Mairead was depressed but she denied this. Mairead was now drinking throughout the day and seldom went out. She asked a neighbour's daughter, who often got her groceries, to buy her alcohol. The teenager did so but gradually Mairead was asking her to buy a bottle of sherry a day. The teenager told her mother, who spoke to Mairead's daughter. Imelda was angry at her mother for embarrassing herself with her neighbours. Mairead denied she was drinking so much but when Imelda checked the bin there were several bottles in it. Mairead had also spent some of her savings on alcohol.

Imelda went to see her mother's GP, with whom Mairead had a good relationship. Mairead admitted to him she was 'drinking a bit'. He discussed with her the seriousness of her abuse and her need to go into hospital to come off the alcohol. Mairead felt there was no point, as she believed she could not cope with living alone without drinking. Her anxiety and loneliness appeared to be at the root of her alcohol abuse. Her GP suggested to Mairead that she discuss this with her daughter. She did and they decided that Mairead would return to live with her, provided she stopped drinking. Six months later Mairead does not drink and is living permanently with Imelda.

CHAPTER 9

LOSS AND BEREAVEMENT

A. ILLNESS THAT MAY LEAD TO DEATH

If a relative becomes seriously ill with a disease (cancer, heart problems, Alzheimer's disease) that may lead to death, you face the possibility of losing her. Her illness will affect you whether she lives with you, in her own home or in a hospital or nursing home.

Such illness can start very suddenly (e.g. heart attack) or come on gradually (e.g. feeling tired, losing weight). Also, the illness may mean the person gets progressively worse, is constantly ill from the beginning or has periods of recovery and then a relapse. At the early stage, you will be asking, 'Will she die now, die suddenly or slowly at some time in the future?' You may also be wondering how incapacitated your relative will be. This will vary from no incapacitation (following a minor heart attack) to some (as occurs in certain forms of cancer) to severe (for someone in the later stages of Alzheimer's disease).

If a member of your family has a long-term illness, you may go through many emotions and reactions.

(1) At the beginning it feels like a **crisis**. The illness is discovered and, following tests, treatment is decided upon by the doctors. You will generally experience many emotions; anxiety, anger, resentment, guilt, desperation may come and go and be mixed with hope, closeness to the ill person, appreciation of life's preciousness and of everyday events. You can feel you have lost 'normal life' as you know it and may grieve for its loss.

It is vital that the family is clear about what the doctors are saying and what they are not saying. Ask for a meeting, if you cannot remember or are unsure what you were told.

When discussing the illness, try to include everyone who is important. Sometimes the one left out is the ill person. If someone has AIDS, secrecy can add to the burden of the illness. Decide who needs to be told and who can provide support.

You may feel better if you get information about the life-threatening illness (e.g. from the Irish Cancer Association) and also about the kinds of resources available (e.g. respite care).

Case 1

Clare (sixty-five years old) became very worried as she had discovered a lump in her breast. She had had a cancerous growth removed from her stomach four years previously. She decided not to tell any of her family, hoping it would not be malignant. She felt afraid she would not overcome the cancer again and angry that it had possibly come back. She attended hospital for a mammogram and the doctor wanted to operate. Clare knew that even if she beat the cancer, life would not be normal for many months. At this point, she told her husband and two daughters. She did not want her son, who lived in Germany, to be told and brought home needlessly.

Three weeks later, Clare had a mastectomy. She was concerned about further spread of the cancer but the surgeon was optimistic. She also felt this was different to her stomach operation as her body was 'mutilated'. She cried a lot while in hospital and asked God to let her live 'at least until Mary's wedding'.

Her husband felt as if it was only yesterday that they had been through this before. He was very frightened Clare would die and he did not ask to see the doctor. Clare's daughters went to see the surgeon, who suggested that he talk to Clare and her family together. A meeting was arranged and the surgeon informed the family that Clare had cancer but it had not spread and no further treatment was proposed.

Clare had to attend regularly for check-ups and found she became very anxious as the date approached. She now attends every year but feels the cancer may recur. She finds life is more precious and believes she has been lucky.

---

(2) The person has been sick for a prolonged period and you feel it is **long-haul**.

There are many demands on you as a carer. You may be exhausted both physically and emotionally. Having initially feared the death of your relative, in time you may wish for her death. This can lead to guilt because you are well and will live. All of these are normal feelings for you in this situation. It is helpful to talk with the other members of the family. If you feel unable to cope, you can attend a counsellor or talk to someone from the organisations (e.g. Alzheimer Society, Multiple Sclerosis Society; see Directory) that know what you are going through. A progressive disease such as Alzheimer's disease or multiple sclerosis involves several losses, each anticipated and grieved as it happens. For example, memory deterioration will progress from the person having difficulty finding her way to the shops, to forgetting who you are, to forgetting who she is.

In illness that can have relapses (asthma, heart disease, diabetes) and cause sudden death, you may feel under strain from the ongoing uncertainty of when an attack could happen. This can affect day-to-day life, especially if the family tries to avoid rows or upsets in case they bring on an attack. You need distinct guidelines from the doctor on the amount of normal stress a person can cope with.

(3) The person is **dying**. It is not always clear when the terminal or end-phase is reached, but for all involved it is now a question of when rather than if. Sometimes doctors continue offering treatments or technology which may prolong life, but can reduce its quality. Your dying relative and your family need quality time. This may mean aiming for effective control of pain, giving up hope of a cure and preparing for death. It necessitates living in the present. You must stay involved with your relative, while accepting that her death is near.

B. DYING AND DEATH

How we face illness and dying will vary from one individual to another. An older person will often have come to accept the idea of her own death; her fears may relate more to the kind of death she will have.

The dying person has many needs. Some are medical/physical while others are emotional. The physical needs include:

113

— adequate fluids
— food that can be eaten
— mouthwashes
— help with personal bathing
— more frequent use of the toilet, commode or bedpan
— being moved regularly to avoid bedsores
— for some people, control of pain.

This last point is one of the major fears of both the dying person and her carer. The Public Health Nurse, GP or Hospice Team can be asked for help with pain control.

The other fears of the dying person are of being kept aimlessly alive by medical technology, enduring a lingering death and being alone as death approaches. You as a carer need to reassure her that you will do all you can to avoid these eventualities. This may involve you or the older person talking to the medical staff about the management of the illness. If you feel you can't be with your relative as death approaches, arrange for another relative or friend to be there.

Here are some common emotional reactions to a fatal illness, though they do not always occur in this order.

Denial: The person denies to herself and to others that she has been told she is dying. Your relative and/or yourself may find denial coming and going. Some people deny to 'protect' those around them whom they think cannot cope. Your relative may die never having accepted that it is about to happen. Do not play along with denial, but do not insist strongly that someone is about to die. Instead, try to be open and sensitive. You can say, 'You are very ill and will not get better,' or, 'Would you believe me if I said you were not dying?'

Anger: Along with and following from denial, the person may feel angry. The anger may be directed at you, the medical staff, relatives, friends or God. She may ask, 'Why me?' 'Why now?' 'Why this way?' 'Why did God let this happen?' Everything is wrong — the food, the bed, the volume of the television, people staying too long or leaving too quickly.

This may be very difficult for you as the carer. It can help if you understand the criticism as part of her anger and not personal to you. Also, don't feel you have to answer the person's questions. What matters is that you are there to share and allow her to express her feelings. Listen sympathetically and respond in a supportive way; that is the most you can do.

You may also feel anger towards your sick relative and/or the medical staff. You also need someone to talk to, who will listen and understand your concerns.

Bargaining: The ill person wants more time and may ask God to give it to her in return for promises of good behaviour. You should not accept that bargaining is possible but help your relative to discuss the reasons that time is important and what can be done about what is worrying her.

Depression: The dying person experiences sadness and loss for all the things she will leave behind — family, home, pets, hobbies and the future plans she may have had. You should not be falsely optimistic but try to listen, understand and acknowledge her grief. This can be difficult for a carer, whose hopes and plans for a future with the ill person are also gone. Sometimes talking about this together, while upsetting, can be healing.

Acceptance: If the dying person comes to terms with her eventual death, she will feel at peace. This does not mean she is happy to be dying, but she accepts it. She will feel able to say goodbye, talk about life after her death and how those she leaves behind are going to cope. She will also be able to let go and allow herself to die when the time comes. You need to accept that death is near and give her permission to die. Remember throughout this time that you do not have to do a lot of talking. Being there is the main thing.

For death to be peaceful, the person needs to be prepared both practically and emotionally. In some cases, in order to know that death is approaching, she will need to be aware of her medical condition. If a person asks whether she is dying, she has a right to be told. She knows she is ill; what she may need to know is how ill and the likely remaining time she has.

Sometimes, as the carer, you may not wish your relative to be informed, because you cannot cope with the idea that she is dying. It may also happen that another member of the family (sister, aunt) is against the ill person being informed. This kind of tension makes the situation more difficult to cope with. If you cannot resolve the differences, it is advisable to discuss the problem with a member of the Hospice Team, your GP or a counsellor.

Practical preparation for death includes making a will. Ideally, everyone should make a will. This is better done by a solicitor than independently at home, as future problems will be avoided.

It may seem easy to write down what you want to happen to

your property and belongings after your death, but precise legal wording is necessary to prevent any misunderstanding of your intentions or family disagreements. If you do not make a will, your spouse will get two-thirds of your estate and the remaining third will be divided equally between your children. If you are unmarried, your nearest blood relatives get your assets. The cost of making a straightforward will is approximately £25.

Sometimes a person will have thought about organising her funeral; if not informed of her probable death, she may not tell anyone of her wishes (e.g. for burial or cremation). In some countries, people plan their own funerals by picking their coffins, flowers, etc. and paying in advance. This option may become more common in Ireland, where it is now available.

Different types of death

SUDDEN DEATH

If your relative dies suddenly, you will be shocked. You may feel unable to believe the person is dead. You may wish you had time to say goodbye. Any opportunities for apologies, sorrow, thanks and love are gone. Sudden death can make grief more difficult.

LINGERING DEATH

This occurs at the end of a long illness, at which point your own emotional and financial resources are likely to be run down. Your social and family life will have been put on hold while you cared for the person at home or spent a lot of time visiting her in hospital, nursing home or hospice. Consequently, you may be relieved at her death, also because her pain and suffering are over. You may feel guilty because of this relief. This is a normal feeling but unnecessary as you have been there for the person and done your best on what will have been a long and difficult journey for you all.

LOSS THAT IS UNCLEAR

In Alzheimer's disease you lose the person you once knew. Carers say, 'She is no longer my mother,' 'She is like a shell of her former self.' The person is there but is psychologically dead. This can be difficult for the carer, especially a spouse, who may have continued to feel close to the person. When the person with dementia dies, there is a large gap for the carer, whose life has revolved around her relative for so many years.

SUICIDE

For families this is a very upsetting kind of death. You may feel puzzled: 'Why did she do it?' You may feel guilty: 'Why didn't I notice something was seriously wrong?' You may feel angry: 'Why did she do this to me?' You may feel a sense of shame and believe you have to cover up the cause of death, though it may help that suicide is no longer a crime in Ireland. It is difficult to grieve after such a death and often families need professional help to overcome the loss.

C. THE FUNERAL

This is a time when there is a public acknowledgment of the death and you are surrounded and supported by family and friends. The funeral helps everyone to accept the reality of the death.

Do not try to protect children and 'vulnerable' family members from the experience. This will make mourning harder. Children need to see the funeral, as excluding them can result in unrealistic and distorted fantasies. Children do not understand that death is permanent until they are seven or eight years old, and younger children ask, 'When is Granny coming back?' It needs to be repeatedly explained that she will not be back.

Talk to the children about the death in simple language, explaining that the person is gone, that part of them is in heaven and their body will go into the ground. If they do not wish to see or touch the dead body, they should not be forced to do so. If you are upset, reassure the children that you are alright, that it is not their fault you are upset. For the funeral it is useful if an adult can be assigned to care for each child and answer her questions, so those in the immediate family are free to respond to their own needs. Children should not be told that the dead person is asleep as they may fear going to sleep themselves. Later, they may need reassurance that you are not going to die or leave them.

People of all ages should be encouraged to attend the funeral. An open coffin helps the reality of the death to be accepted. A public rather than a private funeral allows people to support the family. This also helps the family to accept the death, as people sympathise with them and discuss the dead person. It can be beneficial to the bereaved family if the funeral service is as personalised as possible. If the person you know is spoken about, you realise, 'This is my mother's funeral.'

Costs vary widely depending on the area of the country in which you are holding the funeral and what you require. A funeral in Dublin costs on average £1,500; one in the country approximately £800. Some of this price discrepancy is due to grave prices and opening fees being higher in Dublin. Coffins and other services can also cost more in the capital, the reason given being the higher overheads of Dublin-based firms.

The following is a list of approximate prices for a funeral in Dublin:

Coffin	£300–£900. Average price paid £500–£600.
Habit (if used)	£25–£35
Hearse	£180–£200 (one journey); £480 if used evening and morning. There will be a higher charge for travel from Dublin to the country. For a country burial you can save on cost by employing the country undertaker to bring the coffin from Dublin to the rural area.
Limousine	£75–£95 per trip, i.e. if used for evening removal and morning burial £150–£190. Country funeral directors may not have a car as people traditionally used their own cars.
Hygienic treatment of the body (embalming)	£80–£150 to remove and treat the body. This is carried out within several hours of death in order to assist in the presentation of the body and to facilitate keeping the body for several days prior to burial.
Death notices	£95 per paper
Grave to buy	£400–£1,200
Grave opening	£140–£350
Wreath	£20–£40
Church offerings	£40 to church £10 gratuity to clerk
Organist/Soloist	£40–£50 (if required).

A funeral director can arrange all of the above for you, and can help you word the newspaper notices. You can go to the funeral home to choose the coffin. If the person has died at home, she will be removed on a stretcher which is covered. If she is not being buried in a habit, you supply her clothes — shoes and underwear are not required. The funeral director is obliged to discuss the cost with you prior to the funeral.

The funeral director is paid after the funeral, with some discount if you pay within thirty days. (Other payments — e.g. for church, grave openings — may be requested before the funeral.) If you are dissatisfied with any aspect of the service, complain to the company initially. If you are still not satisfied, you can complain to the Irish Association of Funeral Directors or Consumer Affairs (see Directory).

Funerals can be planned in advance by approaching one of the long-established companies which offer this service. You pay at current prices and there is no increase or further payment when you die.

If someone in your family is terminally ill and likely to die in the near future, it may be helpful to phone some of the local funeral directors and ask for information regarding their services and costs. Some people choose to be cremated rather than buried. Cremation is available only in Glasnevin in Dublin. In Ireland, only a tiny proportion (2.8 per cent) of people take this option. However, it is increasing every year, with approximately 945 in 1993 and 21 cremations a week in 1994. The only religions that forbid cremation are the Orthodox Jewish and Muslim. It is accepted by all the main Christian denominations, and there is an official Catholic service for cremation. There is a chapel at the crematorium and you can hold any type of service, including non-religious, as long as it is dignified.

Only one body is cremated at a time in its own coffin. In California, caskets are hired and bodies are cremated in cardboard boxes.

Cremation is cheaper if you live in Dublin and do not have the additional transport costs.

Cremation	£140
Urn	£25
Certification of cremation	£10

Disposal of the ashes
— privately, no cost
— Columbarium Wall £150 (own niche and name in front of it)
— Garden of Remembrance £120 (burial in a communal vault with the name on it)
— cost of own grave plus £60 placement in Glasnevin Cemetery.

Wreaths can be cremated with the coffin or can remain and may be used to dress local churches. The ashes can be ready for collection within twenty-four hours if required for family who may be returning abroad immediately. You can reserve a place for a relative in the Wall or Garden beside the first urn, like buying a family grave.

All arrangements and payments for cremations are made through the funeral directors. The only exception is a rural funeral director, who pays prior to the cremation.

D. GRIEVING

Common reactions to the threatened loss of a relative as she is dying through illness were described above (see pp. 111ff.). The reactions to the loss at death are very similar. You may experience some but not all of these emotions. You may cope better with one stage than another. You may find yourself having bouts of depression or anger all in one day, possibly even when you thought you were over that feeling or stage. This is part of grieving and is normal if painful.

The first reaction to the news of the death of someone close may be one of **shock and denial**. This may happen even if the death was expected. You may feel like withdrawing, not wanting to see anyone or talk, or you may react as if nothing has happened and go about your work. You may feel like screaming and shouting or indeed laughing. You need time to absorb the shock. It is better not to take medication to sedate you, as it will dampen feelings which you need to express. Don't try to block your feelings as this delays your grieving.

> **Case 1a** Mary
> Mary (eighty years old) describes having heard about her husband's death. 'I knew he was very ill, the hospital were saying he would not recover but they had said that before when his chest

> was bad. My daughter came back from the hospital and told me he was dead. Only half my mind believed it and the other half kept thinking he's still in the hospital, alive. I went upstairs and told the family not to disturb me. I looked out the window for a long time. My daughter came up on and off and asked what I wanted to do about the funeral, I just kept saying, "I'm fine, I'll be down later."' Mary came downstairs to talk to the funeral director but remembers very little of this.

This sense of **numbness** can be a help in coping with the practical arrangements that have to be made. Seeing the body of the dead person may for some people be the beginning of overcoming this. Attending the funeral also helps the reality to sink in. Do not allow the funeral to be rushed; an extra day or two and you may feel better able to cope.

> **Case 1b** Mary
> Mary went to see her husband's body in the funeral home and finally cried. 'I felt desolate, I thought my chest would burst. I didn't want to leave him alone there. I came home and felt physically sick and weak. I said to myself, "How am I going to get through this?" I found my sister a good support, she's a widow.'
>
> Three weeks after the funeral, 'I began to hate the hospital staff. I thought, "Why did they let him die?" I felt angry that they had not told me so that I could have been with him. He was unconscious but I wanted to be there.'

You may next feel very emotional — **sadness, crying, guilt and anger** can all occur. You may miss the person so much that it is painful. There is a feeling of yearning, of wanting to find the person you have lost, and you may not be fully aware of this. You may therefore be restless, having difficulty in relaxing or concentrating, and sleep may be disturbed. You may think you see the person in the street or hear her coming in. You may find that remembering reawakens the grief of previous losses or times of unhappiness. However, remembering is needed to overcome grief and can bring back happy memories which will comfort you. Later, as you remember, you will begin to feel that the person is, in a different way, part of your life again.

Some people are very angry in a way that they have not been before. You may be angry at the doctors, nurses, the priest, God. You may be angry with yourself and repeatedly go over things in your mind, with countless 'if onlys . . . ' — 'If only I had gone upstairs earlier,' 'If only I had called the doctor sooner.' In time you will realise whether there really is anything you need to feel responsible about. Most people's guilt is unnecessary. If you did/said something to hurt the dead person then accept responsibility for it, but do not keep blaming yourself. Continuing to feel guilty means you will not progress in overcoming your grief. Do not bottle up your anger. Try to work through your feelings with someone you can talk to; this may be someone who is not emotionally involved in the loss.

Case 1c Mary

'My sleep was full of vivid dreams of him. I woke up and then a sick feeling came over me as I realised, "He's gone," his side of the bed was empty. I also had disturbing dreams of him calling for me and I'm not there. I felt guilty, I came home for a rest and was not there when he died. I'd wake up and cry or feel anxious and afraid.'

Sometimes family members are angry with each other as the death approaches. This can happen because they spend more time together and old rows and divisions in the family come to the surface again. This may then continue after the death. Also, family members can get angry during their grief, if one person is moving through her grief differently or at a different pace. For example, if one child remains angry for longer and another is feeling lonely, they may find it difficult to support each other. There is a need to be tolerant of other people's ways of grieving. There is no right way to grieve.

You may feel **depressed and apathetic**. You may find it hard to concentrate and may not feel like eating. It may be difficult to sleep or wake up. You may feel very lonely and yet not want to be with other people. You miss the dead person intensely. This can last for several months. The best way to cope is to take one day or one hour at a time and keep busy. This is not an attempt to avoid your grief but to make it more manageable. Break the day into small parts or jobs, e.g. get up and dressed by a certain time, telephone

one person by 2 p.m., etc. Even though you feel depressed you may also experience a sense of pride that you are coping. If you need to learn how to do something your husband or wife may have done — cooking, pumping the car tyres — learn it now. You need to care for yourself physically. Try to eat nourishing meals even if you find cooking for yourself difficult. Take extra rest even if you cannot sleep. Exercise, walking or any sport will help you to relax. Avoid taking alcohol to help you cope. It will not help you deal with your loss and may lead to an alcohol abuse problem. If you are worried about your health see your GP, and if you are emotionally low talk about it.

It is at this stage that family and friends may think that the worst is over, and visit and phone less often. However, it is now that you need company, someone who will listen to you and accept how you feel. You will also need practical help. This may relate to pensions, legal matters, learning to cook or service the car, and so on. Family and friends can help by continuing to call and offer practical assistance.

Case 1d Mary

Ten months later Mary was doing the day-to-day tasks of life but she did not like visiting her family as she had before her husband's death. 'I missed him even more in their houses and I had got used to him not being in our house. Coming back into the empty house after an outing, I missed him even more.'

Christmas occurred at this time. 'It was my first in fifty years without him. I carved the turkey for the first time. I had no heart for it and wanted it to be over as fast as possible. I insisted on staying in my house although my family wanted me to go to them.'

Family and friends should realise that grieving for the dead person may take a long time, for some people at least a year, for others up to two years. This is not surprising, as nearly every part of your life will be affected by the loss: your mental and physical health, your relationship with other people, your daily work. Some bereaved people would say, 'I've never got over it but I've learned to live with it.' Each anniversary, birthday or occasion when the family is together may bring back a sense of loss. It can help if the dead person is spoken about and remembered at these times.

Gradually the sense of depression goes and you may begin to

think of a new life without the dead person. It takes time to do this and each person should be allowed to move at her own pace.

> **Case 1e** Mary
> 'After the first anniversary I felt I should try to look forward. I cleared out the rest of his clothes and asked my son to sort out the tools in the garden shed. I agreed to go on holidays with my sister in the summer and enjoyed them, although looking at other couples reminded me of our holidays together and I missed him then.'

Major decisions like selling your house should be left until this stage, when you are able to make decisions without grief clouding your mind. Don't allow family or friends to hurry you into arriving at decisions. Seek your own independent financial/legal advice.

How you get over your grief will depend not only on your loss but on you as a person, and the amount of support you receive. If you have a good opinion of yourself, are independent and can carry out the everyday tasks, you will find it easier to grieve. It is hard to grieve if there are additional stresses such as unemployment, illness in the family or other deaths.

Here are two widows talking about themselves, one who has completed her grieving and another who has not.

One 66-year-old woman, a year after her husband's death, described herself as: 'Loving to be with people. Enjoying being a meals-on-wheels voluntary worker. Look forward to visiting my grandchildren and daughters. I get lonely but I go out and visit friends.'

The other woman, eighteen months after her husband died, described herself as: 'Miserable, angry with myself and my children. I don't like going out and meeting people. I feel depressed and my health is not good. I'm not getting over all that has happened in the past two years.'

This is the experience of two other people and how they coped with the deaths of their relatives.

Case 2

Bernie (seventy-eight years old) has been a widow for two years and lives alone in her house in Cork city. Her husband, John, died two days after a stroke. Bernie appeared calm but now says she was 'shocked and in a daze'. She could not cry and left all the funeral arrangements to her daughters. She went to the funeral home briefly but does not remember much of this visit. Many friends and relatives called regularly in the weeks after John's death. They found Bernie composed and going about life normally, and thought she was taking John's death very well. Bernie found some of her neighbours crossed the road if they saw her. She felt hurt but understood that they probably did not know what to say. She thought they could just have said, 'How are you? How are you feeling?' Six months after his death, Bernie was very depressed and feared she was 'losing her mind'. She cried all the time, as she then realised that John was dead. Her family, who had cried at the time of and immediately after their father's death, did not understand their mother crying six months later. One of Bernie's neighbours, herself a widow, visited her and listened to her as she talked over and over again about John. She encouraged her to visit his grave, something which Bernie had avoided. She did this for the first anniversary of John's death. This helped her to cope with her grief and come to terms with the loss of John. It took Bernie until the second anniversary to feel she could look towards a life on her own, to begin to do things alone and find new interests.

Case 3

Carmel (seventy-three years old) cared for her brother Jim (sixty-eight) during his illness and death from lung cancer. They lived together on the family sheep-farm ten miles from the nearest town. Jim died within six months of being diagnosed by a specialist in the nearest general hospital. Carmel cared for him at home and received support from the local Hospice Team. While Jim knew he had cancer he did not ask how long he had to live. When he died, Carmel felt a sense of relief, as his suffering was over. She had cried a lot during his illness. She also felt a sense of satisfaction that she had cared for Jim. She was lonely, and concerned about how to run the farm alone.

About three months after Jim's death Carmel got very angry. At first she was angry with the specialist, as she believed Jim might have lived if he had had an operation. At other times she was angry with Jim for smoking and for not going to the doctor sooner — she sometimes felt guilty that she had not insisted on his going. She considered selling the farm but decided to wait a year and employed someone to help her. Carmel felt depressed on occasions but 'kept going', as she thought that was what Jim would have wanted her to do. When the summer came, she visited her neighbours more often. She continued to find the evenings worst, when she felt most lonely. The neighbours had called regularly to her during the winter and spring.

For Jim's first anniversary Carmel organised for his name to be inscribed on the family headstone. She decided to keep the farm for another year. While she believes her life will never be the same again, she has begun to face the future. She worries about getting ill herself and how she would manage if this happened.

If, months later, you are still unable to grieve or cannot move past the stage of being angry or depressed, there are services that can listen and help. Do contact one of them; you may benefit from only one visit (Bereavement Counselling, see Directory).

How can you help a friend who is bereaved?

Be prepared to listen and do not be concerned about saying the right thing. Listening and being there over time is the most important thing you can do. The bereaved person may keep going over the same ground again and again.

Accept that the bereaved person knows what is best for her. Everyone grieves in her own way. If she does not want to talk or go out socially, or rejects your offer of practical help, accept that this is how she is at this time. She may be different in a week or a month.

Talk about the deceased, if the bereaved person wants to. You may irritate her by avoiding this and talking about other things. She may feel you have forgotten her loss, which can add a sense of isolation to her grief.

Allow the person to cry. It is not helpful to say, 'Don't upset yourself,' as the person is then forced to repress her grief.

Don't increase guilt. Try to reassure the person that she did all she could and encourage her not to be harsh and self-critical.

Give practical assistance. The bereaved person may not ask because she does not even think of it. Offer help, and if it is rejected offer it again some time later.

Persist with your listening, support and practical help. Grieving takes a long time, up to two years for many people. As a friend you will be needed for that time.

Remember that celebrations and anniversaries, such as Christmas, Easter, birthdays, weddings, can be particularly painful times for years to come. You can help by making a special effort to contact and/or visit.

CHAPTER 10

YOU AS A CARER

Who receives care?
While the majority of older Irish people are independent and able to care for themselves, 19 per cent living in the community receive care from family and friends. Just over a third need 'a lot of care', the same number need 'some care' and a quarter need 'occasional care'. Most of the people in need of care, their carers and other family members believe that the family is responsible for this care. It is considered preferable to keep the person at home for as long as possible, which accords with older people's own expressed wishes. This also accords with governmental policy, aimed at containing the high cost of residential care.

Which family member gives care?
Society's views on who should care may vary depending on who needs care: mother, father, parent-in-law. It also varies depending on the sex of the carer, the number and sex of siblings. If you are an only child, whether male or female, you are more likely to be the main carer. However, men give less care than women. If you are from an all-female family, you are more likely to be a carer than if all were male. If there are both daughters and sons, daughters are much more likely to be care-givers to their old parents than the sons. Employment can also be a factor in whether you become a carer or not. A woman does not necessarily abandon the carer role if employed; she may give care as well, delegate some care, or 'buy in' care that she would have provided free. In Ireland, 16 per cent of female carers of all age-groups were employed. An employed carer will have more demands on her time and may have to reduce working hours, sacrifice overtime and/or promotion. Some

employed carers experience stress in this situation, a sense of doing both jobs badly and a feeling of guilt.

If you are a carer of an older person you are likely to be a woman (daughter, wife, granddaughter), though some men are carers, particularly of their wives. You are probably over forty and may be older yourself. You may be married and caring for your own children, or indeed have grandchildren. If you are working outside the home, while also caring for an older person, you will have different stresses and difficulties to the carer who is not employed. It is known that carers of all ages and in differing circumstances often have significant health problems, both physical and psychological, due to the tremendous social, physical, emotional and financial pressures involved. The process of taking on a heavy burden of care is usually gradual. If the people live together (spouse or family), caring can begin without any conscious decision being taken.

Stages of caring

It can be helpful to see caring as a journey on which there are four stages. The first is becoming a carer, second the day-to-day caring, third a regular review of caring, and fourth the ending of your caring role.

(1) BECOMING A CARER

Decisions about who becomes a carer need to receive close consideration. This would help carers and the person they are caring for to understand the complexities of their situation and to make the best decision for all concerned. Each family needs to look at possible choices as regards caring for an older relative. What is required at this point is discussion among the whole family, including the older person. The kind and amount of care that is necessary and that can be provided must be examined. Ideally, one or more of the family can then choose to take on the caring role, having looked at the advantages and disadvantages. Typically, the older dependent person is cared for by one individual, who receives little or no help from other family members.

Often the person who feels a duty or feels she is the only one available becomes the carer. The sense of duty can come from a desire to give back what you received; to avoid guilt and maintain your self-esteem and that of others; to fulfil a promise made earlier in life or to a dying parent. For married people their lifelong relationship 'for better or worse' is a strong motivating factor in giving care. Also, some people care not out of a sense of duty but out of strong links between brothers and sisters or gratitude to one's parents. Another motivation is to prevent a relative from being admitted to residential care.

A person who lives nearby or with the older person (e.g. a child who never left the parents' home or a woman who upon widowhood moves to an adult child's home or vice versa) may be more likely to become the carer. The decision is more often gradual than sudden. The older person's health may slowly deteriorate or she may develop memory problems or confusion and grow less able to look after herself. If caring suddenly becomes necessary, it is usually due to:
— an illness or accident
— loss of a partner
— the previous carer giving up or dying.

In this situation some family consultation takes place. The carer is identified. This can be an emotional decision, made without clear knowledge and foresight. Typically, the older person involved does not have a choice as to who becomes her carer, though ideally it should be a choice made by both parties. In some cases, the carer and the person being cared for feel they have no alternative; more do not understand what they are getting involved in.

The following may help you decide
— whether to become a carer
— what you can and cannot do
— what support and services you need.
— Do the two of you get on well together? If you have not up to this point it may be very difficult, if not impossible, to cope with the added stresses involved in a caring situation.
— What are the best living arrangements? Should the older person remain in her own home, move into your home or perhaps into a granny flat attached? If there is a choice, and if the older person can cope with that level of independence, the best option is a 'granny flat'. This way you both have privacy, but the older person can receive support and caring more easily than if you have to travel to her home.
— Think about the financial cost. This may be loss of earnings, as you may not be able to work full-time or do overtime, or may give up your job. It can also involve extra heating costs as older people require a warmer temperature. The need for a special diet

or transport may be an additional financial strain. Major expense may be incurred in modifying or extending your home; this option must be very carefully considered as once the investment is made there may be no money to pay for additional help or residential care if the caring arrangement does not work.

— You need a professional service which will assess the needs of the older person so that care is based on physical, psychological and medical information. You should know about normal ageing and any additional physical and psychological problems your relative may have and their implications for the care she will need.

— You must know how to deal with any medical and emotional problems of the older person. Your GP and Public Health Nurse play a significant role in letting you know what services are available.

— Examine the likely consequences for your marriage, children and social life. Will you have time together and be able to do things together, as a couple and as a family? All carers need a social life but this is particularly important if you are unmarried or living alone with a dependent older person, as you may never get a break from the feeling of having to be there 'on call'.

— The remainder of your family, your friends and the older person's friends can help by letting you know what support and assistance they will give. Actively seek this assistance, let people know you want and welcome it.

— When you know the care that is needed and the help and support available, you can assess the level of care you will have to give. A major dimension of this is how much time caring will require. The time required for a person heavily dependent is eighty-six hours per week, while the average time is forty-seven hours per week. Will you have time for your family and friends and your own leisure activities? Will your own health be able to withstand caring?

When you have considered these factors you will know if your becoming the carer is the best choice. You will also know the amount and kind of care you can give. You must set these limits so that you will not be overburdened, to the detriment of your own physical and mental health. When each family member has the above information and knowledge, hold a family conference to explore the options available. The family needs a definite plan as to which help will be given by whom to the person who will be the carer.

Case 1

Joan (fifty years old) is unmarried and works in Dublin in a senior management position in a firm. Joan's mother, Alice (seventy), lived independently in the family home in Cavan until she had a stroke, which affected her right arm and leg and her speech. Joan has a brother who is married and lives in Westmeath, and a sister who is married, lives in Cork and works part-time outside the home. When Alice was discharged from hospital, Joan took three months' leave of absence from her job. She felt this might affect her position in the company but her brother and sister could not leave their families. Joan's mother made a good recovery from the stroke. Although she was able to walk with difficulty, she was unable to use her right arm for many things. She was very emotional and cried easily and frequently. Her speech was slow and she became frustrated with herself as she often could not find the correct word.

As she was due to return to work and it was now five months since her mother's stroke, Joan discussed the future with her brother and sister. They did not want Alice to go into residential care, but neither of them was prepared to have her live with them. Patricia had never got on well with her mother and knew she could not cope. Jim's wife was not prepared to take on the role of a full-time carer to her mother-in-law as she was looking after her own handicapped child. Joan felt she was expected to give up her job and come back to the family home to care for her mother. She spoke to her mother's GP regarding the length of time she might require care and what services were available. He could not say whether Alice might continue to improve and possibly live independently again. She needed care now. Joan was advised that the only service which would suit her mother was a nursing home.

Joan discussed this with Alice, who did not want to leave her home. She too was hoping Joan would care for her full-time. Joan felt pressurised and guilty because she did not want to do this. She considered having her mother to live with her in Dublin, but as she worked long and irregular hours with frequent travel this was not a solution.

Joan decided she could not be a full-time carer for her mother. She firstly told her brother and sister, who were upset and said she was selfish. Alice said she would stay at home and manage on her own. Joan left her for a few hours, she was unable to manage and accepted that she could not at this point live alone without help.

Joan and her mother agreed that Joan would find a place in a nursing home in Dublin. Her house would not be sold for a year as she might continue to improve and be able to live there or with Joan in the future. Alice had a small pension and Joan agreed to pay the remaining cost of the nursing home.

Joan takes her out to her house almost every Sunday for the day. Her brother and sister visit Alice in Joan's house. They continue to disagree with their mother being in a nursing home. Alice herself is quite happy with the home. She has her own room, enjoys the company of the other residents and can now walk to nearby shops.

(2) DAY-TO-DAY CARING

For some carers the burden can be very great. You may be caring for someone who is very physically frail, or who has problems of incontinence. You may be dealing with difficult behaviour in a person who has dementia or has had a stroke. Your needs at this stage of caring include:

— practical back-up and support from the statutory (Health Board) and voluntary services: home-help, meals-on-wheels, laundry service, provision of aids, regular contact with your GP. The services of an occupational therapist, physiotherapist, psychologist, social worker and other members of the Community Care Services may be required. You may need a break from the older person in your home; short breaks (respite care) can be arranged in a local hospital or residential facility.
— emotional support in coping with the day-to-day caring: this can be provided by your family and friends and possibly a Carers' Support Group (see Directory). If you need professional support, contact a social worker or psychologist.
— financial support: you may be eligible for the Carer's Allowance and may seek financial support from other family members. Of course, the older person should be financially contributing to her own care.

Case 2

Joe (seventy years old) took early retirement ten years ago to care for his wife, Chris. She has had diabetes all her life and had part of her right leg amputated at that time. They married in their forties and have no children so Joe has been caring alone for Chris, who was an only child. Chris had part of her left leg amputated last year and her sight is also failing due to complications of the diabetes. She has found this very difficult to adjust to and is depressed. She uses a wheelchair. Joe finds he is exhausted trying to do everything. Ten years ago he had to learn to shop, cook and clean the house. In the last year he has to help Chris take a bath and dress herself. He says, 'Every day is the same. I don't know how much longer I can go on. My own health is not good, I have chest problems and each year it gets worse. Chris is very low in herself and often does not want to talk. At times she says she would be better off dead. Sometimes I feel like agreeing with her but I often dread the day as what will I do then?'

What is caring like?

The strain you experience as a carer will affect your own well-being. The causes of these feelings of stress, depression, anger, etc. are complex. Caring will feel different for each person. In terms of physical and mental health, sons often suffer less than daughters because they remain more distant from the dependent person. Men establish limits sooner in relation to what they can cope with while maintaining their work and leisure time, and so are less socially isolated. Sons appear to have less difficulty in deciding that parents should go into residential care, though this does not mean they are spared the pain and sorrow of the physical and psychological deterioration of their parents. Also daughters who care are often seen to be doing their duty while sons are judged to be doing more than their duty. They then receive more support and admiration for caring.

As a carer for your dependent relative, you may have one or more of the following feelings at once. Your feelings may also change over time.

Physical strain: Carers report fatigue due to the long hours of work and loss of sleep. Some become ill themselves through the stresses of caring or through physical problems associated with it, e.g. back pain due to lifting a person. Basic training in nursing skills is essential for many carers. You must organise a break for a few hours, a day, a week or a regular holiday to avoid physical burn-out.

Anger: This is a common feeling that carers report towards the older person. You may feel angry that this has happened to you. You may feel angry at your family and the services for not helping enough. You may feel angry if you have looked for a break or for help and the older person refuses, wanting only you to mind her; ask a professional or another family member to talk to her and explain that you both have needs, and that you need this break or back-up if you are to continue caring. Sometimes anger can motivate you to seek practical help but often you may need the emotional support of someone to talk to. This can be obtained in a support group or from relatives and friends.

Grief: This is felt for the losses in your social life and independence, the loss of your job, money, status and friends. You may feel grief at the changes in your relative. Particularly in cases of dementia or stroke, changes in the person's mental and physical state can be difficult to cope with. Talk about this with people in a similar situation. Do not be silent; it can make matters worse and lead to more conflict.

Frustration: You may feel frustration at being tied — caring can seem an endless commitment and responsibility. It is essential to organise regular respite for yourself. Many carers report that they live their lives by the clock. You may be trying to cope with the demands of your older relative, your own job, the needs of children, your husband and your own leisure activities. You may benefit from reviewing the demands and the possibilities for change in any area.

Hurt: You may feel hurt at things the older person says or does. Comments passed about the rearing of your children or how you run your own house, or unfavourable comparison with your sisters or brothers can be hurtful. You should not passively accept this for a 'quiet life'. Express your hurt. If the older person is not mentally impaired, she must be prepared to consider your feelings.

Fear: You may have a fear of the unknown. 'How bad will the situation become? How long will this situation go on? Will I be able to continue caring?' Professionals who understand your relative's illness may be able to answer your questions. You may also fear the death of the person, as your life is so much taken up with caring for

135

her. You could also be financially dependent on her or lose your home when she dies.

Guilt: You may be guilty because at times you resent the person you are caring for and may wish she would die. You may resent those who could help and do not. Guilt makes it difficult for you as the carer to say no. You may think you have not done enough, or feel bad for having taken a break. This can prevent you from setting limits to the caring you give, limits often desperately needed for your mental and physical health. If any professional (GP, nurse, social worker) is involved, ask her to speak to your relative if necessary.

Pleasure: Some people do get a great deal of pleasure from their caring role, and feel love and devotion for their relatives. Some find caring a maturing experience. You are more likely to feel pleasure if you have chosen the caring role, the person is comparatively independent and she lives near you.

The stresses of caring, the failure to set limits and the lack of support services can lead to some carers abusing and neglecting their older relatives (see Chapter 11).

(3) REVIEWING CARING

Caring may go on for many years. The needs of the older person will change over time, e.g. she may become more physically dependent, her behaviour may become more difficult. The changes in the person might result in further stresses on you. Your own health, relationship with your spouse and children, and social life need to be examined as areas that are under strain because of your caring. This review of caring and its costs to your social and family life could be carried out once a year, possibly more frequently if the person is very ill. You must re-examine the need for respite care, for further physical help within the house, for additional aids to help with bathing or feeding or lifting. You may have to call in professionals to assist with this review.

Case 3

Jane (eighty-six years old) lives alone in a suburb of Galway city since she became a widow fourteen years ago. She has arthritis and cannot now walk outside her house. Her daughter Nuala (forty-six) lives two miles away and has been supporting Jane. When Jane's husband died, Nuala visited her every day 'in case

---

she needed anything done'. Initially, Nuala did very little, but over the years she has taken on her mother's shopping, housework and laundry. Nine years ago Jane had central heating installed as she could no longer light a fire. For the past year Nuala has been bathing her mother and calling morning and evening to help her get up and return to bed. Nuala's sixteen-year-old daughter calls into her grandmother to check she is alright and to have a chat a few afternoons a week on her way home from school. A neighbour gives Jane her dinner every day.

Nuala gets support from her sister Ann, who lives in Kerry and phones Nuala weekly. Three times a year Ann stays with her mother for a week and Nuala gets a complete break. For two weeks every year her brother, a priest, comes to stay with Jane. Nuala still has to visit morning and evening as her brother cannot dress and wash their mother.

Nuala is finding visiting and caring for Jane twice a day, seven days a week very tiring. She also worries about her mother during the day and night. Her social life has suffered as she is not free in the evening until 9.30. Her husband is understanding and helps the children with their homework. Nuala finds she is pulled between the needs of her mother and those of her own children.

She is considering having Jane to live in their house. Nuala would then not have to travel, do two lots of shopping and housework and be worried about her. She knows she would not have the total breaks, as even if her sister stayed in the house, her mother would still be there.

Nuala's husband would support her decision of having her mother live with them. He has always liked and got on well with his mother-in-law. They have no bedroom that could be given to Jane and so an extension would be necessary. Jane is prepared to sell her house and pay for the extension. Nuala's sons (eighteen and thirteen) are not so enthusiastic about the prospect. They are aware that they may have to share a bedroom until the extension is built. Also, they think Jane may watch the television in the sitting-room, where they usually have their friends in.

(4) ENDING OF THE CARING ROLE

Caring may end with the death of your relative or with her needing residential care, which can also feel like a bereavement. If the older person has to go into care, you may think you should have been able to go on caring until her death; indeed, the older person may feel this way too. However, you must not feel guilty, you must accept that you have done your best; otherwise your strain continues. Husbands and wives are much less likely than adult children to consider institutional care. A poor relationship between the carer and the person being cared for is a significant factor in deciding on residential care. If the carer feels unhappy with relatives' level of help, she is also more likely to want to discontinue care.

You are still coping with the stress of visiting your relative and possibly contributing financially to her care. You may remain emotionally involved and feel responsible. The nursing home or other institution should allow you to participate in looking after your relative, so diminishing any guilt you feel and improving her quality of care.

A counselling and support service should be available to carers who are coming to terms with their relatives being in residential care or having died. Also, older people and their carers should have easy access to residential care — information and lack of bureaucracy is essential.

If your relative has died, it can be very difficult to pick up the threads of your life. Caring may lead to the loss of your friends and social life and it can be difficult to resume after a break of several years. Some carers, particularly single people, are financially less well off, due to the loss of the older person's income. They may be unable to get employment and find it hard to readjust.

What are the needs/rights of carers?

RECOGNISE YOUR OWN VALUE

You as a carer must value the job you are doing. Recognise your contribution and your own needs. Acknowledge that you cannot care alone and should not push yourself until your own health is on the point of breakdown. Asking for help simply means you are setting limits, and you will not be judged as inadequate by any professionals you may call in. While you may want to remain independent, no one can care alone for a dependent older person.

RESPITE

Many carers in Ireland do not get a break of any kind. As a carer you need respite (hours, days, weeks) to enable you to maintain a normal life, to reduce isolation, to allow you to receive support and to have a social life for yourself and your family. You will also need someone to replace you if you are ill or in hospital. Any respite care must be of high quality, and must also be variable and flexible to meet the needs of your individual situation. It must be reliable and acceptable to the person cared for if it is to be of real help. Check which of the following options are available in your area.

Home-help, care attendants and sitting-in services provide practical support for a short time in the home. Home-helps and care attendants assist with the care of the dependent person; home-helps may also do light domestic tasks. Sitting services stay in the home and perhaps make a drink or take the person to the toilet but do not give personal care.

Day care is often provided in day centres or day hospitals. It does not suit all, but if the older person is fit enough to attend, it can mean a break for the carer. The person might attend each day or perhaps two or three times a week. One drawback of such care is that it is available only during the daytime; it would help if it were more flexible and offered in the evening or at weekends. Transport to and from day care is sometimes a bone of contention; it can be very difficult for a carer to plan her day around transport which could arrive at any time over a one-hour period at collection and return.

Short regular breaks may be possible, where the older person leaves her home. This does not suit everyone: for example, it can be very confusing for someone who has dementia or who is very visually impaired to try to adjust in such a short time. The options of where to go include a residential facility (nursing home, welfare home) or a host family which takes the dependent person regularly for a day, or for up to two weeks.

Relief at home for a few days or weeks can be arranged, where someone comes in and cares for the person. This can supply cover for a holiday or if the carer has to go into hospital. A holiday break for both the carer and the dependent person can help to relieve guilt. Couples may wish to go on holidays together. Parallel to the care provided for the dependent person, the holiday should include a programme for the partner.

Some of these options are not currently open to carers in Ireland. Enquire locally from both the Health Board and voluntary agencies to find out what is on offer.

The Galway Carers' Association publishes a booklet of agencies and services for carers in the county. The Minister for Social Welfare has allocated £500,000 to the Trust Fund for Respite Care, marking at least an initial recognition at government level of its obligation to support carers. Some of this money is being used to establish a directory of respite care services in Ireland. Currently being compiled by Age Action Ireland, this will be available in 1995.

INFORMATION AND TRAINING

Carers need information on normal ageing, the diseases, their causes and the drugs the dependent relative is prescribed. They need easily accessible information on all available services — their existence and how to make use of them. This could be through leaflets and guides for carers, telephone information lines and local contact points for information.

Basic nursing skills — bathing, dressing, lifting, sitting up, turning, changing sheets in an occupied bed — are often a stated need of carers. Some groups have also recommended that carers be trained in assertiveness to enable them to request information, services and support, both from family and from formal service providers. Carers of people with dementia may benefit from training in behavioural management of the difficult behaviours that can arise.

FINANCIAL

The vast majority of family carers express a desire for payment for caring, yet their role is not recognised by the government. Payment of the Carer's Allowance, which was introduced in 1990 and increased in 1993 to £59.20 per week, is very restrictive. To qualify for the full rate, you must be living with your relative and be on a low income. Following means-testing, few people qualify at all, and most of those are on a reduced rate. There is no other form of payment for caring for a dependent person. This highlights the lack of recognition of carers and the contribution they make to caring in the community. Ideally, there should be financial compensation where work is reduced or given up. The carer should not have to pay for medical costs or incontinence wear or equipment. Financial assistance for the necessary adaptation of the home (bathroom) or for increased safety (e.g. grab-rails) should be provided.

LEGAL

Legal services may be needed by carers. Both the carer and the person cared for may need to make wills. It has happened that a single daughter cares for her mother in the family home, which is subsequently willed to another daughter or son. This can mean that a middle-aged or older person, after many years of caring, is left homeless, with no financial independence to start a new life.

Carers may need advice on ward of court procedures or having power of attorney.

COUNSELLING/SUPPORT

Being able to discuss the beginning and ending of caring is very important for the carer, but being able to share the emotional burden is often crucial. Sometimes carers get a lot of emotional support from a home-help or care attendant who has been coming to them over a long period. If there is a Carers' Support Group in the area, this might meet the need (see Directory). If the dependent relative has a particular disease, such as dementia, a support group specifically for this disease may be more useful (e.g. Alzheimer Society, see Directory). Another option being explored is a telephone help-line which could be staffed by volunteers, some of them ex-carers. The Carers' Association has applied for funding for such a service.

A professional counselling service may be required for some carers who are in crisis or experiencing severe stress. A recent Irish report on carers of dementia sufferers (Ruddle & O'Connor 1993) has identified the need for training in stress management skills. Carers need to establish and negotiate their own limits. They need to learn to communicate with the person being cared for and sometimes with the rest of the family about the difficulties of caring. Unfortunately, professional counselling for carers is not readily obtainable from the statutory services.

While it is generally found that where support services are available they are willingly used, it does require changes in the carer. You must recognise your own limits. Then you have to accept the intrusion of strangers into your caring and not feel threatened or in competition with them. Women, because of their strong emotional involvement, may have more difficulty with this than men. The professionals should also respect the carer and see their work as mutual.

The needs of carers are diverse and not all carers need every service. Services must be flexible, accessible and delivered when required. If the service offered is not of a high standard it is unlikely to be used again; an example would be a respite break in a residential facility where the person returns home with some of her clothes missing. The experience of Irish carers of older dependent people is that support from government/statutory services is inadequate. Many of the carers' needs are not met because the service does not exist. An additional problem is that services — particularly if offered by both the state and voluntary organisations — need to be co-ordinated, to avoid overlap and to identify any gaps. Carers must be part of the planning process and therefore need a means of communicating with those who make the policies and provide the services.

EMPLOYMENT

Carers may want to or have to continue working. The main reason is financial. However, work also supplies an interest, a break, enjoyment, companionship, and once a job is given up it can be very difficult to re-enter the market.

Employers can play a role in helping carers to continue working with less stress. They can recognise that carers exist and that it is not just a women's issue, men are carers too. Flexible working hours are of great benefit; a carer can bring the older person to a day centre or for hospital appointments, or can arrange to share care with a relative. A career break can help, especially if an in-touch scheme keeps the carer up to date with changes.

Certain jobs can be done at home and this may suit the needs of those caring for people who do not need constant attention. Some companies will provide computers and fax machines to help a person work at home.

Employers can provide information in the workplace on the voluntary and statutory services that carers may need. Large companies can have their own self-help groups. Small companies can form joint groups with other businesses nearby. Personnel departments and occupational health units can offer counselling about the strain of caring and include it in courses on coping with stress.

A carer may need to be easily contactable and employers can facilitate this, giving her peace of mind. If she is called away from work, the environment should be supportive and understanding. A carer who is employed must have access to alternative sources of care, which will take responsibility during her worktime. She has to feel that she can rely completely on this care.

Carers should have the right to accumulate without financial contribution social insurance rights (illness and old age) for part-time work or when work is given up.

What are the needs of the person being cared for?

A person being cared for often wishes to continue doing as much for herself as she can. However, if she takes longer or is somewhat messy, e.g. in feeding herself, the carer may want to take over. The person being cared for should be encouraged and allowed to be as independent as possible for as long as possible.

The older person should be included in discussions about difficulties if they arise. If these can not be resolved by the family, a professional (social worker, psychologist, counsellor) can be helpful. The person being cared for needs to be treated with dignity, and allowed as much freedom of choice as possible.

The older person should be encouraged to keep up contact and receive visits from friends. She herself should be tolerant and respect the needs of the other people in the house. While it may be very hard for an older person to accept that the carer can no longer look after her and that she must move to residential care, this decision must be made with the welfare of all concerned in mind.

If the older dependent members of our society are to be provided with good-quality care, it must be given in parallel by the family (partner, adult children); formal community services, both statutory and voluntary; various forms of residential care (sheltered housing, geriatric units, nursing homes); and perhaps by a network of neighbours. In this situation, older people and their families would have real choice.

CHAPTER 11

ABUSE OF OLDER PEOPLE

It is generally believed that family care is the best form of care, but in fact not all families can or want to care for older members. This situation can be a source of deprivation and injury.

As a society we have come to accept that violence occurs within the family, in the form of wife-battering and sexual abuse of children. However, we have not yet accepted that older people are abused both within their families and when they are in institutional care. Abuse of older people is different to abuse of children, in that adults have more legal autonomy. It does happen that abused older people will not acknowledge that abuse is taking place and will refuse help. In the USA, which has a longer history of dealing with this problem, there are only very restricted legal powers that can override an adult's right to make decisions for herself. Abuse of older people could be said to arise from a failure of the state to provide them with the financial means to lead an independent life and the opportunity to make their own choices.

Community care policies which depend on family care for older people may contribute to abuse by expecting too much of families or not providing support services and financial rewards (see Chapter 10).

In Britain, 5 per cent of older people are recorded as having experienced verbal abuse, 2 per cent physical abuse and 2 per cent financial abuse. These may not be accurate figures as people may not report the abuse because of embarrassment, shame, and so on. None of the countries of the European Community has a policy of recording family violence against older people.

What is abuse?

There is no agreed definition of abuse and neglect, which can make recognition of abuse difficult. In order to help identify mistreatment of older people, the types of abuse are described:

Psychological abuse and neglect: This type of mistreatment, which causes emotional distress to the victim, includes threatening remarks, insults, and isolation of the person from her friends and family. Another feature is ignoring the older person's concerns and requests. This is usually the first form of abuse, with physical abuse occurring later.

Physical abuse and neglect: This leads to a wide range of injuries and physical symptoms. Examples of this type of abuse include hitting, punching, shaking, tying, sexual assault, not feeding the person properly, not providing necessary medication or over-medicating her.

Financial abuse and neglect: This is the misuse or exploitation of the person's possessions and/or money. It includes threatening the person into handing over her pension or money, and could also involve swindling her out of her home or other assets.

How does the older person respond to abuse?

Quite often, the older person does not see what is happening to her as abuse. She believes that the carer is under stress or has a psychological problem which is causing this behaviour. A person of any age being abused feels very frightened, and may be tearful. She may also be agitated, and find it hard to get to sleep. Many people who have been abused over time become resigned to it, even apathetic.

Where physical abuse is taking place, signs of this may be seen. The person may have bruises, broken bones or fractures. If someone is being confined or restrained, there may be marks on her wrists and legs where she has been tied. If someone is not receiving adequate food, she may be dehydrated, with dry skin, sunken eyes and loss of weight. If she is receiving too much medication, she may appear confused and lacking in responsiveness. If there is financial mistreatment, the person may be unable to pay bills or there may be large or unexplained withdrawals of money from the bank. She may appear to be unaccountably short of money for herself.

Why are older people abused?

The answer to this question is unknown and, as in the areas of child abuse and wife-battering, is likely to be complex. Abuse and neglect occur as part of the interpersonal relationship between the older person and her carer. We look here at this relationship.

For some people, the abuse occurring in their old age is the continuation of a lifelong pattern of family violence. The older person may have been the abuser in earlier life, the adult child now responding in kind. An older person can aggravate the caring situation. Patterns of behaviour that are seen as selfish — self-pity, complaining, feigning illness, reporting the carer to people in authority, e.g. the GP — have been found to contribute to abuse of the older person by the carer. Also, an older person may initiate physical abuse by hitting out, pinching and being verbally abusive to the carer. Again, this may be a continuation of a pattern that has existed throughout their relationship.

Some research indicates that abuse of older people is due to the enormous stress the care-giver is under. While certain studies have concluded that the more dependent the older person, the more likely the relative is to abuse, this has not been proven. Some carers with a heavy burden of caring do not abuse the older person, while others with the same burden do. Studies on the reasons for abuse find that in some cases the abuser is dependent on the older person, financially for her housing needs or because she herself is cognitively impaired or mentally ill. Some research suggests that stressful life events (illness, poor housing, low income, bereavement) unrelated to caring can actually contribute to the person's becoming an abuser.

Who are the abusers?

Both men and women abuse older people. There are more women who are abusers but there are more women who are carers. A high proportion of men abuse, given the number who are carers. So as daughters and daughters-in-law are the main carers, they are the ones most liable to abuse the older person. Abuse of older people takes place in all social classes and in all educational groups. It has been documented in many countries and across several races. The older person may be abused by several members of the family, or by one member, with others aware that it is happening. Abuse is more likely to be inflicted by a close family member living with and caring for the victim: a partner, daughter, son-in-law. It may occur because of psychological difficulties on the part of the carer, e.g. if she is herself depressed or is abusing alcohol or medication.

Who is abused?

Both men and women are the victims of abuse. However, as women live longer and with increasing age become more dependent, they are more likely to be victims. Poor health, disability and some degree of dependency appear to be common in many abused older people. However, others are not suffering from any physical or mental infirmity but are abused as part of a pattern of violence within the family. Some older people may behave in a socially unacceptable, disruptive, manipulative or aggressive way, especially if they suffer from dementia.

An older person who is in residential care can also be neglected and abused. Neglect can occur through inadequate staffing levels and/or training. One example of neglect is the older incontinent person who is not changed as frequently as is necessary for her health and dignity. If there are insufficient staff members to feed a frail or disturbed older person, then neglect is occurring. Abuse can occur if the older person is shouted at and hit for being slow, incontinent or uncooperative. Over-medicating residents to keep them quiet is another form of abuse.

If the older person has family and/or friends who visit regularly, they may become aware of the neglect or abuse. Sometimes they are informed by other residents. Families are upset when they hear this but are sometimes afraid to make a complaint, fearing that their relative will suffer a backlash from the staff or that they will be asked to remove her. There may not be another suitable home in the locality or one that they can afford.

All residential facilities should have a formal complaints procedure of which both residents and families are aware. There should also be a residents' committee in each facility to which a resident is encouraged to bring any complaints.

Case 1

Catherine (eighty-nine years old) had been living alone but near her son prior to developing pneumonia. She spent four weeks in hospital and was somewhat confused due to her chest problems. She was not well enough physically or mentally to go directly home. Her daughter Maura, who lived 170 miles away, spoke to her mother's GP about a suitable nursing home near Catherine's house so her friends, neighbours and son could visit her. He provided her with the names of several in the area and agreed, especially as it was winter, that it was a good idea for Catherine to spend some time in a nursing home.

Maura visited two that had vacancies and chose one to which her mother moved. Catherine appeared to settle in well and said everything was fine. Two weeks later Maura visited her and thought she had lost weight. While her mother reported that she liked the food and was eating, her breakfast tray was untouched at the end of the bed. Staff assured her that Catherine was eating her meals. Maura pointed out that she had needed assistance to eat while in hospital.

Returning the next day at lunchtime, she found Catherine attempting to eat her lunch alone in her room. She was sitting up in bed but had not been able to cut her meat; due to her slight mental confusion she had not asked the staff to do so. With assistance, Catherine ate all her lunch and drank several glasses of fruit juice. On this occasion Maura complained to the person in charge of the nursing home and informed her that her mother was unable to feed herself without help. She also asked whether Catherine should not be up and out of her room for a period each day. The Matron undertook to ensure that Catherine received the help she required to feed and dress herself. Maura believed that the staff should have assessed her mother's ability to care for herself and, at a minimum, observed the uneaten food over the previous two weeks.

Maura alerted the family to the lack of care and a member was present around mealtimes for the next few days. Catherine was receiving the assistance she needed to feed herself. She was also assisted in dressing and walking downstairs to the sitting-room, where residents met each other.

Why does the abused older person not seek help?

An older person may not recognise that she is being abused. She may blame herself for the problems of her abusive relative and think it is the abuser who needs help. She may fear the shame it would bring on her and her family. Once a person is abused, her self-esteem is lowered and it is harder for her to seek help. She may also fear retaliation and even more severe abuse. Finally, in some cases, the abused person is so isolated that she cannot look for help; her abuser may have limited her access to the outside world by not allowing visitors to the house, not allowing access to the telephone or paper or stamps. Alternatively, she may have become isolated as a result of a physical problem, e.g. arthritis, which has limited her mobility.

Case 2

Molly (seventy-nine years old) had arthritis and was visited regularly by the Public Health Nurse to have leg ulcers dressed. Molly's son Joe (thirty-nine) lived with her. He did not want the nurse calling and was reluctant to leave Molly alone with her. Molly seemed agitated but agreed that Joe should stay. One day the nurse saw bruises on Molly's arm, and decided to call next at a time when she knew Joe would be out collecting his Unemployment Assistance. Molly denied there was any problem with her son or any other family member, and attributed the bruising to a fall. The nurse was not convinced. Several weeks later Molly had a black eye. The nurse again called when Joe was out and Molly explained that she had been difficult and Joe had lost his temper. She asked the nurse not to do anything about it. The nurse informed Molly's GP of her suspicion of physical abuse. He visited Molly but she said she felt well and did not agree to a physical examination. She told him Joe had problems but did his best in caring for her. The GP said he would call again and left it open for Molly to ask him to come and see her. It was also suggested that she go into hospital for a rest and treatment of her ulcer, but she declined.

Several weeks later, the nurse noted that Molly had lost weight and her ulcer was disimproving. The GP visited and insisted on Molly being brought to hospital. On admission she was a stone underweight and had bruises on her upper arms. Initially, she denied any abuse or neglect. The medical social worker in the hospital visited Molly regularly and built up a relationship with her. After several weeks, Molly admitted that her son had a gambling problem and took her pension. He did not buy food, and hit and shook Molly when she had no more money to give him. His abuse of Molly began two years previously when he became unemployed and his gambling worsened. He was recently drinking heavily. When interviewed by the social worker, Joe

---

denied his own gambling and any neglect or abuse of his mother. Although Molly owned the house, she was not prepared to tell her son to leave, nor was she prepared to bring any criminal charges. However, she had come to realise that she did not want to return to live with him. Molly had no other children in Ireland and her sister (eighty-one years old) was caring for her husband, who was eighty-five and physically frail. With much support from the social worker, who assisted Molly in examining her options, she decided to go into a nursing home.

Joe was advised to seek help for his alcohol and gambling addictions. He did not but visited his mother regularly in the home. He began to harass her for money, but she informed the staff. Subsequently, he saw Molly only in the sitting-room, where staff were nearby. He was also told that his mother had no money as her pension went towards the nursing-home fees. Since then, he visits Molly very infrequently and she is upset by this. However, she likes the nursing home and has made friends there.

What can be done to help the abused person?

If you have a relative, a friend or a neighbour whom you think is being abused or neglected, you can help in several ways. As a first step, talk to the person, help her to feel less isolated. As she begins to trust you more, you may be able to raise your suspicions with her, though she will probably be very reluctant to admit that abuse is happening. Encourage her to seek help from a solicitor, social worker, the Gardaí or her GP. Although it may be frustrating, continue to visit and talk. If you don't, the abused person will be left even more isolated.

The person may feel very guilty, blaming herself for the abuse. She may feel that, as a good parent, she must put the welfare of the abuser (daughter, son) before herself. She is possibly very concerned about what others would think of her if they knew of the abuse.

Often it is difficult to go on seeing your relative, friend or neighbour if you think she is not helping herself. It takes time, first for her to accept the seriousness of her situation, then to realise that she has options. You could investigate these options for her; even if she does not take them up immediately, she may later.

Offer the victim help in an emergency by supplying a place to stay or at least the knowledge that she can contact you. If the abused person has sought help, she will be trying to rebuild her life. Continue to extend friendship and support.

At present, when a professional suspects that an older person is being abused, there are no Department of Health guidelines for the investigation and management of the case. It is not mandatory to report such abuse. Hostels or refuges should be provided and the legal system should recognise the problem. A person cannot now get a barring order to exclude an adult child living with her. It is possible to get a court injunction but this is a lengthy and expensive process. If assault or fraud is involved, criminal prosecution can be initiated. Victim support groups are required, as well as individual counselling to help the abused person recover.

What can be done to help the abuser?
As there are different types of abuse and mistreatment and different reasons that an abuser does what she does, different types of intervention are needed. An abuser may need help for her own problems, perhaps a drug or alcohol treatment programme. She may need help in getting a job or, indeed, her own accommodation.

In some cases, an abusive carer is under great stress caring for her relative and may need both physical and emotional support. The practical support may be in the form of help in the home, meals-on-wheels, some respite breaks. These may enable the carer to cope better, and perhaps meet some of her own emotional needs. She may also need psychological help and education on alternatives to violence. She may need to review the caring role and her own ability to fulfil it; come to terms with her sense of anger, frustration or despair. She may feel isolated, lonely and with low self-esteem, and these feelings must be addressed in individual counselling or abuse will continue. She may have to limit or cease contact with the person she is abusing. However, some abusers will do so only after legal intervention.

While a small but significant number of older people are abused by their carers in their homes, abuse in institutional care also takes place. Relatives and friends need to be aware of this possibility and take steps to help the older person if they suspect it is happening. This may involve approaching senior nursing staff or the owner of the nursing home.

Abuse and neglect of older people is a serious problem that can result in injury or loss of life. It is likely to continue until the older person can be offered viable alternatives to remaining in the abusing situation.

How can we prevent abuse?

A society which marginalises older people may encourage violence or misuse of power. Age is not a social problem. Older people are active, healthy and a resource to their communities and families. Social policies geared towards keeping them at home for as long as possible accords with what older people and their families want. However, this situation places heavy demands on the family to provide any necessary care and may be stressful. In this context, abuse may occur. Yet family abuse is often a taboo subject, surrounded by secrecy. Prevention of all types of abuse is a challenge to the individual, her family and the broader community.

YOU

Remain in contact with your friends and neighbours and ask them to visit you where you live. Have a friend and confide in her. Participate in activities outside your home to avoid isolation.

Keep regular appointments with your doctor, dentist, hairdresser — it provides contact but also people who can attest to your mental competency. Keep control and records of your financial affairs. Do not transfer your assets to someone in return for care without consulting your solicitor.

Be aware that mistreatment, in the form of threats, humiliation or neglect, is often an early sign of physical abuse.

If you feel neglected or abused, believe in yourself and seek help.

FAMILY

Family members can prevent abuse in the following ways:
— Watch for signs of neglect or abuse of a person who is being looked after at home or in residential care.
— Partake in a family decision regarding care of your relative. Before you become a care-giver examine the reality of the situation and your physical, psychological and financial abilities to cope.
— If you are caring, feeling under pressure and neglecting your relative, acknowledge this and seek help.

COMMUNITY

Everyone should be aware of the possibility of abuse and neglect. This requires public information and education such as is now available regarding child sexual abuse, along with commitment at a political level. The issue should not be sensationalised.

Family carers should be recognised as providing a valuable service, in need of practical and emotional support. However, we must acknowledge that families are not always the best people to give care to their older members.

We should be conscious of the quality of facilities and care on offer in residential institutions.

SERVICES

As a society, we have to accept that abuse and neglect are crimes, and insist on adequate services being provided to the victims and the perpetrators. The problem is not simply solved by criminal prosecution and sanctions. It is a complex issue with medical, social, legal and psychological implications.

A service for reporting of abuse by older people themselves, their carers or others should be available to all, easily accessible and user-friendly. A telephone help-line is a good way for people to begin to discuss the abuse and seek further assistance. Different abusive situations require different solutions — a stressed carer may need support services while an older person abused by a disturbed family member may need to have the carer removed. Abused people will need individual counselling and perhaps self-help groups. There should be a range of services so that admission to residential care is not the only solution.

CHAPTER 12

CRIME AND THE FEAR OF CRIME

Are older people more at risk from crime?
Crime in Ireland is an issue of concern to people of all ages. Fear of crime is an equal if not greater concern. Members of the public believe that crime is on the increase.

Statistics from the Gardaí, while varying from year to year, show that for the past few years the number of indictable crimes (i.e. tried before a judge and jury) has stayed fairly constant at around 90,000 per year. These figures do not include less serious crimes, such as driving without a licence or drunkenness. Also, crimes are not always reported to the Gardaí; estimates of those unreported range from a third to a half of all crimes. This may be because the victim thinks it is not serious enough, believes the Gardaí can do little about it, or is embarrassed or traumatised (e.g. rape). There is also a tendency to report incidents involving financial loss and a possible insurance claim rather than those resulting in pain, injury or fear.

A survey in Ireland (1986) found that 23 per cent of the adult population had been victims of burglary, mugging, theft or indecent assault. The risk of becoming a victim of such a crime is higher in urban than in rural areas. The highest levels were in Dublin, a finding supported by Garda statistics. The lower rates in rural areas may be due to there being less opportunity for crime and more awareness among the community of people's comings and goings.

Surveys in Ireland and other countries have shown that older people are less likely to be the victims of crime than any other group. In general, it is young people, particularly men between the ages of eighteen and twenty-five, who are most frequently the victims, especially of violent crime. Also, the risk of crime is much higher for workers. Even when considering crime committed on the street, older people are less at risk.

Do older people fear crime?

Fear of crime is widespread in society. This fear is due to the fact that the public generally associates crime with violence. For example, whereas Canadian statistics indicate that only 8 per cent of crimes are violent, 75 per cent of Canadians think that over half of all criminal acts are accompanied by violence, i.e. six times more than is actually the case. You are much more likely to be a victim of crime against property (burglary, car theft) than a personal attack (assault, mugging). People feel less safe at night but most crime takes place during the day.

Surveys in Ireland and in other countries have shown that although the rate of victimisation is fairly low among older people, it is they who most often show a fear of crime. Women are more likely to be fearful than men, and people over sixty-five more fearful than younger people. Older people, particularly older women, are more fearful because they perceive themselves to be especially vulnerable in this regard. They may also believe that the outcome will be more serious for them, physically, psychologically or financially.

The health of older people may put them at risk. Ageing is accompanied by a loss of strength and decreased ability to run or walk. Older people may not be able to react as quickly. In addition, some of them may look weak and defenceless, making them attractive targets. When attacked, there is a greater chance of older people being injured, and more seriously injured. This physical trauma must be taken into account, as well as the psychological consequences of victimisation among the elderly. The more serious physical consequences of a push or a fall may lead to their fear of crime.

It is on the street that older people, especially women, are most exposed, particularly as they are much less able to defend themselves. Alone in the street they are a low risk for offenders and so may be victims of theft such as handbag-snatching. Older people often have savings or valuable goods or property which can make them targets for crime. More older people, particularly women, live alone. These factors may increase their feeling of vulnerability to crime. If robbed, they are likely to suffer a greater loss in proportion to their income than other age-groups.

However, while older people may feel more at risk, their lifestyle may actually decrease their likelihood of being victims of crime as, due to health and financial considerations, they may go out less.

Criminals prefer to rob an unoccupied house, so the fact that older people stay in more means they and their property are better protected. This partly explains why the victimisation of older people is proportionately less than that of other age-groups.

Surveys in Britain found that the fears that rose most with age were 'being bothered by strangers' and being mugged. Statistically it is young men who are most likely to be victims of this kind of crime. Older people overestimate the extent to which they are at risk.

Research has shown that an older person who becomes involved in her community, by attending leisure groups and so on, feels safer in her neighbourhood than someone who has no social activities. If a person stays at home alone, her fear and feeling of vulnerability may increase, whereas someone who goes out into her community maintains contact with its reality. She is better able to evaluate the actual dangers in the area rather than responding to exaggerated media reports of the rate of crime and the risk of attack.

What are the effects of crime?

Crime leaves the person and perhaps her family and friends with a sense of loss, whether due to injury or to the emotional consequences.

No one expects to be a victim of crime and so will be shocked and disbelieving: 'I didn't think it could happen to me,' 'I was paralysed,' 'Afterwards everything was a blur.' She may be angry: 'It just wasn't fair.' She may feel anger at the criminal, the police or even herself.

Disorientation and lack of control are common feelings. Concentration may be difficult; the person may be forgetful and feel overwhelmed by her emotions. The person may often be fearful about going out and worried about it happening again. She may feel vulnerable: 'I keep thinking what might have happened.' She may also feel her privacy was invaded.

Sometimes a person feels guilty, blaming herself for not being more careful of her handbag, for not having more locks on the doors, etc. She needs to be reminded that she is not responsible for the crime.

She may experience a sense of isolation, believing that no one understands what she is going through. She may lose trust in other people and in the Gardaí, and feel insecure. Depression may occur. The person may be physically unwell, weak or dizzy. Sleep problems are common.

These reactions are normal and it will take time for the person to feel herself again. Certain events may bring the emotions back, e.g. the arrest and trial of the offender, the anniversary of the crime.

What should you do if you are a victim of crime?

There are various procedures you should follow.

Contact the Gardaí as soon as possible. Prompt reporting increases the chances of detection, and financial compensation requires that you report the crime. If you are burgled don't touch anything.

Medical treatment may be necessary. If it is urgent you can attend the Accident and Emergency department of your local general hospital. If you are a victim of sexual assault or rape, you can attend the Sexual Assault Unit (Rotunda Hospital, Dublin), where specialist teams can treat you and collect necessary evidence. If the treatment is not urgent see your GP and have a check-up. Voluntary Health Insurance does provide cover for treatment of injuries sustained as the result of a crime. However, if you receive compensation from the Criminal Injuries Compensation Tribunal, monies paid by VHI are then repayable to the company.

Support for a victim of crime is very important. If you do not have someone to talk to, or feel you need more help in overcoming the trauma, the Irish Association of Victim Support offers emotional and practical support in your home (see Directory). The Association will also provide advice about your rights and entitlements in areas such as legal aid, courts and compensation.

You may be able to claim compensation if you are a victim of crime.

For crimes against the person (assault, hit and run, mugging, murder, rape and sexual abuse), compensation for expenses incurred or loss of earnings is available from the Criminal Injuries Compensation Tribunal. Since 1986, no compensation is paid for pain and suffering. Personal insurance for your house, business or car may pay compensation. For crimes against property, you can claim for malicious injuries through your Local Authority. Emergency assistance may also be provided by the Community Welfare Officer in your local Health Board Centre.

If your handbag, purse or wallet has been stolen, you will need to do the following:

— Telephone immediately to notify the bank or company of the loss of any credit, cheque or cashpoint card or cheque-book; confirm in writing at a later date. If uncashed cheques or money orders are taken, notify your bank or the issuing authority at once. Apply for a duplicate driving licence; the form is available from your local Garda station or licensing authority.

— If keys to your house, car, garage or place of work are lost, have the locks changed.

— If pension or allowance books are stolen, notify the Department of Social Welfare and inform the Post Office where you draw the allowance.

— Inform the library if your tickets are stolen; otherwise you will be liable for any books taken out on them.

— Cancel and renew any cards, e.g. club membership, bus pass, medical card.

How can you help someone who has been a victim of crime?

A crime can affect not just the victim but her family and friends. Upset at what happened and fearful for the future safety of their relative, they may need help and support. The person herself may need help with basic requirements, e.g. medical treatment or a place to stay for a short time if she feels physically unsafe or her house is uninhabitable. It is not helpful to offer alcohol or tranquillisers. The victim may need help to cancel credit cards, etc. She may also need practical help in going out if she is fearful.

You can help by encouraging the person to talk about how she is feeling. Men and women may handle being a victim of crime differently. For example, after burglary men are more typically angry and become security-conscious, while women are frequently distressed by feelings of contamination. They want to clean and disinfect everything in the house. These different ways of dealing with the trauma may prevent them from understanding each other, and therefore they are less likely to be mutually supportive.

Tell the victim that you are sorry for the loss and hurt she has suffered and that you are glad she was not physically hurt. You can help by saying that she had nothing to do with the fact she was a victim. The Irish Association for Victim Support can give emotional help and practical advice. If criminal proceedings take place, go along to offer support.

Realise that it will take time — weeks to months — for someone to recover from being a victim of crime. Each person will do this in her own way and at her own pace.

Can older people avoid becoming victims of crime?

Older people should certainly be informed of the potential danger of victimisation, but also of their relatively low rate of risk. While it is better to be aware of a possible danger, the information should be conveyed in a calm and practical manner. Older people need to know how to protect their homes against burglary, how to avoid fraud, and how to avoid and deal with crimes that may occur on the street. They should be advised not to be over-trusting with people who call to the house seeking entry or collecting money; to check the identity of callers and never to let a stranger in; always to use a doorchain.

It lessens the sense of vulnerability if the older person feels competent, e.g. by having proper glasses or a hearing-aid, or by being accompanied by friends.

To prevent thefts, older people should be able to opt for having their pensions deposited into a bank account or sent to them in the post. Another way to lessen their vulnerability is to provide company for those who are isolated. A telephone check-in programme would be a source of reassurance, and a way of alerting others if anything happened to them.

Research in other countries found that providing more police generally does not reduce the level of crime but does allow greater assistance to be given to people, which may help with detection and prosecution. Even where there is little prospect of detection, the police can demonstrate concern by recording the incident and offering crime prevention advice.

The Gardaí operate four schemes aimed at preventing crime:

(1) The Neighbourhood Watch Schemes now number 1,500 and are based in urban areas. People are encouraged to watch out for their neighbours with regard to their houses and their safety.

(2) The Community Alert has 500 rural-based schemes. These are run by Muintir na Tíre and the Gardaí. Older or vulnerable people are visited by members of their own communities, and some help may be given with home security.

(3) There are 200 Neighbourhood Gardaí who get to know and visit older people in their areas.

(4) The Garda Crime Prevention Officer will advise on how better to

protect property and person. Contact the local Garda station. A Crime Prevention Room in Harcourt Square displaying equipment is open to the public by appointment.

CHAPTER 13

HOSPITAL

Illness often leads to feelings of vulnerability and helplessness, and pain is common. How you deal with this depends on your way of coping, your past experiences and the practical and emotional support available from family, friends and the professionals involved. We discussed a person's emotional response to a life-threatening illness (see p. 114). People often have a similar response to a major illness or an accident, and we look here at the experience of going into hospital in these circumstances.

As an older person, the greater likelihood of your having an illness increases your chances of needing to attend or enter hospital. Your stay will probably be longer than a younger person's, not only because of the higher incidence of serious illness in your age-group but because of a lack of support from the family or community services. Also, you may be kept in a general hospital because there are insufficient rehabilitation or long-term care facilities.

Certain fears and anxieties often arise. Fear of being dependent on others is heightened when you are ill and needing hospitalisation. Being in hospital can be isolating and disturbing. The surroundings are strange — your bed, meals and routine are missing. You may also be anxious about your physical state. Will you be in a lot of pain during or following tests? Will surgery be a risk to your survival? Will you be in much pain after surgery or other treatments (e.g. radiation therapy or chemotherapy)? Will you be able to live a normal life again? You may also be concerned about medical technology prolonging your life when you are not going to recover.

The best way to help yourself is to get the information you need. Ask questions of the doctors, nurses, physiotherapist, etc. and you will know what you have to cope with. You may find that some of your fears are groundless. Continue asking questions, so you stay informed of your medical condition. Some older people who have an infection or have had surgery become confused. In most cases this will pass; do not assume it is dementia.

An additional worry may be the cost of treatment. You should know your entitlements (see Directory) and, if you have medical insurance, what you are covered for. If you do not, staff are available in the hospital to advise you. Ask for a visit.

Case 1

Paul (seventy-one years old) had never been sick in his life and put this down to his healthy life on the farm he ran. He lived with his brother Aidan, neither was married. He had problems passing water for several years but did not go to his GP. Finally the pain was very severe and he went to see the doctor, who told him he would have to go into hospital for a few days. Paul wanted to put this off as he was needed on the farm. His doctor told him it could be serious and he had to go when he was called by the local hospital.

Paul was concerned at having to go into hospital. He found being in a ward with other men strange. He felt very embarrassed at being physically examined by doctors, particularly female doctors. He was very restless with nothing to do all day and the food was not 'his type'. He went through the tests and hoped he would 'get out with a few tablets to fix him up'. However, the news was bad; the doctor told him he had cancer of his prostate gland and it had spread.

Paul was told he would have an operation and this frightened him. He was not afraid of the pain but of being confined to bed and unable to care for himself. He told no one how he felt. He did not ask if he would die but thought, 'I'll talk to Dr Ward when I get home.' He was not afraid of dying but was afraid of a painful death. Also, Aidan would not be able to care for him or run the farm, as an accident a few years ago had left him with a head injury. After surgery, Paul woke up with a drip in his arm and a drainage bag for his urine. He felt helpless and very embarrassed. A nurse explained that both of these were temporary, which helped. Paul recovered well but asked no questions. He went to a nursing home for two weeks, then returned home. He did not go to his GP: 'I'll leave well enough alone.' He had no private insurance but paid his hospital bills for private care by cheque.

Some people have anxieties about life outside the hospital. If you are resident in a home, your concerns may be whether your room is still there for you or whether you will be too sick to go back. When you go into the home find out the policy. Some homes will keep a room as long as it is paid for, others will keep it if your return is likely. Sometimes, your room may be used by someone for a short stay. If this occurs, what will happen to your belongings?

If you are admitted to hospital in an emergency, you may be concerned about someone you are caring for. Tell the social worker in the hospital and help may be arranged for the person at home.

Coming out of hospital means another change and adjustment. While happy to be leaving the hospital, you or your carer may feel insecure without the reassurance and support. Most people leave hospital needing further care and time to recover fully. Again, you should get clear information regarding medication, level of activity and exercise, and possible length of time for recovery. You also need to know who to contact if a problem arises — your GP, Public Health Nurse, occupational therapist or the hospital; and to be aware of any necessary follow-up treatment, e.g. physiotherapy, speech therapy.

Case 2

Moira (sixty-five years old) was admitted suddenly to her general hospital following a road traffic accident. She was on her way home when she was knocked down crossing the road. In the ambulance her main thought was, 'I hope I don't die, there is no one to care for Frank.' Frank, her husband (sixty-eight), had emphysema and was on oxygen at home. He was not able to cook, light the fire or wash himself without help.

Moira had no internal or head injuries but she had bad bruising, a broken leg and was in shock. She was in hospital for a week. She found it difficult to move around on crutches. Her main concerns were Frank and the fact that she was in a single room and unsure whether her private health insurance would cover this. The morning after the accident, she asked the Sister on the ward to phone Frank. He was fine and their daughter was caring for him. Moira was worried as her daughter was employed and had two young children — how long could she care for Frank? Moira was recovering well physically but was upset. She was not eating or sleeping, worrying about Frank and how they would cope when she went home. The social worker saw Moira and explained they

---

could have a home-help who would come every morning and evening, to help with the housework and shopping and get Frank up and back to bed. This was a great relief to Moira. Someone from the hospital accounts department also discussed Moira's insurance cover with her. Her major concerns dealt with, Moira could concentrate on recovering from the traumatic accident both physically and mentally.

The Department of Health in 1992 produced *A Charter of Rights for Hospital Patients*. It covers rights in the area of access to services when attending hospital, as well as personal rights.

Access to services includes your right to be admitted in an emergency or to be transferred to another hospital for a medical procedure; your right to receive notice of cancellation and, in this event, to an early appointment date. As an out-patient, you have the right to receive confirmation within a reasonable time of a first appointment and to see at least a senior doctor on this visit.

In hospital, you have the right to courtesy, privacy and respect for your religious beliefs, and the right to receive visitors. You are entitled to information regarding your test results, and the purpose, method, likely duration and expected benefit of treatment. You should be informed of possible pain or discomfort, risks and side-effects of any proposed treatment. You have a right to confidentiality in respect of medical records. You can request to have your records made available to you; if the hospital considers this could seriously damage your physical or mental health it will usually ask your GP to communicate the information. You have the right to refuse to participate in the teaching of medical students or to take part in clinical trials or research. You have the right to make a complaint and, if it is not resolved satisfactorily, to refer the matter to the Hospitals Complaints Committee.

After discharge, you and your GP have the right to information on your condition, treatment, medication and further treatment.

The Patients' Charter is just an aspiration. It is not legally binding and there are no ministerial regulations in place. It is only as good as the hospital which operates it, and much is left to the individual professional and her interpretation of the guidelines. Further work is needed to develop the Charter, to make it specific and clear about the services hospitals must provide for their patients.

CHAPTER 14

Staying Put or Moving

A. WHY IS CHANGE NECESSARY?

Changes in your life may become necessary if you or your carer can no longer manage as things are.

You may have become more physically frail. Like most people, you will probably want to remain as independent as possible and stay in your own home. Sometimes relatives may think you are at risk because you are weaker and/or do things (decorate, drive, use dangerous tools) they think you should not. Their response may be to suggest that you live with them or move into a nursing home. Many older people reject these suggestions. The anxieties of relatives need to be balanced with people's right to take some risks in order to remain independent. Often, additional precautions can be taken, e.g. larger mirrors on the outside of the car or a reorganised kitchen or help in the home with heavy cleaning. You and your relatives should aim for a balance between the need for safety and the desire for independence.

Change may also become necessary if you become confused or incontinent or you want more company. Your carer may feel she cannot continue to give you the same care or cannot cope with your new needs. The problems may lie in your house; it may lack running water, be too big to heat or too isolated.

If you are clear about what your current problems are, you can explore the options.

B. WAYS OF STAYING PUT

We look first at ways to help you remain in your home or to provide help to your carer.

(1) If the problem is that your home lacks a toilet and/or bathroom and running water, there are schemes aimed at improving these conditions for people living alone. The Task Force on Special Housing Aid can be contacted through the Health Boards and organisations such as Alone, St Vincent de Paul and Social Service Councils.

Case 1

Peg (eighty years old) is single and has lived alone in a small village since the death of her sister. She is in excellent health and goes out daily to shop and to attend Mass. Her income is the old age pension. Her house was in poor repair with rotting windows, no indoor toilet and an open fire for heating. In order for Peg to remain at home, and to decrease her risk of contracting hypothermia and of falling going to the toilet in bad weather or at night, the Task Force installed new windows and a bathroom. The St Vincent de Paul contributed to the installation of electric storage heaters.

---

(2) If you are renting and being asked for a higher rent, you may get assistance under a special scheme. If you live in a formerly controlled dwelling, you may qualify for a rent allowance. The new rent must have been set by the District Court or by the Rents Tribunal, which was established in August 1983. The property-owner must register your tenancy with the Local Authority. For this allowance, which is means-tested, apply to the Department of Social Welfare.

(3) If you or your relative could remain in the house if it were adapted or improved with aids, approach the Community Occupational Therapist or Physiotherapist, who will assess your needs. There is usually a waiting-list for this service. The length of time you have to wait will depend on where you live and how urgent your need is. The consultation is free. Equipment may be available free of charge to medical-card holders; others have to

purchase it. If you have a long-term illness, you may be entitled to some pieces of equipment. The Health Board may contribute some money for adaptations to your home. Apply before any building takes place.

(4) Personal care or help for the carer within the home may make it easier to continue living there. Home helps can provide assistance in your home on a daily basis. Contact the National Social Service Board for the name of your local Home Care Organiser. The availability of the service varies greatly, and anyone who can afford it may be asked to contribute towards the cost. Some areas of the country have care attendants; ask the Public Health Nurse about this possibility.

(5) Help outside the home is found in day centres/day care centres. These are run by a variety of bodies, including the Social Service Centres and the Health Boards. The Alzheimer Society runs day centres in Dublin and throughout the country (see Directory). There are also some day hospitals for older people, run by the Health Boards. Your GP would be able to assess your need for this and inform you of availability.

If as a carer you need a longer break, you may be able to arrange it, either regularly throughout the year (e.g. one week in four) or for holidays only. Contact your GP or Public Health Nurse about this service.

C. MOVING — WHERE TO?

If you or your relative have considered the above to help you remain in your house or with the carer, and decided that a move is the best option, the next step is to see what best meets your needs, what is available and what you can afford. The options are as follows:

(6) If your major problem is financial, in that the cost of running and maintaining your house is too great, you may be able to sell your house and buy a smaller one, giving you some extra money on which to live. Currently, no financial institution in Ireland offers the scheme whereby you stay in your home and are paid a sum

of money annually, and the institution owns all or part of the house upon your death.

Alternatively, you may have to move to a house that is not necessarily cheaper but, for example, is nearer family or in town, is a bungalow or convenient for support services. An option in some parts of the country may be to buy a house in a retirement complex. These houses/apartments are designed for older people, with safety features, hand-rails in bathrooms, etc. An alarm system is usually available. Some are built near a private nursing home to which you may be able to transfer if you are unable to live independently in the future. You need to examine carefully the conditions of purchase and the costs of the care provided.

Case 1

Catherine (seventy years old) and Thomas (seventy-three) lived in their own large two-storey, four-bedroom house in Dublin. They lived on an Occupational Pension and an Old Age Contributory Pension. Both were independent in caring for themselves but had some health problems. Thomas had a chronic chest condition, making it hard for him to climb the stairs; and Catherine had arthritis, which was making cleaning the house and walking a half-mile to the local shops increasingly difficult.

They discussed getting help in the house and installing a stair-lift for Thomas. However, the help on a long-term basis was going to be a significant drain on their finances. Also, the cost of heating the house was substantial. Catherine did not drive and did not want to learn. She wanted to continue doing her own shopping although her daughter was prepared to do it for her.

Catherine and Thomas considered moving but Catherine was concerned about losing her neighbours and friends who lived locally. They looked for a small bungalow but there was none suitably located nearer to the shops and church. They also went to see some purpose-built apartments for older people but they were too far from their family and friends.

One year later, the auctioneer with whom they had investigated moving contacted them. A small estate of two-bedroom bungalows was being built quite near their house. It was a quarter-mile from the shops. A bus stopped almost beside the estate. Catherine hoped it was near enough to keep in touch with her

---

neighbours and friends. She could continue to attend the flower club of which she had been a member for many years. They could afford to buy it and have additional money if they needed practical help at a later date. They would also be able to visit their son in Australia.

They discussed some changes with the builder: raising the plug sockets, installing grab-rails, fitting sink and shower with controls that were easy to turn on. The shower was a walk-in one with a seat.

(7) If you are unable to purchase, you may be eligible for Corporation or County Council Sheltered Housing. Home-owners are generally not eligible for Local Authority Sheltered Housing. This form of sheltered housing has a warden or a twenty-four-hour alarm system. There may be communal facilities where a meal is provided. You apply for this housing and are assessed and allocated points. You should then make an appointment to see the Housing Adviser, who can tell you your chances of obtaining accommodation. If you get an offer of a place, go and see it before you accept the key. Rent is payable on this form of accommodation.

Private sheltered housing (e.g. Altadore in Glenageary, Respond in Cork) is also available. Apply to the organisation running the scheme. Again, rent is payable. Some schemes will consider you if you own your own house.

If you become in need of permanent care, you have to move from this type of accommodation.

(8) If you cannot live alone, your Health Board may have a 'Boarding Out' option, where you go and live permanently with a family.

(9) Welfare Homes, run by the Health Boards, provide accommodation for older people who need a high level of care. They are also referred to as Geriatric Homes or Homes for the Aged. Each Health Board lists them in the telephone directory. There are usually waiting-lists for places. Admission would require a full medical assessment, often by a consultant in geriatric medicine. Payment of a portion of your pension is required.

(10) Nursing homes provide accommodation to people who need a high level of care. They are run by voluntary groups or private individuals and vary in the residents they will accept. Some will take only people who are independent, while others will take those more dependent. Some homes will take people with dementia while others will not. Many nursing homes will have a waiting-list, so enquire about this. You can ask for a brochure from the homes which are within visiting distance for you and your family and friends; proximity to shops and facilities is also important. Check if they are on the list of approved nursing homes available from the Health Boards. Payment is made directly to the home.

Good nursing homes are those that emphasise:
— rehabilitation rather than a custodial model of care
— the residents' needs, and their involvement in the daily life of the home.

Size may also be important. They should be split into sub-units of twenty-five to give a homely feel to the people living there. The homes should be placed in the community, in towns and in the city areas where people have lived, not on the outskirts. It is also possible to make nursing homes more open and integrated into the community by providing access (meals and cultural events) to non-residents, including younger people.

Matching your needs to the homes will give you a short-list. These institutions can be contacted and a visit arranged. On this visit, and perhaps during a short trial stay, you should consider the following factors:
— Does the home seem comfortable and clean, with an absence of odours? Is it geared to your level of disability (e.g. is there a lift)? Is the home suitable for someone who may wander off? Is it easy to find your way around? Are there signs and notices to help?
— Are the residents treated as individuals? Are you spoken to by the Matron/Head or are your relatives spoken to about you? Are the residents addressed with respect and not patronised?
— Are the staff trained? Do they seem helpful and friendly? Do they have experience of someone with Alzheimer's disease? Are they supervised? Are they offered training and development?
— How many people are in the home? With how many people will you be sharing the sitting-room, dining-room, bathroom and toilet?
— Will you have privacy? Do staff knock on the bedroom door

before they enter? Is it possible to share a room with your partner?

— Will you have a single room? If not, is your area screened off?
— May you bring some belongings: radio, TV, favourite chair, photographs, ornaments? Where can you keep them safely and privately?
— What is the daily routine and what choices will you have? May you take a bath when you want to, make tea, decide what time to go to bed at? What about the menu, times and places where meals can be eaten? May alcohol be taken?
— What arrangements are there for laundry? Do you do it yourself or pay an extra cost?
— How do you get medical, chiropody and hairdressing services and send and receive letters?
— Are there restrictions on visiting? Is there a place to receive visitors in private? May you have an overnight guest to stay? Do staff talk to visitors about residents in front of them?
— Are there activities (bingo, card-playing, musical events, reminiscence groups, occupational therapy) arranged in the home? Are you allowed to do any small tasks that you may enjoy? May you attend activities outside?
— May you go away for weekends or holidays? Is there any reduction in charge for this?
— If you are ill or have an accident and have to stay in hospital, what happens to your place?
— If you become very ill or confined to bed or severely demented, will you be able to remain in the home?
— Do you as a resident have any say in the running of the home and the planning of your own care?
— May you smoke in the home, or if you need a smoke-free environment, is it available?
— May you make telephone calls in private when you want to?
— Is there a grievance procedure and a residents' committee?

You may make your decision about a home while being aware of possible drawbacks. Talk about these rather than pretending they do not exist. If as a carer you are choosing for a person with dementia, do not exclude her but take her to visit the homes. Do not expect her to make a choice from memory, but she may be able to express a preference.

The decision regarding nursing-home care should be discussed by all the family, though often it is left to the carer. If families share the decision-making, the carer may feel less guilty and the older person may accept she can no longer be cared for at home. Families often need to share the considerable financial cost of a nursing home. The Health Boards may pay a subsidy towards the cost and the person may have a pension but this will leave a shortfall of between £100 and £200 per week (see Nursing Homes, Directory). The older person may need to sell her investments and assets, perhaps even her home. It may be necessary to change her will.

The decision is made and the day of moving has arrived. As a carer, always go with your relative. Help her unpack and settle in. Talk to the staff. When the time comes to go, say a brief goodbye and leave. It can be helpful if one of the staff is there with your relative.

Case 2

James (eighty-nine years old) was a physically frail man who was cared for by his wife until her death. He then went to live with his daughter Anne (fifty-nine). However, a year later his daughter found it very difficult to manage as he really needed two people to assist him out of bed and to walk. He needed to be washed. He was able to feed himself, hold lively conversations and watch television.

With his agreement, James's daughter arranged for him to go into a local nursing home when her daughter was getting married. James did not like his stay there, his main complaint being that he had to share a room and many of the people there had dementia.

As James became more physically dependent, there were days when Anne found it easier to leave him in bed. He subsequently found it more difficult to get up. Neither James nor Anne wanted anyone coming into the house to help with him.

Finally his daughter told James she could no longer adequately care for him at home. She was very upset and felt guilty. He accepted the situation and agreed to go into a nursing home. He had the proceeds of the sale of his house, which would cover the cost.

Anne telephoned several local nursing homes seeking a single room. One home had one available. She went to see it and it was unsuitable. The home was a three-storey building and there was no lift to bring James to the sitting-room or dining-room. She then went to visit two more, which had places sharing with one other person. One home was bright and clean, with trained staff. She could visit her father anytime and take him out for days. James would also be able to remain there until his death. However, the bedroom was extremely small with little space between the two beds, and the only place for the visitor to sit was on the commode. There was one sink beside what would have been James's bed, which both people used. She knew James would not have accepted these circumstances. There was a waiting-list of approximately one year for a single room, with current residents being given preference.

Anne went home to James feeling dispirited. They discussed the situation and decided to try for a home further away. This would mean fewer visits to James but appeared to be the best solution. She went to see three more nursing homes, now also seeking one with a telephone in the bedroom so she could phone her father regularly. The best option was a shared bedroom and a room which was adequate in size. The bathroom, which was equipped with aids, was next door. It was a single-storey building and had a large garden. James would have his breakfast in bed, then be assisted to wash and dress. Dinner and tea were served to everyone in the dining-room. The staff were friendly and aimed to create 'a home from home'. James was free to come and go as he pleased. However, he would have to change his GP as the nursing home was too distant from his current one.

Following a discussion with Anne, James decided to try this nursing home for one month.

For a carer, a relative going into a home can be very difficult, especially if the older person does not want to go or does not realise, due to dementia, that she will be staying there. Many relatives feel guilty. You must accept you have reached the limits of your ability to care for your relative at home. Some of your stresses are gone, but you may be sad and upset. It may feel like a loss and you can go through a period of grief. If you have spent many years as a carer, this can be a very empty time in your life. Whereas up to this, you may have been needed constantly and had a busy routine, now you have time and do not know what to do with it. You need several months to build a new life, to get well rested, develop new interests and have time for yourself, your family and friends.

For a while, the guilt may be there every time you visit. By continuing to visit, you are helping your relative cope with her loss. You are also giving her support and a sense of belonging. If you do not visit, you may feel more or less guilty. Your relative may put pressure on you to visit more often than you think you can. Do not promise what you cannot deliver. Tell the person when to expect you, and if you have to cancel a visit let her know.

As an older person, having considered all the options, you can decide what is best suited to your needs, to stay put or move. You will have to look for the services you require. Your GP or Public Health Nurse will be aware of some of these. Another source of information is the headquarters of your Health Board or local Community Care headquarters (see Directory or consult the telephone directory).

SECTION III
DIRECTORY

VOLUNTARY AND STATUTORY SERVICES AND BENEFITS

This is an alphabetical listing of organisations by title, ignoring 'the' and 'an'. If you cannot find the organisation you are looking for, check the Index under the relevant subject-matter.

ABBEYFIELD (Dublin) SOCIETY LTD,
Avon Cottage, Hainault Park, Foxrock, Dublin 18.
Tel. (01) 2893122.
Abbeyfield House,
29 Seapoint Avenue,
Monkstown, Co. Dublin.
Tel. (01) 2801314.
Provides accommodation for active older people.

ACTIVE RETIREMENT ASSOCIATIONS: See FEDERATION OF ACTIVE RETIREMENT ASSOCIATIONS

ADULT EDUCATION
Adult education is run by many second-level and some third-level institutions. Most second-level institutions give substantial reductions in fees to senior citizens.

ADULT EDUCATION ORGANISERS' ASSOCIATION,
Adult Education Officer,
Vocational School, Battery Rd, Longford.
Tel. (043) 45474.
Promotes the development of adult education and gives a collective expression to the views of adult education organisers.

AGE ACTION IRELAND,
114/16 Pearse St, Dublin 2.
Tel. (01) 6771930/6779892,
fax 6715734.
A non-governmental organisation acting as a network for organisations and people providing services for older people and their carers in Ireland, and as a development agency promoting better policies and services. Its main aim is to improve the quality of life of

175

older people, especially those who are most vulnerable and frail, by enabling them to live full, independent and satisfying lives. Main activities include:

(1) running a library and information service on all aspects of ageing and older people, which anybody can contact
(2) publishing a monthly bulletin
(3) organising conferences and seminars
(4) undertaking pilot projects to develop examples of good practice.

Membership is open to all organisations and individuals dealing with older people and their carers. At present there are working groups on respite care, education and training, education for death and dying, and cross-border co-operation. Age Action is represented on the Steering Group to establish a Dementia Services Centre. Other groups are being set up on rural issues, research, community alarm systems, day care, community care and ageing in developing countries. It publishes a Directory of Services for Older People in Ireland and is preparing a national directory of respite care services (available 1995). It has received a grant to promote the University of the Third Age in Ireland.

AGE ALLIANCE IRELAND,
 c/o Age & Opportunity,
Carmichael House,

North Brunswick St, Dublin 7.
Tel. (01) 8723311,
fax (01) 8735737.
Operates to enhance collectively the well-being of its affiliates through seeking the implementation of the Irish Congress of Trade Unions and European Charters, and advance the interests — economic and social — of retired and older people. Its main objectives are to act as a forum for the views of its constituent organisations; to present these views to government, international, national, local, statutory, voluntary and other agencies; to promote mutual support between constituent organisations.

AIDS HELPLINE
Cork: Tel. (021) 276676.
Mon.–Fri. 10 a.m.–5 p.m.
Dublin: Tel. (01) 8724277.
Mon.–Fri. 7–9 p.m., Sat. 3–5 p.m.
Galway: Tel. (091) 66266
Mon.–Fri. 10 a.m.–12 noon,
Thurs. 8–10 p.m.
Limerick: Tel. (061) 454554.
Sat. 2.30–5 p.m.
Sligo: Tel. (071) 70743.
Mon.–Fri. 6–7 p.m.
Western Health Board Aids Information: Tel. (091) 25200.
Wed. 10 a.m.–1 p.m, 7–10 p.m.
Provides information on HIV and AIDS and other sexually transmitted diseases, in a non-judgmental and confidential manner.

AIM GROUP FAMILY LAW
INFORMATION, MEDIATION
AND COUNSELLING,
32 Upr Fitzwilliam St,
Dublin 2. Tel. (01) 6616478.
Mon.–Fri. 10 a.m.–12 noon.
Operates a legal information
and referral centre for people
with marital and family problems, and a mediation service
for couples wishing to separate.

ALCOHOLICS ANONYMOUS,
109 South Circular Rd,
Leonard's Corner, Dublin 8.
Tel. (01) 4538998.
After hours tel. (01) 6795967.
Community Centre, Monkstown
Ave. 7–10 p.m.
Tel. (01) 2808723.
Fellowship of men and women
alcoholics. There are many
branches throughout the country; see local newspapers for
meetings or contact the above
number for your local area. For
alcohol and other addictions,
community treatment is provided by addiction counsellors (see
Health Boards).

ALCOHOLISM — GENERAL
INFORMATION,
Health Promotion Unit,
Hawkins House, Dublin 2.
Tel. (01) 6714711.

ALCOHOLISM — RESIDENTIAL
TREATMENT CENTRES
Clare: Bushy Park, Treatment &
Recovery Centre, Ennis.
Tel. (065) 40944.
Cork: Tabor Lodge, Alcohol,

Drug & Gambling Treatment
Centre, Belgooly.
Tel. (021) 887110.
Dublin: The Rutland Centre Ltd,
Addiction Treatment,
Knocklyon House, Knocklyon
Rd, Dublin 16.
Tel. (01) 4946358/4946972/
4946761.
Mayo: Hope House, Foxford.
Tel. (094) 56888.
Tipperary: Aiséirí, Townspark,
Cahir. Tel. (052) 41166.
Wexford: Aiséirí, Roxborough.
Tel. (053) 41818.
For adults, including older people.

AL-ANON,
Information Centre, 5 Capel St,
Dublin 1. Tel. (01) 8732699.
Fellowship of men and women
whose lives have been or are
being affected by another person's compulsive drinking.
Contact the above number for
your local support group.

ALONE,
1 Bermingham Place,
Kilmainham Lane, Dublin 8.
Tel. (01) 6791032.
Aims to promote awareness of
elderly people's problems, res-
cue those in need, visit and
provide with necessities of life.
Refers cases to the Task Force
on Special Housing Aid for the
Elderly and monitors same.

ALZHEIMER CARE CENTRE,
Swords Rd, Whitehall, Dublin 9.
Tel. (01) 8374444.
Purpose-built centre, provides

day care, holiday/weekend care and long-term care in additional facilities in Highfield and Hampstead Hospitals. There is a family support group which is open to all carers, even if they do not have someone attending the facilities.

ALZHEIMER SOCIETY OF IRELAND,
St John of God Hospital, Stillorgan, Co. Dublin.
Tel. (01) 2881282. Mon.–Fri. 9.30 a.m.–5 p.m. for information. In Dublin there are six support groups and two day care centres and a respite care centre for Alzheimer patients at Temple Hill, Blackrock, Co. Dublin. There are thirty support groups throughout the rest of the country. These groups provide information for relatives and carers. Referrals are through GPs, Public Health Nurses, social workers or directly through the family. There must be a firm diagnosis of Alzheimer's disease or dementia for entry to day centres. Contact the above telephone number for the support group nearest you.
DAY/RESPITE CARE CENTRES
Blackrock Day Care, Temple Hill, Blackrock, Co. Dublin. Tel. (01) 2887572. Mon.–Fri. 10 a.m.–4 p.m. Respite (overnight) Mon.–Thurs (incl.).
Sybil Hill Day Care, Sybil Hill Rd, Raheny, Dublin 5. Tel. Patsy Downes

(01) 8328222. Mon.–Fri 10 a.m.–4 p.m.
Limerick Day Care, Mount Convent Day Centre, O'Connell Avenue, Limerick. Tel. (061) 313456. Thurs. 10.30 a.m.– 4 p.m.
Cork Day Centre, Deer Park, Friar's Walk, Cork. Tel. (021) 311698. Fri. 10 a.m.–4 p.m.
Navan Day Centre, Kells Rd, Navan. Tel. (046) 27007. Wed. & Fri. 10 a.m.–4 p.m.
Waterford Day Centre, c/o Social Service Centre, Spring Garden Alley, Lady Lane, Waterford. Tel. Annette (051) 50491. Wed. & Fri. 10 a.m.–4 p.m.
REGIONAL OFFICES
Dublin, national office:
St John of God Hospital, Stillorgan, Co. Dublin.
Tel. (01) 2881282. Mon.–Fri. 9.30 a.m.–5 p.m.
Limerick: Bishop's Palace, Church St, King's Island, Limerick. Tel. (061) 313456. Mon.–Fri. 10.30 a.m.–12 noon. Wed. 8–9.30 p.m.

AONTAS: THE NATIONAL ASSOCIATION OF ADULT EDUCATION,
22 Earlsfort Tce, Dublin 2. Tel. (01) 4754121/4754122. Independent national organisation representing all aspects of adult education. Aims to develop a system of lifelong learning accessible to all adults regardless of age, sex, income or

location, and especially those who are socially or educationally disadvantaged. Membership is open to individuals and organisations.

AOSTA (ASSOCIATION OF SERVICES TO THE AGED), 19 Clover Lawn, Skehard Rd, Blackrock, Cork.
Tel. (021) 292157.
Co-ordinating group for those working with older people on a voluntary or statutory basis. Publishes a directory of organisations.

APPLICATION FORMS
A large number of application forms are stocked by your local library and Citizens' Information Centre. These include Social Welfare forms, such as free travel, free TV licence, old age pensions, medical card, widow's pension, motor taxation forms, passport forms and many more.

ARTHRITIS FOUNDATION OF IRELAND,
1 Clanwilliam Sq., Grand Canal Quay, Dublin 2.
Tel. (01) 6618188. Mon.–Fri. 9.30 a.m.–1 p.m, 2–5 p.m.
Raises money to further research, education and patient care for this disease. There are several branches throughout the country. Contact the above for the centre nearest you and for information leaflets.

ASSOCIATION FOR COUNSELLING: See IRISH

ASSOCIATION FOR COUNSELLING

ASSOCIATION FOR THE DEAF: See NATIONAL ASSOCIATION FOR THE DEAF

ASSOCIATION OF IRISH WIDOWS: See NATIONAL ASSOCIATION OF WIDOWS IN IRELAND

ASSOCIATION OF OCCUPATIONAL THERAPISTS OF IRELAND (AOTI),
c/o UVOH, 29 Eaton Sq., Monkstown, Co. Dublin.
Tel. (01) 4730320.
Provides a list of members throughout the country.

ASTHMA SOCIETY OF IRELAND,
24 Anglesea St, Dublin 2.
Tel. (01) 6716551.
Tues.–Thurs. 10 a.m.–12.30 p.m., 2–4 p.m.
Provides information and advice.

AWARE,
St Patrick's Hospital, James's St, Dublin 8. Tel. (01) 6775423.
147 Phibsboro Rd. Tel. (01) 8308449.
Help-line (01) 6791711.
Assists people suffering from depression and elation. Provides both factual information about the disorders and supportive group therapy sessions. Fosters an increased public awareness of the nature, extent and consequences of the disorders. Promotes research into the caus-

es and the effective treatment of depression and elation.

BEREAVEMENT COUNSELLING
Offers support and non-directive counselling to enable people to deal with their grief. The basic service, which is free, consists of one-to-one counselling by appointment. Volunteers may also be available for telephone and emergency counselling sessions.
Carlow: (0503) 31063
Cavan
Sr Lily, Convent of Mary, Station Rd, Cootehill, Co. Cavan. Tel. (049) 52151.
Clare
Clare Bereavement Counselling Group, Clarecare, Harmony Row, Ennis. Tel. (065) 28178. Group support for those suffering bereavement. Meetings at the above address.
Cork
Alison Mc Comish, Community Resource Centre, Glengarriff Rd, Bantry.
For those bereaved by suicide: Teresa Melia, meetings at 2 Tuckey St, Cork. Write to PO Box 162, Cork.
Donegal
Seamus Gordon, General Hospital, Letterkenny. Tel. (074) 25888.
Dublin
Bereavement Counselling Service, PO Box 1508, Dublin 8. Tel. (01) 6767727. Meets at St Ann's Church, Dawson St,

Dublin 2. Mon. & Wed. 7.45–9.45 p.m. Also at: Augustinian Fathers, St Augustine's, Ballyboden. Tel. (01) 4944966. Mon.–Fri. Baldoyle, Dublin St. Tel. (01) 8321367/8391766. Malahide, tel. (01) 8450122. Mon.–Fri.
Raheny Social Service Centre. Tel. (01) 8313700. Mon.–Fri. Rathcoole Day Care Centre. Tel. (045) 62129. Mon.–Fri. Rialto Parish Centre, Old School House, SC Rd, Dublin 8. Tel. (01) 4539020. Mon.–Fri. 9.30 a.m.–5 p.m. Tuesday morning by appointment.
Servite Oratory, Rathfarnham Shopping Centre. Tel. (01) 4936300. Mon.–Fri. 10.30 a.m.–5.30 p.m.
Wicklow
Wicklow Bereavement Support Group, Queen of Peace, Vevay Rd, Bray. Tel. (01) 2822360/2867303/ 2862346.
People who have been through the bereavement experience offer a confidential 'listening ear' to people in grief.
Wicklow Bethany Support Group, c/o Breeda Shine, Main St, Wicklow; Fr P. Dowling PP, Parochial House, Wicklow. Tel. (0404) 67196/67444/ 69234/67905/69554 (or any priests of the parish).
Listens and offers support to the bereaved. Available to call to people's homes.

BEREAVEMENT SOCIETY —
COPING WITH GRIEF,
c/o Leslie Marron, Secretary,
5 Cuil Fearna, Mullinarry,
Carrickmacross, Co. Monaghan.
National Bereavement Help-line
(042) 62341.
Self-help group of bereaved
people who meet regularly to
share their grief. Aims (1) to
help newly bereaved to cope
with their grief; (2) to make
society aware of needs of
bereaved. Professional back-up
available. Confidential. Book-
lists and leaflets.

BLIND PENSION,
Pensions Services Office, Dept
of Social Welfare, College Rd,
Sligo. Tel. (071) 69800 or (01)
8748444.
A blind person may be entitled
to a Blind Pension subject to a
means test. Further information
available from the above
address. See Leaflet SW 76 from
the Dept of Social Welfare.

BODY POSITIVE,
24/6 Dame St, Dublin 2.
Tel. (01) 6712363.
Support group for people with
HIV/AIDS.

BRABAZON TRUST,
2 Gilford Rd, Dublin 4.
Tel. (01) 2691677/2698038/
2694061.
Brabazon Trust House.
Tel. (01) 2691677.
Provides sheltered accommoda-
tion for older people in its

complex in Sandymount.
Relieves needs by grants, fuel
and heating allowances.

BRITISH DEPARTMENT OF
HEALTH AND SOCIAL
SECURITY,
War Pensioners' Welfare
Service, Hume House,
Pembroke Rd, Dublin 4.
Tel. (01) 6601122.
Irish Life Building, South Mall,
Cork. Tel. (021) 272080.
(The Cork office deals with the
counties of Cork, Kerry and
Waterford only.)
Provides a welfare service to
disabled ex-UK service mem-
bers and advice to UK national
insurance recipients. Medical
treatment for the accepted dis-
ability includes hospitalisation,
supply of limbs/appliances.
Advice on social security matters
to general callers.

CAIRDE,
One-to-One Befriending for
HIV/AIDS,
25 Mary's Abbey, off Capel St,
Dublin 7.
Tel. (01) 8730006.

CANCER SOCIETY: See IRISH
CANCER SOCIETY

CARE FOR DUBLIN'S OLD
FOLK LIVING ALONE,
Carmichael House, North
Brunswick St, Dublin 7.
Tel. (01) 8735702. Mon.–Fri.
9 a.m.–5 p.m.
Aims to provide necessities of
life and additional comforts to

needy aged living alone. Visiting, food, fuel, clothes, bed-clothes. A specialty of the organisation is to seek out and care for old people living in bad conditions.

CARE OF THE ELDERLY COMMITTEES

Clare

Clarecare is a community organisation offering counselling and encouraging self-help. It employs twenty professional staff, who provide a range of services. Services for the elderly include: home-help, visiting, holidays and outings, meals and general care. There are five offices in Clare:

Ennis: Harmony Row, tel. (065) 28178.

Kilrush: Community Centre, tel. (065) 51269.

Shannon: Town Centre, tel. (061) 364704.

Killaloe: Molua Centre, tel. (061) 76346.

Spanish Point: Convent of Mercy, tel. (065) 84005.

Cork

For the Care of the Aged Committee, city and county visiting services, Community Associations and Community Care Groups dealing with older people, consult the AOSTA directory.

Bantry Homes for the Aged Association, c/o Jim O'Sullivan, The Pharmacy, New St, Bantry.

Day care centres

Vincent O'Leary, Boyce St, Cork. Tel. (021) 965511.

Catherine Colgan, Windmill Rd, Cork. Tel. (021) 274776.

Roaches Buildings, Sr Patricia, Assumption Convent. Tel. (021) 501407.

Dublin: See CARE FOR DUBLIN'S OLD FOLK LIVING ALONE

Galway

Barna-Furbo Senior Citizens' Committee, c/o Rose Brosnan, Truskey East, Barna. Tel. (091) 92296. Organises meals-on-wheels, Christmas party, summer outings, visits to older people, help in cases of urgent need.

Clarinbridge Social Services Group, Mrs Mc Namara, Strabally, Clarinbridge. Tel. (091) 69045.

CARER'S ALLOWANCE

This is a means-tested payment for carers on low incomes who live with and look after certain people who need full-time care and attention. For more information see Leaflet SW 41 from the Dept of Social Welfare or contact Carer's Allowance Section, Dept of Social Welfare, College Rd, Sligo. Tel. (071) 69800 or (01) 8748444.

CARERS' ASSOCIATION, St Mary's Community Centre, Richmond Hill, Rathmines, Dublin 6.

Tel. (01) 4974498. Mon.–Fri.
9 a.m.–5 p.m.
Aims to represent the relatives
who provide care for older people at home by supplying
information/advice and by lob-
bying for services. Also
publishes a quarterly newsletter,
Take Care, and plans to establish a respite care service.

CARERS' SUPPORT GROUPS
Run by the Eastern Health
Board for carers of older peo-
ple. Meetings, which include
information sessions and group
support, are held monthly in
Dublin, from 7.45–9.45 p.m., in
the following centres:
Northside: Clonliffe College,
Dublin 3.
Westside: St James's Day
Hospital, Dublin 8.
Southside: Baggot St
Community Hospital, Dublin 4.
For more details phone
Catherine Mc Cann
(01) 6681577.

CATHOLIC MARRIAGE
ADVISORY COUNCIL (CMAC),
All Hallows College, Dublin 9.
Tel. (01) 8371151.
In fifty-five centres throughout
Ireland, CMAC offers pre-mar-
riage preparation courses; a
counselling service for those
experiencing difficulties in their
close relationships; information
on all methods of family planning and instruction in natural

methods; marital sexual therapy.
See telephone directories for all
local branches.

CHIROPODISTS: See IRISH
CHIROPODISTS' ASSOCIATION,
SOCIETY OF CHIROPODISTS
OF IRELAND

CHIROPODY
Most chiropodists give discounts
to those over sixty-five. Consult
the Golden Pages for addresses
of chiropodists. The Health
Boards may provide a chi-
ropody service for medical-card
holders over sixty-five; likewise
many Social Service Centres.
Ask at your local Health Centre
or Social Service Centre.

CITIZENS' INFORMATION
CENTRES
There are about eighty centres
in cities and towns throughout
the country. They provide free
and confidential information to
the general public on a wide
range of services and entitlements, e.g. health, social
welfare, taxation, housing, consumer affairs, as well as on local
organisations and facilities.

COMMUNITY CARE SERVICES
(see also p. 210)
Community care services are
organised and provided locally.
There is wide variation in the
level of services on offer. In
some areas, they are provided
by the Health Board either

directly or through voluntary organisations; in other areas, some of the services may be exclusively voluntary and some are not available at all.

You can find out more about what is available locally by asking at your local Health Centre, Social Service Centre, Citizens' Information Centre, library, or your doctor.

CONSUMER AFFAIRS/FAIR TRADE OFFICE,
Shelbourne House, Shelbourne Rd, Dublin 4.
Tel. (01) 6606011, administration tel. (01) 6613399.
The Director of Consumer Affairs and Fair Trade has powers in relation to consumer information and protection, monitoring competition, safety of certain goods, and a number of other areas.

You may complain about false or misleading claims regarding goods, services and prices, and the Director may prosecute the traders concerned or apply for a court order to get misleading advertisements withdrawn or amended. The Director monitors the Sale of Goods and Supply of Services Act and may prosecute traders for breaches.

CONSUMERS' ASSOCIATION OF IRELAND,
Consumer Personal Service, 45 Upr Mount St, Dublin 2.

Tel. (01) 6612293.
A voluntary body which provides a service whereby consumers may have their complaints dealt with relatively cheaply. It caters for consumers who have to take legal action to enforce their rights. The consumer pays a fixed fee of £19 for the service.

COUNCIL FOR THE STATUS OF WOMEN,
32 Upr Fitzwilliam St, Dublin 2.
Tel. (01) 6615268.
National representative body for over seventy women's organisations. Lobbies government on wide range of issues of concern to women. Provides information and support to women and their organisations, highlights and combats cases of discrimination. Enquiries welcome. Publishes *Council News* (quarterly). List of other publications available.

CROSS CARE,
The Red House, Clonliffe College, Dublin 3.
Tel. (01) 8360011/5.
Supplies a wide range of services for older people, mainly in the region of information and advice for both older people and their carers as regards assistance and entitlements. Counselling is available for both bereavement and transitional trauma, e.g. illness, retirement. Also networks with all other agencies involved with older

people, e.g. EHB. It operates a positive health promotion from a holistic point of view. It provides reading material for other professionals in the area and offers facilities to students involved in geriatric research.

DEATH

The duty of registering all deaths which take place in the district is the responsibility of the local Registrar (see General Register Office of Births, Deaths and Marriages). Details registered are the date and place of death, the name, surname, sex, conjugal status, age and occupation of the deceased, and the cause of death. The cause of death is usually certified by the medical practitioner who attended the deceased in her last illness. Where a post-mortem or inquest has been held, a Coroner's Certificate as to the cause of death is sent to the Registrar.

DEATH GRANT,
Dept of Social Welfare,
Ballinalee Rd, Longford.
Tel. (043) 45211.
A lump sum payable on the death of a person who has paid enough Social Insurance Contributions or the spouse or dependent child of an insured person. Only insurance contributions paid since 1970 are of value for this grant. See Leaflet SW 46 from the Dept of Social Welfare.

The claim may be made by the personal representatives of the deceased or, if there are none, by the person responsible for the funeral expenses. Further information and application forms from your Community Welfare Officer or the above address (see also Bereavement Counselling above).

DENTAL CARE,
Treatment Section, Dept of Social Welfare, St Oliver Plunkett Rd, Letterkenny, Co. Donegal.
Tel. (01) 8748444 or (074) 25566.
Dentists on the Social Welfare panel have application forms. Medical-card holders are entitled to treatment from the Health Boards.

DISABLED DRIVERS'
ASSOCIATION,
Ballindine, Co. Mayo.
Tel. (094) 64266/64054.
Carmichael House, North Brunswick St, Dublin 7.
Tel. (01) 8721671.
Provides information and support services on all matters relating to disabled driving.

DUBLIN CENTRAL MISSION,
Social Aid Centre, 7 Marlborough Place, Dublin 1.
Tel. (01) 8742123/8744668.
Offers accommodation for older people.

DUBLIN COUNCIL FOR THE AGED,
c/o Chairperson, 9 Dorden Pk, Booterstown, Co. Dublin.
Umbrella group for a number of voluntary and statutory organisations involved with older people in Dublin. Aims for improvement of services. Supplies information and advice.

DUBLIN INSTITUTE OF ADULT EDUCATION,
1/3 Mountjoy Sq., Dublin 1. Tel. (01) 8787266/8743251.
Provides adult education courses and develops community adult education programmes in association with local groups. Literacy scheme trains tutors, arranges one-to-one tuition, assists local groups.

DUBLIN WELL WOMAN CENTRE,
35 Lr Liffey St, Dublin 1.
Tel. (01) 8728095/8728051.
Mon–Fri. 9 a.m.–8 p.m., Sat. 10 a.m.–5 p.m.
73 Lr Leeson St, Dublin 2. Tel. (01) 6610083/6610086. Mon.–Fri. 9 a.m.–8 p.m., Sat 10 a.m.–5 p.m., Sun. 10 a.m.–1 p.m.
Provides a variety of professional, confidential and sympathetic health services for women. Offers a wide range of counselling services on relationships, sexual problems, pregnancy, menopause, etc. It also runs a mail-order service for such items as condoms, books, vibrators.

ENERGY ACTION,
20 Lr Dominick St, Dublin 1.
Tel. (01) 8723737.
A charity which services mainly the Dublin area but has repaired houses on Tory Island and in Donegal.

EPILEPSY ASSOCIATION: See IRISH EPILEPSY ASSOCIATION

FAMILY PLANNING SERVICES LTD,
67 Pembroke Rd, Dublin 4.
Tel. (01) 6609860/6609988/6683714/6681108.
78A/79 Lr George's St, Dún Laoghaire, Co. Dublin. Tel. (01) 2841666.
Provides family planning clinics, information and publications. A mail-order service is available.

FEDERATION OF ACTIVE RETIREMENT ASSOCIATIONS,
Shamrock Chambers, 59/61 Dame St, Dublin 2.
Tel. (01) 6792142.
The active retirement movement is for active women and men who are retired and who wish to engage in educational, cultural, sporting and social activities of their own choice and so make retirement a meaningful and enjoyable phase of life. There are eighty branches throughout the country.

FINANCIAL INFORMATION SERVICES CENTRES (FISC),
87/9 Pembroke Rd, Dublin 4.

Tel. (01) 6682044.
Provides free confidential financial advice to people or organisations unable to afford the professional services of accountants. Gives lectures; makes representation on tax anomalies; runs centres open to the public — usually in conjunction with Citizens' Information Centres; answers written queries.

FREE LEGAL ADVICE CENTRES, 49 South William St, Dublin 2. Tel. (01) 6794239.
Provides advice mainly but will provide representation for Social Welfare appeals and unfair dismissal. In conjunction with the Citizens' Information Centres and at specific times, the Centres are open to the general public.

REGIONAL BRANCHES

Cork
Blackpool Community Centre. Tel. (021) 501787. Mon. 7.30–9.30 p.m.
Education Rights Centre, 5 Churchfield Ave. Tel. (021) 307969. Tues. 8–9 p.m.
St Vincent de Paul, 2 Tuckey St. Tel. (021) 270444. Wed. 8–9.30 p.m.

FREE SCHEMES (electricity, telephone rental and free travel)
The Electricity Allowance and Television Licence schemes provide a certain amount of free electricity and a free licence for a black and white television. You pay the difference if you have a colour television. If you qualify for the fuel allowance, you will be entitled to a free colour television licence from the next renewal date. You may be entitled to these if you are aged sixty-six or over and getting a pension or other payment from the Department of Social Welfare. To claim, complete a FEA 1 form — available from the Department — and send it to your nearest ESB office. If you qualify for an Electricity Allowance, you are entitled to a free television licence, which you can get at your local Post Office. Widows aged sixty and over whose deceased spouses qualified for the schemes will retain entitlement, assuming they meet all the other conditions. It is expected that this provision will also become available to widowers. In the case of the Electricity Allowance, pensioners aged seventy-five and over retain eligibility even if they no longer live alone. The free travel companion pass will be extended to all wheelchair-users who qualify for free travel. See Telephone below.

FRIENDS OF THE ELDERLY, 25 Bolton St, Dublin 1. Tel. (01) 8731855.
A voluntary, non-denominational organisation. Activities include home and hospital visit-

ing, entertainment, home improvements, transport and holidays for older people. It organises outings and parties and runs a club which meets weekly. Full-time staff work in close co-operation with volunteers, relatives and other statutory organisations to meet a wide range of needs.

GALWAY CARERS'
ASSOCIATION,
c/o UCG Community, Education & Resource Centre, Island House, Galway.
Tel. (091) 24411.
Publishes a booklet providing names, addresses, telephone numbers and opening hours of voluntary, statutory and private agencies and services relevant to carers in Galway. Available from the above address.

GENERAL REGISTER OFFICE OF BIRTHS, DEATHS AND MARRIAGES,
Joyce House, 8 Lombard St East, Dublin 2.
Information Service, tel. (01) 6711863.
Dublin Records, tel. (01) 6711968.
Provincial Records, tel. (01) 6711000. Mon.–Fri. 9.30 a.m. –12.30 p.m, 2.15–4.30 p.m.
A death certificate is needed for insurance purposes and for the Death Grant benefit. Deaths may be registered in the rest of the country through local County Councils. See your local telephone directory.

GLASNEVIN CREMATORIUM,
Glasnevin Cemetery, Finglas Rd, Dublin 11.
Tel. (01) 8301133.
If you wish to discuss any aspect of cremation, or arrange to purchase a place for the ashes, contact John Kinahan at the above address. The cremation is organised by the funeral director you engage.

GROW,
Community mental health movement
South and national headquarters: 11 Liberty St, Cork. Tel. (021) 277520.
Dublin: 167 Capel St, Dublin 1. Tel. (01) 8734029.
South-east: Ormonde Home, Barrack St, Kilkenny. Tel. (056) 61624.
Midlands: Community Health Centre, Bury Quay, Tullamore, Co. Offaly. Tel. (0506) 51284.
Mid-west: 27 Mallow St, Limerick. Tel. (061) 318813.
Weekly meetings emphasise self-help/mutual help approach to mental health and the development of personal resources. Twelve-step programme of growth to maturity in avoiding and recovering from mental breakdown. Anonymous and confidential.

HEALTH BOARDS: See p. 210

HEALTH SERVICES

Different health services are available to people on different incomes.

Two categories are defined:

(1) Medical-card holders

There are income guidelines for the issue of a medical card, so you will have to undergo a means test.

People who are receiving a Social Security Pension from another EC country but not from Ireland are entitled to a medical card regardless of their means provided they are not employed or self-employed here. This entitlement arises because of EC regulations. When assessing your entitlement under EC regulations, the Health Board may enquire into your sources of income to ascertain whether you come under the regulation — this is not the same as a means test. People who receive both an Irish pension and a pension from another EC country must pass a means test.

If you have a medical card, you are entitled to free GP services, free prescribed drugs and medicines, free in-patient and out-patient hospital services, free dental, optical and aural services (although these last may not always be available).

There is no appeals system for medical cards. You can write to the Chief Executive Officer of the Health Board and state your case.

(2) Non-medical-card holders

Everyone is entitled to free treatment and maintenance in a public ward but is subject to daily charges from some groups (£20 a day to a maximum of £200 per year, and other charges after thirty days for non-medical-card holders who do not have dependants).

HOSPICE CARE: see IRISH HOSPICE FOUNDATION

ILEOSTOMY AND COLOSTOMY ASSOCIATION OF SOUTHERN IRELAND, Curravilla, Greenfield, Maynooth, Co. Kildare. Tel. (01) 6285968.
Aims to help people who have had, or are about to have, an ileostomy/colostomy operation to return to a fully active and normal life. Organises hospital/home visits by volunteers who have completely recovered.

INCORPORATED LAW SOCIETY OF IRELAND, Blackhall Place, Dublin 7. Tel. (01) 6710711, fax (01) 6710704.
Representative body of solicitors, operates under charter. Makes regulations on standards, conduct, discipline, legal education, etc. Administers a compensation fund for losses suffered by clients through defaulting solicitors.

IRISH ARTHRITIS AND
RHEUMATISM ASSOCIATION:
See ARTHRITIS FOUNDATION
OF IRELAND

IRISH ASSOCIATION FOR THE
BLIND: See NATIONAL
COUNCIL FOR THE BLIND OF
IRELAND

IRISH ASSOCIATION OF CARE
WORKERS,
PO Box 1729, Dublin 3.
Promotes the welfare, education
and rehabilitation of people
receiving residential and day
care.

IRISH ASSOCIATION OF
CHARTERED PHYSIO-
THERAPISTS,
c/o Royal College of Surgeons,
St Stephen's Green, Dublin 2.
Tel. (01) 4780200.
Provides a list of its members
throughout the country.

IRISH ASSOCIATION FOR
COUNSELLING,
11 Rock Hill, Blackrock, Co.
Dublin.
Tel. (01) 2780409.
Provides a list of accredited
counsellors.

IRISH ASSOCIATION OF
FUNERAL DIRECTORS,
c/o Tom Sharkey, National
Secretary, Barrick St,
Ballaghaderreen, Co.
Roscommon.
Tel. (0907) 60031.
This is a self-regulatory body to
whom you may complain about

services from members.

IRISH ASSOCIATION OF
OLDER PEOPLE,
Room G02, University College,
Earlsfort Tce, Dublin 2.
Tel. (01) 4750013.
Association for those who are
55-plus. The main objective is to
change existing attitudes to ageing. Also aims to enhance the
quality of life for the over-55s by
creating new and more positive
images of ageing.

IRISH ASSOCIATION OF
SPEECH AND LANGUAGE
THERAPISTS,
4 Greenmount Office Park,
Harold's Cross, Dublin 6.
Tel. (01) 4730398.
Provides a list of members and
also advice and information
related to speech therapy.

IRISH ASSOCIATION FOR
VICTIM SUPPORT,
Head Office, 29/30 Dame St,
Dublin 2.
Tel. (01) 6798673, fax (01)
6793839.
Provides support and practical
assistance by:
— lending a sympathetic ear
   and providing the opportunity for the crime victim to talk
   about her experience in strict
   confidence
— providing information and
   advice to the crime victim
   about rights and entitlements
   in matters such as compensation, legal aid, the courts, etc.

— providing advice about security, insurance, health and counselling services
— articulating and highlighting, in society generally, the viewpoint of crime victims
— being available to accompany and support the person attending court, and providing rooms in the Four Courts, Dublin.

The Association may also be contacted at:

Carlow, commencing 1994
Cork: c/o George Glendon, 4 Garfield Tce, Wellington Rd. Tel. (021) 505055.
Dublin East: c/o Garda station, Dún Laoghaire. Tel. (01) 2801285.
Dublin South: 512 Main St, Tallaght. Tel. (01) 4599511.
Dublin North: Clontarf, tel. (01) 8327988.
Donnybrook: a new branch, contact Head Office for phone number.
Louth: Dundalk, tel. (042) 26752.
Westmeath: Athlone, tel. (0902) 73344.
Wexford: c/o Joan Nally, Bunclody. Tel. (053) 77011.
Wicklow: Arklow, tel. (0402) 31060.

IRISH CANCER SOCIETY,
5 Northumberland Rd, Dublin 4. Tel. (01) 6681855.
70 Lr George's St, Dún Laoghaire, Co. Dublin. Tel. (01) 2843589.

Cancer Help-line Freefone 1800-200700.
Freefone Cancer is operated by professional staff who will answer any query about cancer.

Carlow
Carlow Cancer Home Care Group, South Eastern Health Board, Athy Rd, Carlow. Tel. (0503) 31804.
Care and visiting of cancer patients in their own homes and support service for families of cancer victims.

IRISH CHIROPODISTS' ASSOCIATION,
c/o Patrick Mortell, tel. (01) 8309708.
Can provide a list of members countrywide.

IRISH COUNTRYWOMEN'S ASSOCIATION,
54 Merrion Rd, Dublin 4. Tel. (01) 6684052/6680453.
Freefone 1800-652652.
Aims to develop and improve the conditions of rural life in Ireland. Holds meetings, lectures, courses, demonstrations, competitions, etc. Guilds throughout the country; for your local branch see telephone directory.

IRISH DEAF SOCIETY,
Carmichael House, North Brunswick St, Dublin 7.
Tel. (01) 8725748. Mon.–Fri 9 a.m.–5 p.m.
Promotes the welfare of deaf people. Information, coun-

selling, interpreting services and sign-language teaching available. Educates the public through seminars, lectures and talks. For pensions write to Dept of Social Welfare, 157/64 Townsend St, Dublin 1. Tel. (01) 8786444.

IRISH DIABETIC ASSOCIATION, 76 Lr Gardiner St, Dublin 1. Tel. (01) 8363022. Mon.–Fri. 10 a.m.–5 p.m.
Provides help for people with diabetes, particularly newly diagnosed, to understand their treatment.

REGIONAL BRANCHES
Donegal: F. Morris, Convoy, Donegal. Tel. (074) 47147.
Galway: R. Winters, 12 Blackthorn Park, Renmore, Galway. Tel. (091) 53048.
Limerick: N. Barrett, 70 Stoneyhurst, Dooradoyle, Limerick. Tel. (061) 28610.
Offaly: B. Quinn, Bunateen, Screggan, Tullamore. Tel. (0506) 41663.
Tipperary: P. Hegarty, Kilmacomma, Clonmel. Tel. (052) 21607.
Waterford: Anne-Marie Cusack, Fairways, Newtownhill, Tramore. Tel. (051) 86905.

IRISH EPILEPSY ASSOCIATION, Head Office, 249 Crumlin Rd, Dublin 12.
Tel. (01) 4557500.
Provides a social work service, education and advisory service and Epi-Alert bracelets.

IRISH FAMILY PLANNING ASSOCIATION
Centres
5/7 Cathal Brugha St, Dublin 1. Tel. (01) 8727173.
59 Synge St, Dublin 8. Tel. (01) 6682420.
Medical Centre, Level 3, The Square SC, Tallaght. Tel. (01) 4597685.
Educational Resources Centre
36/7 Lr Ormond Quay, Dublin 1. Tel. (01) 8725033. Operates a mail-order service and stocks a wide range of books.

The Association provides a comprehensive contraceptive and women's health service, including special services for women suffering from Pre-Menstrual Syndrome or the menopause. A confidential postal service is also available. Runs sex education courses for professionals and parents and provides speakers and audiovisual material for youth and women's groups. Book Centre has a wide selection of books on family planning, relationships, sexual problems, women's health and sex education. Counselling for sexual problems is available.

IRISH FEDERATION OF WOMEN'S CLUBS, 11 St Peter's Rd, Dublin 7. Tel. (01) 8680080.

Promotes the education, cultural advancement and welfare of women through membership of women's clubs.

IRISH HARD OF HEARING ASSOCIATION,
c/o St Joseph's, Brewery Rd, Stillorgan, Co. Dublin.
Assists in the information of small groups of people hard of hearing. Provides counselling in relation to lip-reading, wearing of hearing-aids. Promotes installation of loops, etc.

IRISH HOSPICE FOUNDATION,
64 Waterloo Rd, Dublin 4.
Tel. (01) 6603111.
Hospice care combines symptom control with psychological, emotional and spiritual support for the family as well as for the patient who is terminally ill with cancer or other illness. The service includes home care, in-patient care, day care, bereavement counselling, training and educational programmes. Available in many counties. For an up-to-date list contact the above address.

IRISH KIDNEY ASSOCIATION,
Donor House, 156 Pembroke Rd, Ballsbridge, Dublin 4.
Tel. (01) 6689788.
Support group which looks after the welfare of all in chronic renal failure and sponsors research into its causes and effects. Provides financial help and counselling to patients and

their families. Arranges holidays with nursing for dialysis patients.

IRISH MOTOR NEURONE DISEASE ASSOCIATION,
Carmichael House, North Brunswick St, Dublin 7.
Tel. (01) 8730230, fax (01) 8735737. Mon.–Fri. 9 a.m.–5 p.m.
Aims to make people aware of this disease, to remove the isolation felt by sufferers, to help patients and their families with counselling and funding where necessary. Advises on disease and Social Welfare problems. Supplies aids considered necessary by Community Occupational Therapists. Visiting and occasional financial aid where required is available.

There may be a local support group near you so contact the above telephone number for further information.

IRISH RED CROSS SOCIETY,
Headquarters, 16 Merrion Sq., Dublin 4.
Tel. (01) 6765135/7.
Provides training in first aid, cardiac pulmonary resuscitation, home nursing care of the elderly, first aid and emergency services at public events.

IRISH WHEELCHAIR ASSOCIATION,
24 Blackheath Drive, Clontarf, Dublin 3.
Tel. (01) 8338241.
Aims to ensure members can

193

live normal lives. Services include provision of social workers, occupational therapists, holidays, sports, transport, advice about wheelchairs. Contact nearest office for local details.

REGIONAL OFFICES

Cork: Sawmill St, Cork. Tel. (021) 966350.
Donegal: The Mall, Ballyshannon. Tel. (072) 52333.
Galway: Hession Buildings, 35/7 Dominic St, Galway. Tel. (019) 65598.
Kilkenny: Parnell St, Kilkenny. Tel. (056) 62775.
Limerick: Social Service Centre, Henry St, Limerick. Tel. (061) 313691.

LEGAL ADVICE

Legal Aid Board, 47 Upr Mount St, Dublin 2.
Tel. (01) 6615811, fax (01) 6763426.
Provides the services of solicitors at a low charge (means-tested). Helps with legal problems.

REGIONAL BRANCHES (Mon.–Fri. 10 a.m–12.30 p.m, 2–4 p.m.)

Cork
24 North Mall, Cork. Tel. (021) 300365.
1A South Mall, Cork. Tel. (021) 275998.

Dublin
45 Lr Gardiner St. Tel. (01) 8787295.
9 Lr Ormond Quay. Tel. (01) 8724133.

Aston House, Aston's Place. Tel. (01) 6712177.
517 Main St, Tallaght. Tel. (01) 5511519.
St Canice's Precinct, 44/9 Main St, Finglas. Tel. (01) 8640314.
Galway: 5 Mary St, Galway. Tel. (091) 61650.
Kerry: 6 High St, Tralee. Tel. (066) 26900.
Limerick: Unit F, Lock Quay, Limerick. Tel. (061) 314599.
Louth: The Laurels, Dundalk. Tel. (042) 30448.
Mayo: Humbert Mall, Main St, Castlebar. Tel. (094) 24334.
Sligo: 1 Teeling St, Sligo. Tel. (071) 61670.
Waterford: 5 Catherine St, Waterford. Tel. (051) 55814.
Westmeath: Northgate St, Athlone. 10 a.m.–12.30 p.m, 2–4 p.m. Tel. (0902) 74694.

PART-TIME LAW CENTRES

Carlow: St Catherine's, Social Service Centre, St Joseph's Rd. Tel. (0503) 31063/31354. Open on the first, third and fourth Wednesdays of every month.
Clare
Clarecare, Harmony Row, Ennis. Tel. (065) 28178. Open on the fourth Tuesday of every month. Kilrush Community Centre, Toler St. Tel. (065) 51269. Open on the second and fourth Monday afternoons of every month.
Cork: Health Centre, O'Brien St, Mallow. Tel. (022) 21484. Open fourth Monday of every month.

Donegal: Donegal County Hospital. Tel. (074) 26177. Open on the first Friday of every month.

Dublin

Town Hall, The Square, Balbriggan. Tel. (01) 8787295. Open on the third Tuesday of every month.

Citizens' Information Centre, Blanchardstown. Tel. (01) 8212666. Contact Centre for information.

Kerry: Citizens' Information Centre, St Anne's Rd, Killarney. Tel. (064) 32297. Open on the first and third Tuesday afternoons of every month.

Kildare: Co. Kildare Centre for the Unemployed, 5 Edson Hall, Main St, Newbridge. Tel. (045) 21685. Open on the first Thursday of every month.

Kilkenny: Kilkenny Social Service, Waterford Rd. Tel. (056) 21685. Open on the first and third Tuesdays of every month.

Louth: Drogheda Community Services Centre, Fair St. Tel. (041) 36084/33490. Open on the first and second Tuesdays of every month.

Mayo

Ballina Community Centre, Teeling St. Tel. (096) 24334. Open on the first Monday of every month.

Health Centre, Ballyhaunis. Tel. (091) 61650. Open on the fourth Tuesday of every month.

Monaghan: Social Service Centre, Broad Rd. Tel. (047) 82290. Open on the first Friday of every month.

Roscommon: Health Centre, The Crescent, Boyle. Tel. (079) 62164. Open on the first Monday of every month.

Tipperary

North Tipperary Community Services, Loreto House, Kenyon St, Nenagh. Tel. (067) 31800. Open on the first and third Tuesdays of every month.

Thurles Community Social Service, Rossa St. Tel. (0504) 22169. Open on the second Tuesday of every month.

Citizens' Information Centre, 14 Wellington St, Clonmel. Tel. (0504) 22267. Open on the first, third and fourth Fridays of every month.

Wexford: Wexford Community Services Centre, St Bridget's Centre, Roche's Rd. Tel. (053) 23819. Open on the first and third Wednesdays of every month.

MARRIAGE COUNSELLING SERVICES LTD,
24 Grafton St, Dublin 2.
Tel. (01) 8720341.
Provides a non-denominational marriage counselling service, a sexual dysfunction clinic, marriage preparation courses, relationship counselling and an education service to schools, professional groups, etc.

MASTECTOMY: See REACH TO RECOVERY

MEALS-ON-WHEELS
This service is generally provided by voluntary organisations. Contact your local Health Centre, Social Service Centre or Citizens' Information Centre.

MEDICINES
PRESCRIBED DRUGS AND MEDICINES BENEFIT
Medical-card holders
Holders are entitled to prescribed drugs and medicines free of charge on production of medical card. There are certain exceptions; your GP will be aware of the current list.
Long-term illness
Anyone suffering from any of the following can obtain necessary drugs and medicines free of charge: mental handicap, phenylketonuria, cystic fibrosis, haemophilia, cerebral palsy, epilepsy, diabetes mellitus, multiple sclerosis, muscular dystrophy, Parkinson's disease, acute leukaemia, spina bifida and hydrocephalus.

MENDED HEARTS
(Cardiac Support Group), 52 Bettyglen, Dublin 5. Tel. (01) 8314576.
A group of people who have had heart surgery and wish to support others, and their families, who are facing surgery. Visits to hospitals where patients are awaiting heart

surgery. Home visits on request. Enquiries will be answered by telephone or letter.

MENTAL HEALTH ASSOCIATION OF IRELAND, Mensana House, 6 Adelaide St, Dún Laoghaire, Co. Dublin. Tel. (01) 2841166, fax (01) 2841736.
A national voluntary organisation with over sixty local mental health associations working throughout the country. The membership includes mental health professionals and ordinary lay people who provide care, support and friendship for the mentally ill. The MHAI produces a range of booklets, leaflets and other publications on specific and general subjects. It has developed an original approach to community mental health education. Adult education courses on relationships and positive lifestyles are run in co-operation with vocational education authorities. You can become involved in the care of the mentally ill by contacting your local MHA. For further details contact the above office.

MOTOR NEURONE SOCIETY: See IRISH MOTOR NEURONE DISEASE ASSOCIATION

MS IRELAND
(The Multiple Sclerosis Society of Ireland), 2 Sandymount Green, Dublin 4. Tel. (01) 2694599. Help-line

1800-233233. Mon.–Fri.
10 a.m.–5 p.m.
Provides a help-line, counselling services and six Community Workers, a number which it hopes to increase.

MS Care Foundation
The National MS Care Centre, 65 Bushy Park Rd, Rathgar, Dublin 6.
Tel. (01) 4906234.
Offers short-time respite care and disability management to people with MS and other neurological disabilities. The centre is recognised by the VHI and is also open to medical-card holders. Referral is from GPs, Public Health Nurses, carers and individuals themselves.

NATIONAL ASSOCIATION FOR THE DEAF,
Mary Nicholas House, c/o St Joseph's, Cabra, Dublin 7.
Tel. (01) 8388124/8388129/8388131.
Provides a social work service and technical aids service for those with hearing problems.

NATIONAL ASSOCIATION OF HOME CARE ORGANISERS,
Kilbarrack Health Centre, Dublin 5. Tel. (01) 8391221.
Association of those who arrange home-help/home care where required. A list of organisers is available from the National Social Service Board.

NATIONAL ASSOCIATION OF WIDOWS IN IRELAND,
12 Upr Ormond Quay, Dublin 7.
Tel. (01) 6770977/6770513.
Annual membership fee of £4.
The Association is non-sectarian and non-political. Over 65 per cent of members are over sixty years old and most of the activities are geared to their needs.
The NAWI has fifty-one branches throughout Ireland; contact Dublin Head Office for details of local branches and counselling service. There is special therapy for the newly bereaved and the not-so-young widow. A bereavement service with trained counsellors offers support to people coping with loss. Volunteers are available for telephone and one-to-one counselling by appointment.

REGIONAL BRANCHES
Galway: Galway Bereavement Support Group, Jesuit House, Sea Rd, Galway. Tel. (091) 67208. Meets Mon. 8.30 p.m.
Kilkenny: Kilkenny Bereavement Association, c/o Villa Marie, Talbots Inch, Kilkenny; Sr Pius or Miss O'Leary, St Luke's Hospital, Kilkenny. Tel. (056) 21133.
Limerick: Limerick Bereavement Counselling, c/o Social Service Centre, Henry St, Limerick. Tel. (061) 314111.

NATIONAL BACK PAIN ASSOCIATION, (Irish Branch),
c/o St Jude, 6 Lois-na-Sithe, Milford Grange, Castletroy, Co. Limerick.

Supports research into causes of back pain and helps to prevent it through education and information.

NATIONAL COUNCIL FOR THE BLIND OF IRELAND,
45 Whitworth Rd, Drumcondra, Dublin 9.
Tel. (01) 8307033.
Voluntary organisation providing a nationwide social work service (forty-four full-time social workers) to visually impaired people. The social worker will check that the person is getting all the relevant benefits and will link her up with day centres, Public Health Nurses, meals-on-wheels. Provides a counselling service, information service for aids and benefits. Teaches Braille and daily living skills. Mobility training leading to independent travel for a visually impaired person. Provides a volunteer reader service. Publishes information leaflets, video, staff development package of five videos. Operates on a county-to-county basis. Contact the above office or see your local telephone directory.

NATIONAL COUNCIL FOR THE ELDERLY,
Corrigan House, Fenian St, Dublin 2.
Tel. (01) 6766484/5.
Aims to advise the Minster for Health on all aspects of the welfare of the aged, either on its own initiative or at the request of the Minister. Has a list of its own publications.

NATIONAL FEDERATION OF PENSIONERS' ASSOCIATIONS,
c/o Irish Congress of Trade Unions, 31 Parnell Sq., Dublin 1.
Tel. (01) 7384513.
Umbrella group for thirty-two pensioners' associations countrywide. Aims to improve pensioners' rights and benefits.

NATIONAL REHABILITATION BOARD, 25 Clyde Rd, Ballsbridge, Dublin 4.
Tel. (01 6684181, fax (01) 6609935.
Provides an Independent Living Service including technical aids and access. Hearing Centre, tel. (01) 8747727. Operates a national hearing aid service. Publishes NRB reports. Leaflets, brochures and reports are generally available on request, in Braille and on tape.

NATIONAL SOCIAL SERVICE BOARD (NSSB),
71 Lr Leeson St, Dublin 2.
Tel. (01) 6616422,
fax (01) 6616422.
Publications: *Entitlements for the Elderly, Come and Stay Awhile, Guide for Home Helps.* Provides training for the Citizens' Information Centres. Advises the Minister for Health on the development of social services generally. Promotes

greater accessibility, public awareness and co-ordination of social services, and encourages the development of schemes in local communities to disseminate information and advice on these services.

NURSING HOMES
Summary of NSSB (1993), *Relate*, 19 (12):
The Health (Nursing Homes) Act came into effect on 1 September 1993 and contained a whole new system for the registration of nursing homes and for paying subventions for people who move into nursing homes. While it clarifies matters for new applicants for subventions, the rules remain complex for existing residents.

If you are going into a nursing home, you must apply for a subvention before you actually take up residence. The exception to this rule is if you entered the home before 1 September 1993, in which case you may apply for a subvention at any time. If you go in after that date without applying for a subvention, you must generally wait two years before applying unless you were admitted because of a genuine emergency.

When the application is received, the Health Board investigates your level of dependency and your means and then decides what, if any, subvention

is payable. You may get a subvention if the Health Board considers that you are 'sufficiently dependent to require maintenance in a nursing home' and you are unable to pay any of the cost.

An assessment is first made of your level of dependency. You and your relatives will be interviewed for this assessment. If you are considered dependent, you may be offered a place in an institution run by the Health Board. If you are not offered a Health Board place and are in need of care, you will then be categorised as having a medium, high or maximum level of dependency.

In the means test, the Health Board looks at the income and assets of you and your spouse. They do not at this stage examine the means of other family members. Income from all sources in the previous year is taken into account, PRSI contributions and any levies payable are deducted and the rest is assessed. If you are married, your means are assessed as half of the joint means of the two of you.

Also taken into account is the value of assets such as house property, stocks and shares, money, interest in a company, business, farm or land, life insurance or endowment polices, valuables held as investments and value of equipment of a business or machinery, excluding a car. The first £6,000 of the value of assets is disregarded.

If the value of your assets, excluding your principal private residence, exceeds £20,000, the Board may refuse to pay a subvention. They may also refuse a subvention if the principal private residence is worth over £75,000 and is not occupied by your spouse, a son or daughter under twenty-one or in full-time education, or a relative who is receiving the DPMA, Blind Pension, Disability Benefit, Invalidity Pension or Old Age Non-contributory Pension, and your income is £5,000 or more per annum.

If you are considered to be dependent and if you meet the requirements of the means test, you may be entitled to a subvention. Once your entitlement is established, the Health Board then looks at your circumstances to decide the amount of the subvention. Your 'circumstances' for these purposes mean the capacity of any children over twenty-one and living in Ireland to contribute towards the cost of your nursing-home care. There are specific rules for determining whether your adult children are expected to contribute. If they are, there are no explicit rules determining how

much. There is no legal obligation on the children to pay.

The maximum rates of subvention are as follows:
Medium dependency: £70 per week
High dependency: £95 per week
Maximum dependency: £120 per week.

If your means, as assessed by the Health Board, are equal to or less than the current rate of Old Age Non-contributory Pension, you will get the maximum subvention appropriate to the level of dependency. If they are greater than the pension, the subvention may be reduced by the excess amount. This is the case if you take up residency in a nursing home after 1 September 1993. If you were already in a nursing home at that date, the maximum subvention may be further reduced by reference to the actual amount you pay to the nursing home at that date or at the date you applied for the subvention.

If your means and circumstances are assessed as being less than the current rate of the Old Age Non-contributory Pension, the maximum subvention may be increased — this is unlikely to arise very often in practice.

You must be told by the Health Board of the outcome of your application within eight weeks of applying, or of providing the necessary information if that is later. If you get no subvention or you get less than the maximum, you must be told of the grounds for the decision and of your right to appeal the decision within twenty-eight days. You are entitled to seek a review every six months.

The Act obliges nursing homes to register with a Health Board. Standards of care are stipulated in relation to accommodation, food, care, activities for recreation, privacy, reasonable time to receive visitors, safety standards, hygiene and nutrition. Each person must have a contract of care which includes details of the services to be provided and the fees to be charged. The regulations also deal with staffing levels, the standard of accommodation, the maximum numbers allowed, safety standards, kitchen and sanitary facilities.

NURSING SERVICE
Health Boards employ Public Health Nurses, one of whose main duties is the care of older people. The service they provide is normally free of charge to everyone over sixty-five and to all medical-card holders. Contact your local Health Centre for details.

OFFICE OF THE OMBUDSMAN, 52 St Stephen's Green, Dublin 2. Tel. (01) 6785222.

Established by the government, this investigates complaints relating to administrative actions of government departments and offices, Local Authorities, Health Boards, Telecom Éireann and An Post.

OPTICAL SERVICES,
Social Welfare Services Office, Optical Benefit, St Oliver Plunkett Rd, Letterkenny, Co. Donegal.
Tel. (074) 25566 or (01) 8748444.
The Dept of Social Welfare provides Optical Benefit for insured workers and their dependent spouses when the required number of contributions have been made.
In addition:
(1) Any person who is entitled to Social Welfare optical benefit at old age pension age, i.e. those who have enough contributions, retain the entitlement for life. People who are receiving Invalidity Pension or Long-term Disability Benefit would normally also be entitled to these benefits. Treatment is provided by private opticians (ophthalmic surgeons).

(2) Medical-card holders are entitled to optical treatment from the Health Board. Treatment may be provided by either the Board or private opticians — the Health Board

decides which. If you are entitled to Optical Benefit, application forms are available from the above address or from your local library. Medical-card holders should apply to the local Health Centre.

PARKINSON'S ASSOCIATION OF IRELAND,
Carmichael House, North Brunswick St, Dublin 7.
Tel. (01) 8722234.
Freefone 1800-359359.
Aims to support and comfort sufferers of Parkinson's disease and their relatives; to collect and disseminate information on the disease and to fund research. A newsletter is published every two months.

PASSPORTS,
Passport Office, Molesworth St, Dublin 2.
Tel. (01) 6711633 Mon.–Fri. 9.30 a.m.–4.30 p.m. All necessary information on getting a passport on tel. (01) 6797600.
Issues passports to Irish citizens. Persons aged sixty-five and over may obtain a three-year passport which costs £10.
Application forms from your local Garda station.

PENSIONS
Old Age Contributory Pension
Retirement and Old Age Contributory Pensions are paid on the basis of people's social insurance record. They are not subject to a means test. To qualify for Old Age Contributory Pension you must be aged sixty-six or over. For more information see Leaflet SW 18 from the Dept of Social Welfare. Application forms are available from the Pensions Services Office, College Rd, Sligo. Tel. (071) 69800 or (01) 8748444.
Survivor's Contributory Pension (Widows/Widowers)
This is payable on either one's own social insurance record or that of one's spouse.
Application forms and further information are available from the Survivor's Contributory Pension Section, Pensions Service Office, College Rd, Sligo. Tel. (071) 69800 or (01) 8748444.
Invalidity Pension
This is payable instead of Disability Benefit to an insured person who has been incapable of working for at least twelve months and will continue to be incapable of work for a further twelve. At age sixty-six you may transfer to Old Age Contributory Pension if that would be to your advantage. When you have been on Disability Benefit for at least a year, you may get an application form from the Invalidity Pension Section, Social Welfare Services Office, Ballinalee Rd, Longford. Tel. (043) 45211 or (01) 8786444.

Old Age Non-contributory Pension

This is paid to a person aged sixty-six or over who satisfies a means test and who does not qualify for a contributory pension. For more information see Leaflet SW 16 from the Dept of Social Welfare. Application forms are available from the Pensions Services Office, College Rd, Sligo. Tel. (071) 69800 or (01) 8748444.

Widow's Non-contributory Pension

This is payable to a widow who satisfies a means test and does not qualify for a Survivor's Contributory Pension. Application forms and further information are available from the Widow's Non-contributory Pension Section, Pensions Services Office, College Rd, Sligo. Tel. (071) 69800 or (01) 8748444.

Farm Retirement Scheme

Summary of NSSB (1994), *Relate*, 21 (5):

Payment of a pension to farmers aged between fifty-five and sixty-six who have been farming for at least ten years and who retire from farming and transfer (sell, lease or give as a gift) their farms — minimum five hectares — to farmers who by acquiring new land will expand their holdings.

The rate of pension payable will be at a basic 4,000 ECUs per annum (approximately £3,200 at present) plus 250 ECUs (£200) per hectare up to a maximum of 10,000 ECUs (£8,000) for a farm of twenty-five hectares or more.

It will be payable for a maximum of ten years. It will not be payable beyond the retired farmer's seventieth birthday.

There is also a scheme for retiring agricultural workers aged between fifty-five and sixty-five. The rate of payment will be 2,500 ECUs (£2,000). It is not payable beyond the retired worker's sixty-fifth birthday. The worker must have spent at least half her working time farming in the five past years and have worked in the retiring farmer's farm full-time for two years in the previous four years. She must undertake to stop farm-work completely and have paid PRSI contributions since at least 30 July 1992. No more than two workers per agricultural holding may qualify.

The scheme is being administered by the Department of Agriculture and Teagasc has a role in assessing entitlement. Further information is available from local offices of both organisations or from the Irish Farmers' Association, Irish Farm Centre, Bluebell, Dublin 12. Tel. (01) 4501166.

All Social Welfare payments (Retirement Pension, Pre-retirement Allowance, Old Age

Pension, Invalidity Pension) will be paid for six weeks after the death of the recipient.

PEOPLE'S COLLEGE OF ADULT EDUCATION AND TRAINING,
32 Parnell Sq., Dublin 1.
Tel. (01) 8735879.
Aims to stimulate, satisfy and co-ordinate the demands for adult education and offers a wide range of courses.

PEST CONTROL
The Pest Control service is usually run by the environmental sections of the Health Boards and offers free extermination of rats, mice, bugs. Free disinfection service available for senior citizens.

POISONS INFORMATION SERVICE,
Beaumont Hospital, Dublin 9.
Tel. (01) 8379964/8379966.
Twenty-four-hour information service.

PSYCHOLOGICAL SOCIETY OF IRELAND,
13 Adelaide Rd, Dublin 2.
Tel. (01) 4783916.
Provides a list of registered psychologists throughout the country.

RAPE CRISIS CENTRE,
70 Lr Leeson St, Dublin 2.
Tel. (01) 6614911.
Provides a support system for people who have been victims of rape/sexual assault or incest.

Both group and individual counselling are available.
REGIONAL BRANCHES
Clonmel: Tel. (052) 24111.
Cork: Tel. (021) 968086.
Galway: Tel. (091) 64983.
Kilkenny: Tel. (056) 51555 or Freefone 1800-478478.
Limerick: Tel. (061) 311511.
Tralee: Tel. (066) 23122.
Waterford: Tel. (051) 73362.

REACH TO RECOVERY,
5 Northumberland Rd,
Dublin 4.
Tel. (01) 6681855.
Helpful and supportive programme for women who are about to have or have recently had breast cancer surgery. Organises a phone-in on the first Wednesday of every month, 11 a.m.–4 p.m., where volunteers are available to speak to callers. Also encourages the use of Cancer Freefone — dial 10 and ask the operator for the service, free throughout the country.

RENT
Private tenancies
Under the Supplementary Allowance Scheme, it may be possible to get some assistance towards the cost of rent. This is a discretionary scheme so there is no absolute right to an allowance.

As a rule, anyone whose only income is a Social Welfare payment (not including Pay-related Benefit) has a chance of getting some assistance. Apply to the Community Welfare Officer at your local Health Centre. Tax relief is allowed for rent paid to a private landlord by persons aged fifty-five or over, subject in a year to a maximum of £750 for single and/or widowed people and £1,500 for a married couple. Applications should be made on a special form available from the Tax Office.

De-controlled dwellings
A rent allowance may be paid to a tenant whose rent has increased because of the de-controlling of her tenancy after July 1982. The landlord must register the tenancy with the Local Authority.

This is means-tested. Apply to the Dept of Social Welfare, Ballinalee Rd, Longford. Tel. (043) 45211 or (01) 6779122.

RETIREMENT HOME INFORMATION SERVICES LTD, 158 Stillorgan Rd, Dublin 4. Tel. (01) 2691832.
Aims to provide information on retirement, sheltered or nursing-home accommodation, mainly in the greater Dublin area.

RETIREMENT PLANNING COUNCIL OF IRELAND, 27/9 Lr Pembroke St, Dublin 2. Tel. (01) 6613139.
Promotes the concept of early preparation for retirement to eliminate the problems and remove the fears, anxieties and uncertainties associated with that period of life after work. Organises pre-retirement courses.

RHEUMATISM: See ARTHRITIS FOUNDATION OF IRELAND

SAMARITANS, 112 Marlborough St, Dublin 1. Tel. (01) 8727700.
Works for the prevention of suicide and befriends the lonely, despairing and suicidal. Telephone any time, day or night. Call in daytime or evening or write.
REGIONAL BRANCHES
Athlone: 3 Court Devenish. Tel. (0902) 73133.
Cork: Coach St. Tel. (021) 271323.
Ennis: Kilrush Rd. Tel. (065) 29777.
Galway: 14 Nun's Island. Tel. (091) 61222.
Limerick: 20 Barrington St. Tel. (061) 412111.
Newbridge: 3 Macelwain St, Tel. (045) 35299.
Sligo: 12 Chapel St. Tel. (071) 42011.
Tralee: 44 Moyderwell. Tel. (066) 22566.
Waterford: 13 Beau St. Tel. (051) 72114.

SENIOR CITIZENS' GROUPS
These exist in many areas and their activities are usually of a social nature. Ask at your local library, Social Service Centre or

Citizens' Information Centre for addresses.

SEX AIDS
These are available from:
Bliss Products, Castle Everest Centre, Bray. Tel. (01) 2863441.
Harmony Products, 5 Bridge St, Dundalk, Co. Louth. Tel. (042) 33066.
Utopia, 164 Capel St, Dublin 7, tel. (01) 8729045; 1 South Richmond St, Dublin 2, tel. (01) 4781095. Also operates a mail-order service.

SEXUAL ASSAULT TREATMENT UNIT, Rotunda Hospital, Dublin 1. Tel. (01) 8730700.
Service provided in Rotunda Hospital for teenagers and adults.

SHARE
(Schoolboys Harness Aid for Relief of Elderly),
19 Dyke Parade, Cork.
Tel. (021) 273977.
Aims to help the elderly poor of Cork by raising funds for building projects and visiting.

SOCIAL WELFARE
The Department of Social Welfare operates Social Welfare Offices in many areas. See telephone directory for the address of your nearest office.

When consulting the Department, always state the type of pension/allowance you are receiving and quote your pension/allowance number.

Summary of Social Welfare allowances is available from the Department or your local Citizens' Information Centre. The Social Welfare Appeals Office is at D'Olier House, D'Olier St. Tel. (01) 6718633.

The following leaflets may be of benefit to those reaching pensionable age and are available free of charge.

Subject	Leaflet number
Pre-retirement Allowance	SW 80
Retirement Pension	SW 18
Old Age Contributory Pension	SW 18
Old Age Non-contributory Pension	SW 16
Mixed Insurance Pro-rata Pension	Fact Sheet
EC Pro-rata Pension	Fact Sheet
Irish/Austrian Social Security Agreement	SW 79
Irish/Canadian Social Security Agreement	SW 84
Irish/Australian Social Security Agreement	SW 87
Irish/United States Social Security Agreement	SW91
Free Travel	SW 40
Electricity & Television Licence	SW 39
Natural Gas Allowance	SW 81
Bottled Gas Refill Allowance	SW 55
National Fuel Allowance	SW 17
Carer's Allowance	SW 41
Living Alone Allowance	SW 36
Survivor's Contributory Pension	SW 25
Checklist for Pensioners	SW 10
Blind Person's Pension	SW 76
Death Grant	SW 46
Telephone Rental Allowance	SW 45

SOCIETY OF CHIROPODISTS
OF IRELAND,
5 Wicklow St, Dublin 2.
Tel. (01) 6777486.
Members are permitted to treat
patients on chiropody cards, i.e.
persons over sixty-five who
hold a medical card. Talks can
be arranged on request.

SOCIETY OF ST VINCENT DE
PAUL,
8 New Cabra Rd, Dublin 7.
Tel. (01) 8384164/8384167/
8308219.
Aims to help the needy and visits people in their homes.
Provides holidays and fuel for
older people. For your local
branch contact one of the above
telephone numbers.

SOROPTIMIST INTERNATION-
AL (Republic of Ireland),
c/o Michael Mc Mahon & Son,
O'Connell Sq., Ennis, Co. Clare.
Tel. (065) 28307.
Aims to heighten public awareness of carers' rights; to identify
and meet their needs; to provide
respite care and training.

STROKE SCHEME: See
VOLUNTEER STROKE SCHEME

TAX
Age Allowance
In addition to the normal tax
allowances, an Age Allowance is
granted to people over the age
of sixty-six. You should claim
this four months before your
sixty-sixth birthday. Allowance

for a single person is £200 and
for a married couple £400. In
the case of a couple, the
allowance is given where either
spouse is over sixty-six.

Exemption limits are not tax-
free allowances; they are limits
below which you are not liable
for tax. If your income is slightly
above the limit, you may get
marginal relief. If your income is
below the limit or not much
above, inform your Tax
Inspector. The exemption limits
for 1994/5 are as follows:

Single/Widowed

Under 65	66–74	75+
£3,600	£4,100	£4,700

Married couple

Under 65	66–74	75+
£7,200	£8,200	£9,400

TELEPHONE
Telephone Rental Allowance is
available to certain pension and
Social Welfare recipients who
live alone. It is also available to
someone receiving a pension
and being cared for by a recipient of a Carer's Allowance.
Pensioners aged seventy-five
and over who no longer live
alone will retain eligibility for
the Allowance. Telecom Éireann
provides telephone aids for the
hard of hearing. Information
and application forms are available from Post Offices or from
the Dept of Social Welfare,
College Rd, Sligo. Tel. (071)
69800 or (01) 8748444.

THRESHOLD
(National Housing Advisory and Research Service)
Provides information and advice on all matters pertaining to housing, especially landlord/tenant problems, Local Authority housing, house purchase problems. Also helps or refers to appropriate agency those who are homeless.
REGIONAL BRANCHES
Dublin
Capuchin Friary, Church St, Dublin 7. Tel. (01) 8726311. Mon.–Fri. 9.30 a.m.–5 p.m. Tues. 6–8 p.m.
52 Lr Rathmines Rd. Tel. (01) 4964634. Mon.–Fri. 9.30 a.m.– 5 p.m. Thurs. 6–8 p.m.
Cork: Tel. (021) 271250.
Galway: Tel. (091) 63080.

TURNING POINT,
Positive Health Centre,
23 Crofton Rd, Dún Laoghaire, Co. Dublin
Tel. (01) 2800626/2807888, fax (01) 2800643.
Offers a holistic health programme, complementary to orthodox medicine, involving support and therapeutic groups, autogenics, diet education, and counselling with individuals, couples and families. Aimed at those experiencing life crises, such as severe illness — cancer in particular.

VINCENT DE PAUL SOCIETY:
See SOCIETY OF ST VINCENT DE PAUL

VOLUNTEER STROKE SCHEME, 249 Crumlin Rd, Dublin 12.
Head Office: Tel. (01) 4557455.
Northside: Tel. (01) 8481059.
Southside: Tel. (01) 966770.
Ring Mon./Wed./Thurs. 10.30 a.m.–12.30 p.m.
There are nine branches throughout the rest of the country; contact Head Office for their telephone numbers. Aims to help people who suffer from speech and allied problems as the result of a stroke. It offers each patient a small team of volunteers who will visit singly for about an hour at a time on a regular weekly basis. It provides a club where people can meet and be helped further. It organises outings. The scheme is based on the experience gained by volunteers, supported by doctors, nurses and speech therapists who work with stroke sufferers.

WILLS
See the *Making a Will* leaflet published by the Incorporated Law Society of Ireland, available at your local library and from the Arthritis Foundation of Ireland.
   The record of wills is held at the Registry of Deeds, Henrietta St, Dublin 7. Tel. (01) 8748911.

WOW
(Wonderful Older Women), c/o Age & Opportunity, Carmichael House, North

Brunswick St, Dublin 7. Tel. (01)
8723311.
An older women's network is
currently being established to
address and tackle issues which
concern them. If you are interested in this new association
and would like more information, contact the above address.

HEALTH BOARDS

There are eight Health Boards throughout the country. The Eastern Health Board, because of the size of the area, is subdivided into ten districts. The rest are subdivided on a county-by-county basis.

EASTERN HEALTH BOARD
Covers Dublin city and county, Wicklow and Kildare.

Administrative Headquarters
Dr Steevens' Hospital, Dublin 8. Tel. (01) 6790700.

Register of Births, Deaths and Marriages, 8 Lombard St, East, Dublin 2. Tel. (01) 6711968/ 6711974.

MIDLAND HEALTH BOARD
Covers Laois, Offaly, Westmeath and Longford.

Administrative Headquarters
Arden Road, Tullamore, Co. Offaly. Tel. (0506) 21868.

OFFICES FOR THE REGISTRATION OF BIRTHS, DEATHS AND MARRIAGES
Laois: Dublin Rd, Portlaoise. Tel. (0502) 21135.

Longford: Co. Clinic, Longford. Tel. (044) 46211.
Offaly: Arden Rd, Tullamore. Tel. (0506) 41301.
Westmeath: Co. Clinic, Mullingar. Tel. (044) 40221.

MID-WESTERN HEALTH BOARD
Covers Clare, Limerick, Tipperary North Riding.

Administrative Headquarters
31/3 Catherine Street, Limerick. Tel. (061) 316655.

OFFICES FOR THE REGISTRATION OF BIRTHS, DEATHS AND MARRIAGES
Clare: Bindon Street, Ennis. Tel. (065) 28525.
Limerick
City: St Camillus's Hospital. Tel. (061) 326677.
County: Newcastle West. Tel. (069) 62545.

NORTH-EASTERN HEALTH BOARD
Covers Cavan, Louth, Meath and Monaghan.

Administrative Headquarters
Navan Rd, Kells, Co. Meath. Tel. (046) 40341.

OFFICES FOR THE REGISTRATION OF BIRTHS, DEATHS AND MARRIAGES
Cavan: Gate Lodge, General Hospital. Tel. (049) 61399.
Louth
Market Street Road, Dundalk. Tel. (042) 32287.
Health Centre, Peter St, Drogheda. Tel. (041) 38615.
Meath
The Courthouse, Trim. Tel. (046) 31512.
Co. Infirmary, Navan. Tel. (046) 23209.
Monaghan: NEHB, Rooskey, Monaghan. Tel. (047) 81333.

NORTH-WESTERN HEALTH BOARD
Covers Donegal, Leitrim and Sligo.

Administrative Headquarters
Manorhamilton, Co. Leitrim. Tel. (072) 55123.

OFFICES FOR THE REGISTRATION OF BIRTHS, DEATHS AND MARRIAGES
Donegal
North Donegal, Co. Clinic, Letterkenny. Tel. (074) 24576.
South Donegal, St Joseph's, Stranorlar. Tel. (074) 31038.
Leitrim: Community Care, Carrick-on-Shannon. Tel. (078) 20308.
Sligo: Markievicz House, Sligo. Tel. (071) 60222.

SOUTH-EASTERN HEALTH BOARD
Covers Carlow/Kilkenny, Tipperary, Waterford and Wexford.

Administrative Headquarters
Lacken, Dublin Road, Kilkenny. Tel. (056) 51702.

OFFICES FOR THE REGISTRATION OF BIRTHS, DEATHS AND MARRIAGES
Tipperary: St Vincent Health & Day Care Centre. Tel. (062) 51207.
Waterford: Tel. (051) 55296.

SOUTHERN HEALTH BOARD
Covers Cork city and county and Kerry.

Administrative Headquarters
Cork Farm Centre, Dennehy's Cross, Cork. Tel. (021) 545011.

OFFICES FOR THE REGISTRATION OF BIRTHS, DEATHS AND MARRIAGES
Cork
18 Liberty St, Cork. Tel. (021) 275126.
Co. Council Offices, Mallow. Tel. (022) 21123.
Courthouse, Skibbereen. Tel. (028) 21299.
Kerry: Regn. Office, Ardnaweely, Killarney. Tel. (064) 32251.

WESTERN HEALTH BOARD
Covers Galway, Mayo and
Roscommon.

Administrative Headquarters
Merlin Park Regional Hospital,
Galway. Tel. (091) 751131.

OFFICES FOR THE REGISTRATION OF
BIRTHS, DEATHS AND MARRIAGES
Galway: Community Care
Offices, 25 Newcastle Rd.
Tel. (091) 28966.
Mayo: Town Hall, Castlebar.
Tel. (094) 23249.
Roscommon: Tel. (0903)
26518/26604/26665.

At the Administrative
Headquarters of each Board,
you can find the Chief Executive
Officer, and the Programme
Managers of each of these three:
(1) General Hospital Care
    Programme
(2) Special Hospital Care
    Programme
(3) Community Care Programme

(1) GENERAL HOSPITAL CARE
PROGRAMME
Responsible for the provision of
in-patient and out-patient
hospital services, including
ambulance and transport
services. Can be divided into
four main categories:

(i) general hospital services
(ii) services for the elderly
(iii) ambulance and transport
    services
(iv) central services (medical

treatment outside Ireland,
nursing-home subvention, EC
entitlements when abroad).

(2) SPECIAL HOSPITAL CARE
PROGRAMME
Responsible for the provision of
services for the mentally ill and
mentally handicapped,
alcoholism services, child
psychiatry services and forensic
services.
   Some Health Boards provide
a specialist Psychiatry of Old
Age Service for older people
who have mental health
problems (e.g. depression,
anxiety) or dementia with
behavioural problems. It is
delivered by psychiatrists,
nurses, clinical psychologists,
occupational therapists and
social workers.
   These services are provided
either directly by the Health
Board or by arrangement with
other agencies, including
voluntary organisations.

(3) COMMUNITY CARE
PROGRAMME
Comprises those services and
related welfare services which
provide care outside hospitals
and other institutions.
   For the purpose of
administration and organisation
of services, each Health Board
has divided its area into
Community Care Areas. To find
out about the availability of any
service, contact the

Administrative Headquarters of the Board. If it is a service in Community Care, you may get the information from your Health Centre, in the green pages of the telephone directory or your Director of Community Care.

SERVICES PROVIDED BY THE HEALTH BOARDS

GENERAL MEDICAL SERVICES SCHEME/CHOICE OF DOCTOR SCHEME

A person eligible to receive Free General Practitioner services for herself and dependants registers with the doctor of her choice, provided that doctor has entered into an agreement with the relevant Health Board and is prepared to accept the patient on to her panel. Except in certain circumstances, the doctor chosen must not live more than seven miles from the patient nor have already a patient list in excess of the maximum number allowed. When an eligible person does not succeed in obtaining registration, the Health Board arranges to have her entered on a doctor's panel. Drugs, medicines and appliances supplied under the Scheme are provided through retail pharmacies. In most cases, the doctor gives the completed prescription form to the patient, who takes it to any pharmacy that has an agreement with a

Health Board. In rural areas, where a doctor has a centre of practice three miles or more from the nearest retail pharmacy participating in the Scheme, the doctor dispenses for those patients served from the centre who opt to have their medicines dispensed by her.

NURSING SERVICE

Provides home nursing for people in need of regular nursing care — particularly the old and infirm. The range of services is as follows:
— visits to people in their homes and nursing service if required
— nursing care, support and guidance for physically disabled people so as to maximise independence
— nursing aids to medical-card holders
— maintenance of a register of all older people (over sixty-five) in the area.

Public Health Nurses

Care of older people is a major element of a Public Health Nurse's work. She maintains a register of older people in her district and visits each on a regular basis. These visits can include a contribution of some or all of the following duties:
— dressings
— injections
— bed-baths
— management of incontinence
— arranging support services,

e.g. meals-on-wheels, chiropody, laundry
— liaising with Social Service Councils
— arranging the supply of appliances.

The Public Health Nurse also prepares reports in relation to applications for day-care services, home-help services, Housing Aid Scheme and residential care.

Liaison Nurses

The Liaison Nurse acts as a facilitator between hospital and community-based services. She provides an information channel, implements planned discharges, establishes a one-to-one relationship with patients and familiarises herself with any special treatment required after discharge.

Twilight Nursing Service

This is an extension of the Public Health Nursing (daytime) Service to night-time, weekends and early hours. The Service is of benefit to terminally ill patients and those who suffer from chronic disease.

A specially trained nurse provides a Continence Advice Service to people who need it.

The Palliative Care Nurse provides pain control and advice for people with terminal illnesses, and counselling for families affected.

To apply for this Service contact the Public Health Nurse through your GP or hospital. It is provided on the basis of need.

SPEECH THERAPY SERVICE
Laryngectomy

Patients who have had a laryngectomy because of cancer need immediate speech therapy and should have a pre-operative visit.

Neurological disorder

Patients who have disorders such as Parkinson's disease, multiple sclerosis, motor neurone disease require assessment and management, including advice and help with alternative means of communication, e.g. technological aids.

CVA (Stroke)

These patients are referred by medical consultants for assessment and management.

OCCUPATIONAL THERAPY SERVICE
Occupational therapy is one of the many disciplines and services available to disabled and handicapped people, their carers and other professionals. It facilitates the disabled and elderly to achieve maximum independence and to become as fully integrated as possible in the community.

Much of the Community Occupational Therapist's work centres on the assessment for and the provision of housing adaptations and technical aids and appliances, including wheelchairs. The range of technical aids available is extensive and continually expanding. The occupational therapist's full role involves considering alternative means of achieving the maximum level of functioning in the task in question, both inside and outside the home. The work can also include the treatment of medical/surgical conditions. The therapist would advise the family on the management of the older person's physical functioning.

OTHER SERVICES

Physiotherapy

Assessment and treatment of physical problems of older people at home in the areas of mobility, respiratory complaints (chest) pertaining to neurological or orthopaedic conditions.

Home-help

Apply through your local Public Health Nurse. The home-help service is designed to help people to remain living independently in their homes. The home-help performs various household tasks for the older or infirm person, e.g. dressing and washing, setting fires, preparing meals, shopping.

Care Attendants also give assistance with personal needs.

Chiropody

The Health Boards may provide a chiropody service for medical-card holders over sixty-five. Ask at your local Health Centre.

Counselling services

Supplied in areas relating to substance abuse, bereavement, alcoholism, incest, unplanned pregnancies, AIDS, wife-battering, etc.

Day care is provided in each of the Health Board areas, sometimes on a voluntary basis or offering specialist care, e.g. for Alzheimer's sufferers. Some areas have day hospitals, and the Eastern Health Board has a mobile day hospital. Day hospitals cater for people who are attending the psychiatric service.

Welfare Homes and residential centres are provided for older people who, although ambulant, are incapable of independent living but do not require constant medical or nursing care. You must be referred by your GP, Public Health Nurse or hospital consultant. You are then assessed and, if eligible, placed on a waiting-list in order of priority. To be admitted to a Welfare Home, you must be over sixty-five, mobile and requiring a low level of nursing care, and need admission because of social reasons.

Respite care is a relatively

new service aimed at elderly people who are being cared for at home to give their carers a short break. Admission to this service depends on assessment; contact your Public Health Nurse.

Boarding out is a scheme aimed at older people who can no longer live alone but do not require extended residential care, as well as those suitable for discharge from hospital who have nowhere to go or whose relatives are unable to care for them. It offers older people the opportunity to remain in their localities, with people they know and trust, in living conditions which provide shelter, food, warmth and companionship.

Hospice care is available in many areas of the country; see Directory.

As Superintendent Registrar, each Health Board has important statutory functions in the registration of births, marriages and deaths and is responsible to the Registrar-General for the effective operation of the registration system in its area through local registrars.

The Housing Aid Scheme/Task Force ensures that older people living alone are in comfortable, waterproof accommodation. In recent years, priority has been given to improving the security of houses against forced entry and installing smoke detectors as a precaution against fire, when requested. Work carried out includes repairs and the provision of water, toilet and shower/bath.

Pest control is provided by the Health Boards.

BIBLIOGRAPHY

SECTION I NORMAL AGEING

1 ATTITUDES TO AGEING

Barta Kvitek, S.D., B.J. Shaver, H. Blood & K.F. Shepard (1986), 'Age bias: physical therapists and older patients', *Journal of Gerontology*, 41 (6), 706–9.

Braithwaite, V.A. (1986), 'Old age stereotypes: reconciling contradictions', *Journal of Gerontology*, 41 (3), 353–60.

Commission of the European Communities (1993), *Age and Attitudes — Main Results from a Eurobarometer Survey*.

Darwin, J. (ed.), *Against Ageism, Research Project*, Newcastle-Upon-Tyne, England.

Gibson, H.B. (1992), 'Psychosocial factors affecting the emotional lives of older people' in *The Emotional and Social Lives of Older People*, London: Chapman & Hall.

Glass, J.C. Jr, R.D. Mustian & L.R. Carter (1986), 'Knowledge and attitudes of health-care providers towards sexuality in the institutionalised elderly', *Educational Gerontology*, 12, 465–75.

Hesse, K.A., E.W. Campion & N. Karamouz (1984), 'Attitudinal stumbling blocks to geriatric rehabilitation' (special article), *Journal of the American Geriatrics Society*, 32 (10), October, 747–50.

Jones, S. (1986), 'The elders: a new generation', *Ageing and Society*, 6, 313–31.

Keller, M.L., E.A. Leventhal & B. Larson (1989), 'Ageing: the lived experience', *International Journal of Ageing and Human Development*, 29 (1), 67–82.

Liebman, T.H. (1984), 'We Bring Generations Together!', *Young Children*, September, 70–5.

Midwinter, E. (1991), *Out of Focus: Old Age, the Press & Broadcasting*, London: Centre for Policy on Ageing.

National Council for the Elderly (1993), *Bearing Fruit, A Manual for Primary Schools*, No. 30, Dublin.

National Council for the Elderly (1993), *In Due Season, A Manual for Post-primary Schools*, No. 30, Dublin.

Nishi-Strattner, M. & J.E. Myers (1983), 'Attitudes towards the elderly: an intergenerational examination', *Journal of Educational Gerontology*, 9, 389–97.

Office of Ageing (1991, Nov.), 'Community Attitudes to Ageing: Resource Paper No. 1, Facts about Ageing', cited in *Bulletin on Ageing* (1992), No. 3, United Nations Office at Vienna, Centre for Social Development and Humanitarian Affairs.

Power, B. (1987), *Attitudes of Young People to Ageing and the Elderly*, Report No. 16, National Council for the Aged, Dublin.

Retsinas, J. (1986), 'Geriatric myths reconsidered', *American Family Physician*, 33 (3), 187–91.

Sanders, G.F., J.E. Montgomery, J.F. Pittman & C. Balkwell (1984), 'Youth's attitudes toward the elderly', *Journal of Applied Gerontology*, 3 (1), 59–70.

Saul, S. (1983), *Aging: An Album of People Growing Old*, New York: John Wiley & Sons.

Schonfield, D. (1982), 'Who is stereotyping whom and why?', *The Gerontologist*, 22 (3), 267–72.

Scrutton, S. (1990), 'Ageism, the foundation of age discrimination' in E. Mc Ewen, *Ageism, The Unrecognised Discrimination*, England: Age Concern.

Seefeldt, C. & S.R. Keawkungwal (1986), 'Children's attitudes towards the elderly in Thailand', *Educational Gerontology*, 12, 151–8.

Signori, E.I., D.S. Butt & J.F. Kozak (1982), 'Attitudes toward the aged of persons under and over the age of forty', *Canadian Counsellor*, 16 (3), 173–9.

Taher, Z., J. Mirle & P. Jarvis (1990), 'Children's attitudes towards elderly individuals: a comparison of two ethnic groups', *International Journal of Ageing and Human Development*, 3, 161–74.

Tyler, W. (1986), 'Structural ageism as a phenomenon in British society', *Journal of Educational Gerontology*, 1 (2), 38–46.

United Nations Office at Vienna (1992), *Bulletin on Ageing*, No. 3, Centre for Social Development and Humanitarian Affairs.

Wood, Tierce J. & W.C. Seelbach (1987), 'Elders as school volunteers: an untapped resource', *Educational Gerontology*, 13, 33–41.

2 FACTS ON AGEING

Central Statistics Office (1991), *Census Population of Ireland*, Dublin: Government Stationery Office.

Central Statistics Office (1992), *Labour Force Survey*, Dublin: Government Stationery Office.

Central Statistics Office (1993), *Census '91 Summary Population Report — 1st Series*, Dublin: Government Stationery Office.

Donovan, K. (15 March 1993), 'Brightening up the golden years', *The Irish Times*.

Eastern Health Board (1989), *Services for the Elderly — A Policy Document*.

Fahy, T. (1993), *A Profile of Health and Well-being among the Over-65s: Preliminary Findings of a National Survey*, paper presented at the Conference to Promote Health and Autonomy for Older People, Dublin: National Council for the Elderly.

Kelleher, C. (1993), *Measures to Promote Health and Autonomy for Older People: A Position Paper*, No. 26, Dublin: National Council for the Elderly.

O'Shea, E. (1993), *The Impact of Social & Economic Policies on Older People in Ireland*, Report No. 24, Dublin: National Council for the Elderly.

O'Sullivan, T. (1993), 'Health fact sheet (5)', Health Services Unit, Dublin: Institute of Public Administration.

Walker, A., J. Alber & A-M. Guillemard (1993), *Older People in Europe: Social and Economic Policies*, Commission of the European Communities.

INCOME

Commission of the European Communities (1993), *Age and Attitudes — Main Results from a Eurobarometer Survey*.

Dane Age Association (1993), *Travel and Culture: Access to Concessions by Older People in Europe*, Dane Age Association/EC Commission.

Hunt, E.H. (1990), 'Paupers and pensioners: past and present', *Ageing and Society*, 9 (4), 407–30.

Laczko, F. (1990), 'New poverty and the old poor: pensioners' income in the European Community', *Ageing and Society*, 10 (3), 261–77.

O'Shea, E. (1993), *The Impact of Social & Economic Policies on Older People in Ireland*.

Victor, C.R. (1989), 'The myth of the WOOPIE: poverty and affluence in later life', *Geriatric Medicine*, 19 (12), 22–6.

HOUSING

Butler, A. (1986), 'Housing and the elderly in Europe', *Social Policy & Administration*, 20 (2), 136–52.

Central Statistics Office (1993), *Census '91 Summary Population Report — 1st Series*.

Irish Council for Social Housing (1992), 'Housing for the elderly', Dublin: The Housing Centre.

O'Shea, E. (1993), *The Impact of Social & Economic Policies on Older People in Ireland*.

Walker, A. et al. (1993), *Older People in Europe: Social and Economic Policies*.

Wheeler, R. (1986), 'Housing policy and elderly people' in C. Phillipson, A. Walker & A. Gower (eds), *Ageing and Social Policy: A Critical Assessment*, Aldershot: Gower.

3 PHYSICAL ASPECTS OF NORMAL AGEING

Whelan, B.J. & R.N. Vaughan (1982), *The Economic and Social Circumstances of the Elderly in Ireland*, Paper No. 110, Dublin: The Economic and Social Research Institute.

HEARING

Ham, R.J., J.M. Holtzman, M.L. Marcy & M.R. Smith (1983), *Primary Care Geriatrics*, Bristol, England: John Wright.

Mulrow, C.D., C. Agiular, E. Endicott, R. Velez, M.R. Tuley, W.S. Charlip & J.A. Hill (1990), 'Association between hearing impairment and the quality of life of elderly individuals', *Journal of the American Geriatrics Society*, 38, 45–50.

National Association for the Deaf, leaflets.

Olsho, L.W., S.W. Harkins & M.L. Lenhardt (1985), 'Aging and the auditory system' in J.E. Birren & K.W. Schaie (eds), *Handbook of the Psychology of Aging*, New York: Van Nostrand Reinhold Co.

Salomon, G. (1986), *Hearing Problems and the Elderly*, Danish Medical Bulletin, 33, Supplement No. 3.

VISION

Botwinick, J. (1984), *Aging and Behavior* (3rd ed.), New York: Springer Publishing Co.

Deckert, J., R.J. Ham, M.R. Smith & C. Long (1983), 'Some common problems of the elderly' in R.J. Ham et al., *Primary Care Geriatrics*.

Disabled Living Foundation (1979), *The Elderly Person with Failing Vision*, England.

Kline, D.W. & F. Schieber (1985), 'Vision and aging' in J.E. Birren & K.W. Schaie (eds), *Handbook of the Psychology of Aging*.

Mc Call, R.F., *Communications Barriers in the Elderly*, England: Age Concern.

PHYSICAL

Donovan, K. (17 January 1994), 'The fitness gap', *The Irish Times*.

Fried, S., D. Van Booven & C. Mc Quarrie (1993), *Older Adulthood — Learning Activities for Understanding Aging*, USA Health Professions Press Inc.

Grimley, Evans J., M.J. Goldacre, M. Hodkinson, S. Lamb & M. Savory (1992), *Health: Abilities and Well-being in the Third Age*, Research Paper No. 9, Carnegie UK Trust.

Kelleher, C. (1993), *Measures to Promote Health and Autonomy for Older People: A Position Paper*.

Wiener, J.M., R.J. Hanley, R. Clarke & J.F. Van Nostrand (1990), 'Measuring activities of daily living: comparisons across national surveys', *Journal of Gerontology*, 45 (6), 229–37.

SLEEP

Albert, M.S. & M.B. Moss (eds) (1988), *Geriatric Neuropsychology*, London: Guildford Press.

Leng, N.R.C. (1990), *Psychological Care in Old Age*, London: Hemisphere Publishing Corporation.

Morgan, K. (1987), *Sleep and Ageing*, London: Croom Helm.

Morgan, K., H. Dallosso, S. Ebrahim, T. Orie & P.H. Fentern (1988), 'Characteristics of subjective insomnia in the elderly living at home', *Age & Ageing*, 17 (1), 1–7.

Morin, C. & S.R. Rapp (1987), 'Behavioural management of geriatric insomnia', *Clinical Gerontologist*, 6 (4), 15–23.

SEXUALITY

Baikie, E. (1984), 'Sexuality and the elderly' in I. Hanley & J. Hodge (eds), *Psychological Approaches to the Care of the Elderly*, London: Croom Helm.

Brecher, E.M. (1984), *Love, Sex and Aging, A Consumer Union Report*, Boston: Little Brown & Co.

Fried, S. et al. (1993), *Older Adulthood – Learning Activities for Understanding Aging*.

Gibson, H.B. (1992), *The Emotional and Sexual Lives of Older People, A Manual for Professionals*, London: Chapman & Hall.

Greengross, W. & S. (1989), *Living, Loving and Ageing*, England: Age Concern.

Grimley, Evans J. et al. (1992), *Health: Abilities and Well-being in the Third Age*.

Health Education Bureau (1991), *The Menopause*, Dublin: Dept of Health.

Hendricks, J. & C.D. (1978), 'Sexuality in later life' in V. Carver & P. Liddiard (eds), *An Ageing Population*, England: Open University Press.

Kay, R.A. (1993), 'Sexuality in the later years', *Ageing and Society*, 13, 415–26.

Masters, W.H. & V.E. Johnson (1981), 'Sex and the aging process', *Journal of the American Geriatrics Society*, 26, 385–9.

Mohr, D.C. & L.E. Beutler (1990), 'Erectile dysfunction: a review of diagnostic and treatment procedures', *Clinical Psychology Review*, 10, 123–50.

Starr, B.D. & M.B. Weiner (1981), *The Starr-Weiner Report on Sex and Sexuality in the Mature Years*, New York: McGran.

Thienhaus, O.J., E.A. Conter & H.B. Bosmann (1986), 'Sexuality and ageing', *Ageing and Society*, 6, 39–54.

ACCIDENTS AND SAFETY

Blake, A.J., K. Morgan, M.J. Bendall, H. Dallosso, S.B.J. Ebrahim, T.H.D. Orie, P.H. Fentern & E.J. Bassey (1988), 'Falls by elderly people at home: prevalence and associated factors', *Age & Ageing*, 17, 365–72.

Central Statistics Office (1991), *Fourth Quarterly and Yearly Summary, Department of Health Vital Statistics*, Dublin: Government Stationery Office.

Eastern Health Board (1992), *Coping with Falls*, Carer Leaflet No. 5, Customer Services, Dr Steevens' Hospital, Dublin 8.

Eastern Health Board (1992), *Safety in the Home*, Carer Leaflet No. 6, Customer Services, Dr Steevens' Hospital, Dublin 8.

Grimley, Evans J. et al. (1992), *Health: Abilities and Well-being in the Third Age*.

Ham, R.J., J. Pattee & M.L. Marcy (1983), 'Accidents in the elderly' in R.J. Ham et al., *Primary Care Geriatrics*.

Hooker, S. (1976), *Caring for Elderly People: Understanding and Practical Help*, Report No. 81, London: Routledge & Kegan Paul.

Itoh, M., M. Lee & J. Shapiro (1984), 'Self-help devices for the elderly population living in the community' in T.F. Williams, *Rehabilitation in the Aging*, New York: Raven Press.

Kennedy, J.C. (1986), 'Car choice for the elderly or disabled: features to consider', *Geriatric Medicine*, December, 34–9.

Ochs, A.L., J. Newberry, M.L. Lenhardt & S.W. Harkins (1985), 'Neural and vestibular aging associated with falls' in J.E. Birren & K.W. Schaie (eds), *Handbook of the Psychology of Aging*.

Report of the Kellogg International Work Group (1987), *The Prevention of Falls in Later Life, Danish Medical Bulletin*, 34, Supplement No. 4.

Sheppard, D. & M.I.M. Pattinson (1986), *Transport and Road Research Laboratory: Interviews with Elderly Pedestrians Involved in Road Accidents*, Southampton: Hobbs.

Sterns, H.L., G.V. Barrett & R.A. Alexander (1985), 'Accidents and the aging individual' in Birren & Schaie (eds), *Handbook of the Psychology of Aging*.

Wynne-Harley, D.W. (1991), *Living Dangerously: Risk-taking, Safety and Older People*, London: Centre for Policy on Ageing.

MEDICINES

Bender, K.J. (1990), *Psychiatric Medications*, London: Sage Publications.

Blair, P. (1991), *Know Your Medicines* (2nd ed.), England: Age Concern.

Cartwright, A. & C. Smith (1988), *Elderly People, Their Medicines and Their Doctors*, London: Routledge.

Herxheimer, A. (1976), 'Sharing the responsibility for treatment', *The Lancet*, 2, 1294.

Lorenc, L. & A. Branthwaite (1993), 'Are older adults less compliant with prescribed medication than younger adults?', *British Journal of Clinical Psychology*, 32, 485–92.

Rivers, P. (1992), *Managing Your Medicines*, London: Help the Aged.

4 PSYCHOLOGICAL ASPECTS OF NORMAL AGEING

Bassett, M., B. Brady, T. Fleming & T. Inglis (1989), *For Adults Only: A Case for Adult Education in Ireland*, Dublin: AONTAS.

Bayles, K.A. & A.W. Kasznaik (1987), *Communication and Cognition in Normal Ageing and Dementia*, London: Taylor & Francis.

Botwinick, J. (1984), *Aging and Behavior.*

Coleman, P.G. (1992), 'Personal adjustment in late life; successful ageing', reviews in *Clinical Gerontology*, 2 (1), 67–78.

Coleman, P.G., C. Ivani-Challian & M. Robinson (1993), 'Self-esteem and its sources: stability and change in later life', *Ageing and Society*, 13, 171–92.

Grimley, Evans J. et al. (1992), *Health: Abilities and Well-being in the Third Age.*

Hart, L. (1993), *Adult Education and Social Change*, Council for Cultural Co-operation, Council of Europe.

Hoyer, N.J. & K. Hooker (1989), 'The psychology of adult development, and ageing: new approaches and methodologies in the developmental study of cognition and personality' in N.J. Osgood & H.L. Santz (eds), *The Science & Practice of Gerontology*, London: Greenwood Press.

International Association of Third Age Universities (1992), 'The Third Age University', *Bulletin on Ageing*, No. 3, 5–6.

Jenkins, T.S., N.J. Roberts & J.N. Johnson (1983), *Mental Health & Aging, A Guide to Training & Program Development*, V.K. Windsor, Psychological Assessment Resources.

Kausler, D.H. (1985), 'Episodic memory: memorizing performance' in N. Charness (ed.), *Age and Human Performance*, New York: John Wiley & Sons.

Kelly, P. (1992), *Living & Learning: Older Open University Graduates*, England: Open University Press.

Labouvie-Vief, G. (1985), 'Intelligence and cognition' in J.E. Birren & K.W. Schaie (eds), *Handbook of the Psychology of Aging.*

Masoro, E.J. (1989), 'The biology of ageing' in Osgood & Santz (eds), *The Science & Practice of Gerontology.*

Open University V205 Course Team (1985), *Birth to Old Age, Health in Transition*, England: Open University Press.

Poon, L.M. (1985), 'Differences in human memory with aging: nature, causes and clinical implications' in Birren & Schaie (eds), *Handbook of the Psychology of Aging.*

Rott, C. & H. Thomae (1991), 'Coping in longitudinal perspective: findings from the Bonn longitudinal study on ageing', *Journal of Cross-cultural Gerontology*, 6, 23–40.

Schaie, K.W. (1989), 'The hazards of cognitive ageing', *The Gerontologist*, 29 (4), 484–93.

Schuller, R.T. & A.M. Bostyn (1992), *Learning: Education and Information in the Third Age, Carnegie Inquiry into the Third Age*, Research Paper No. 3, Carnegie United Kingdom Trust.

Senior Studies Institute (1993), *Lifelong Learning: Responsive to the Community*, Canada.

Twining, C. (1991), *The Memory Handbook*, Oxon: Winslow Press.

Ulatowska, H.K. (ed.) (1985), *The Ageing Brain: Communication in the Elderly*, London: Taylor & Francis.

5 SOCIAL ASPECTS OF NORMAL AGEING
(i) RELATIONSHIPS

Aizenberg, R. & J. Treas (1985), 'The family in later life: psycho-social and demographic considerations' in J.E. Birren & K.W. Schaie (eds), *Handbook of the Psychology of Aging*.

Antonucci, T.C. (1985), 'Personal characteristics, social support and social behavior' in R.H. Binstocke & Shanas (eds), *Handbook of Aging & the Social Services*, New York: Van Nostrand Reinhold Co.

Biegel, D., B.K. Shore & E. Gordon (1984), *Building Support Networks for the Elderly, Theory and Application*, London: Sage Publications.

Brubaker, T.H. (1985), *Later Life Families*, London: Sage Publications.

Commission of the European Communities (1993), *Age and Attitudes — Main Results from a Eurobarometer Survey*.

Daly, M. & J. O'Connor (1984), *The World of the Elderly: The Rural Experience*, Dublin: National Council for the Aged.

Duck, S. (ed.) (1990), *Personal Relationships and Social Support*, London: Sage Publications.

Fahy, T. (1993), *A Profile of Health and Well-being among the Over- 65s: Preliminary Findings of a National Survey*.

Finch, J. & J. Mason (1990), 'Filial obligations and kin support for elderly', *Ageing and Society*, 10 (2), 151–75.

Fogarty, M.P. (1986), *Meeting the Needs of the Elderly*, Ireland: European Foundation for the Improvement of Living and Working Conditions.

Gordon, C. (1988), *The Myth of Family Care, The Elderly in the Early 1930s*, Discussion Paper No. 29, The London School of Economics.

Hawley, D. & J.D. Chamley (1986), 'Older persons' perceptions of the quality of their human support systems', *Ageing and Society*, 6, 295–312.

Horkan, M. & A. Woods (1986), *This Is Our World: Perspectives of Some Elderly People on Life in Suburban Dublin*, Report No. 12, National Council for the Aged, Dublin.

Hyde, V. & Gibbs, I. (1993), 'A very special relationship: grand-daughters' perception of grandmothers', *Ageing and Society*, 18, 83–96.

James, A., W.L. James & H.L. Smith (1984), 'Reciprocity as a coping strategy of the elderly: a rural Irish perspective', *The Gerontologist*, 24 (5), 483–9.

Jerrome, D. (1990), 'Frailty and friendship', *Journal of Cross-cultural Gerontology*, 5, 51–64.

Jerrome, D. (1991), 'Loneliness: possibilities for intervention', *Journal of Ageing Studies*, 5 (2), 195–208.

Langer, N. (1990), 'Grandparents and adult grandchildren: what do they do for one another?' *International Journal of Ageing and Human Development*, 31 (2), 101–10.

National Council for the Elderly (1993), *Bearing Fruit, A Manual for Primary Schools*.

National Council for the Aged (1984), *The World of the Elderly: The Rural Experience*.

O'Higgins, K. (1990), *Kinship and Ageing in Ireland*, Reprint No. 89, Dublin: The Economic and Social Research Institute.

Peterson Warren, A. & J. Quadagno (eds) (1985), *Social Bonds in Life: Ageing and Interdependence*, published in co-operation with The Midwest Council for Social Research in Ageing, London: Sage Publications.

Power, B. (1984), *Old and Alone in Ireland*, Dublin: Society of St Vincent de Paul.

Retsinas, J. (1986), 'Geriatric myths reconsidered'.

Russell, J. (1983), 'Attitudes of elderly people living alone', *The Irish Journal of Psychology*, 1, 1–12.

Sauer, W.J. & R.T. Coward (eds) (1985), *Social Support Networks and the Care of the Elderly*, New York: Springer Publishing Co.

Smith, P.K. (1993), 'Being a grandparent', *Clinical Psychology Forum*, 59, 2–5.

Talbott, M.M. (1990), 'The negative side of the relationship between older women and their adult children: the mother's perspective', *The Gerontologist*, 30 (5), 595–603.

Walker, A. et al. (1993), *Older People in Europe: Social and Economic Policies*.

Wenger, C. (1983), 'Loneliness: a problem of measurement' in D. Jerrome (ed.), *Ageing and Modern Society*.

Wenger, G.C. & S. Shahtahmasebi (1991), 'Survivors: support network variation and sources of help in rural communities', *Journal of Cross-cultural Gerontology*, 6, 41–82.

Whelan, B.J. & R.N. Vaughan (1982), *The Economic and Social Circumstances of the Elderly in Ireland*.

Whelan, C.T. & B.J. (1988), *The Transition to Retirement*, Paper No. 138, Dublin: The Economic and Social Research Institute.

Willmott, P. (1987), *Friendship Networks and Social Support*, Report No. 666, London: The Policy Studies Institute.

(ii) WORK AND RETIREMENT

Berry-Lound, D. (1992), *Is Retirement Working? Retirement Plus — A Review of UK Corporate Retirement Policies*, England: Re Action Trust.

Braithwaite, V.A. & D.M. Gibson (1987), 'Adjustment to retirement: what we know and what we need to know', *Ageing and Society*, 7, 1–18.

Clarke, R.J. (1988), 'The future of work and retirement', *Research on Ageing*, 10 (2), 169–93.

Dempsey, A. (1986), *What Are You Doing with the Rest of Your Life? Retirement in Ireland*, Dublin: Retirement Planning Council of Ireland.

European Foundation for the Improvement of Living and Working Conditions (1985), *Retirement, A Time of Transition*, Ireland.

European Foundation for the Improvement of Living and Working Conditions (1993), *News from the Foundation*, No. 36, Ireland.

Grimley, Evans J. et al. (1992), *Health: Abilities and Well-being in the Third Age*.

Howard, J.H. & J. Marshall (1983), 'Retirement adaptation — what research says about doing it successfully', *Business Quarterly*, Summer, 29–39.

Irish Congress of Trade Unions (1993), *Guidelines on Retirement Planning*, Dublin.

National Council for the Aged (1982), *Retirement: A General Review*, Report No. 2, Dublin.

National Council for the Aged (1983), *Retirement Age: Fixed or Flexible?*, Seminar Proceeding, Report No. 4, Dublin.

National Social Service Board (1993), *Now's the Time, Volunteering Opportunities for Older People*, Dublin.

Nusberg, C. (1986), 'Early retirement ubiquitous in western nations', *Ageing International*, 26–32.

O'Shea, E. (1993), *Older People in Europe, Social and Economic Policies*, National Report Ireland, European Community Observatory.

Phillipson, C. (1983), *New Directions in Pre-retirement Education*, England: Beth Johnson Foundation.

Rapid Reports Eurostat (1993), *Older People in the Labour Market During the Eighties*, Luxemburg.

Retirement Planning Council of Ireland (1993), *Planning for Retirement: Statement of Best Practice*, Ireland.

Wheller, T.R. (1986), *Pre-retirement Training/Education — Are We Leading or Following?*, England: George Spencer Memorial Fund.

SECTION II PROBLEMS AND THEIR EFFECTS

6 INCONTINENCE

Browne, B. (1978), *Management for Continence*, England: Age Concern.

Burgio, K.L., K.L. Pearce & A.J. Lucco (1989), *Staying Dry, A Practical Guide to Bladder Control*, Baltimore: Johns Hopkins University Press.

Campbell, A.J., J. Reinken & Mc Cosh (1985), 'Incontinence in the elderly: prevalence and prognosis', *Age and Society*, 14, 65–70.

Eastern Health Board (1992), *Helping with Bladder Problems*, Carer Leaflet No. 8, Customer Services, Dr Steevens' Hospital, Dublin 8.

Garfield, C.P., R.J. Ham, M.R. Smith & J.M. Holtzman (1983), 'Genito-urinary and sexual problems of the elderly' in R.J. Ham et al., *Primary Care Geriatrics*.

Long, M.L. (1985), 'Incontinence', *Journal of Gerontological Nursing*, 11 (1), 30–41.

Mares, P. (1990), *In Control: Help with Incontinence*, England: Age Concern.

Stokes, G. (1987), *Incontinence and Inappropriate Urinating, Common Problems with the Elderly Confused*, Oxon: Winslow Press.

7 DISEASES WITH PSYCHOLOGICAL CONSEQUENCES
ALZHEIMER'S DISEASE AND OTHER DEMENTIAS

Alzheimer Society of Ireland (1986), *Carer's Handbook* (5th reprint).

Copeland, J.R.M., I.A. Davidson, M.E. Dewey, B. Gilmore, B.A. Larkin, C. Mc William, P.A. Saunders, A. Scott, V. Sharma & C. Sullivan (1992), 'Alzheimer's disease and other dementias, depression, pseudodementia: prevalence, incidence, three-year outcome in Liverpool', *British Journal of Psychiatry*, 161, 230–9.

Coyne, A.C., W.E. Reichman & L.J. Berbig (1993), 'The relationship between dementia and elder abuse', *American Journal of Psychiatry*, 150 (4), 643–6.

Fisher, J.E. & L.L. Cartensen (1990), 'Behaviour management of the dementias', *Clinical Psychology Review*, 10, 611–29.

Grimley, Evans J. et al. (1992), *Health: Abilities and Well-being in the Third Age*.

Hope, R.A. & C.C. Fairbourn (1990), 'The nature of wandering in dementia: a community-based study', *International Journal of Geriatric Psychiatry*, 5, 239–45.

Kelly, M. (1993), *Designing for People with Dementia in the Context of the Building Standards*, Dementia Services Development Centre, University of Stirling, Scotland.

Mace, N.L., P.V. Robins, B.A. Castleton, C. Cloke & E. Mc Ewen (1981), *The 36-hour Day*, 1981 (1st ed.), Baltimore: Johns Hopkins University Press; 1985, England: Hodder & Stoughton, Age Concern.

Miller, E. (1992), 'Psychological approaches to the management of memory impairment', *British Journal of Psychiatry*, 160, 1–6.

Miller, E. & R. Morris (1993), *The Psychology of Dementia*, New York: John Wiley & Sons.

Report of the Working Party on Services for the Elderly (1988), *The Years Ahead: A Policy for the Elderly*, Dublin: Government Stationery Office.

Twining, C. (1991), *The Memory Handbook*.

Ware, C.J.G., C.C. Fairbourn & R.A. Hope (1990), 'A community-based study of aggressive behaviour in dementia', *International Journal of Geriatric Psychiatry*, 5, 337–42.

Woods, R.T. (1989), *Alzheimer's Disease*, London: Souvenir Press.

ACUTE CONFUSIONAL STATE

Albert, M.S. & M.B. Moss (eds) (1988), *Geriatric Neuropsychology*.

Ham, R.J. & M.R. Smith (1983), 'The confused elderly patient' in R.J. Ham et al., *Primary Care Geriatrics*.

Leng, N.R.C. (1990), *Psychological Care in Old Age*.

PARKINSON'S DISEASE

Ham, R.J. et al. (1983), *Primary Care Geriatrics*.

Holden, U. (1988), *Neuropsychology and Ageing*, London: Croom Helm.

Hooker, S. (1976), *Caring for Elderly People: Understanding and Practical Help.*

Knight, R.G, H. Godfrey & E.J. Shelton (1988), 'The psychological deficits associated with Parkinson's disease', *Clinical Psychology Review*, 8, 391–410.

Leng, N.R.C. (1990), *Psychological Care in Old Age.*

Ring, H.A. & M.R. Trimble (1991), 'Affective disturbance in Parkinson's disease', *International Journal of Geriatric Psychiatry*, 6, 385–93.

STROKE

Albert, M.S. & M.B. Moss (eds) (1988), *Geriatric Neuropsychology.*

Allman, P. (1991), 'Depressive disorders and emotionalism following stroke', *International Journal of Geriatric Psychiatry*, 6, 337–83.

Hooker, S. (1976), *Caring for Elderly People: Understanding and Practical Help.*

Leng, N.R.C. (1990), *Psychological Care in Old Age.*

8 PSYCHOLOGICAL PROBLEMS

DEPRESSION

Ames, P. (1991), 'Epidemiological studies of depression among the elderly in residential and nursing homes', *International Journal of Geriatric Psychiatry*, 6 (6), 347–54.

Baldwin, R.C. & D.J. Jolly (1986), 'The prognosis of depression in old age', *British Journal of Psychiatry*, 149, 574–83.

Beats, B., R. Levy & B. Sahakian (eds) (1991), 'Affective disorders in old age', *International Journal of Geriatric Psychiatry*, 6 (whole issue).

Benbow, S.M. (1991), 'ECT in late life', *International Journal of Geriatric Psychiatry*, 19, 401–6.

Bender, K.J. (1990), *Psychiatric Medications*, London: Sage Publications.

Benedict, K.B. & D.B. Nacoste (1990), 'Dementia and depression in the elderly: a framework for addressing difficulties in differential diagnosis', *Clinical Psychology Review*, 10, 513–37.

Blazer, D. (1989), 'Current concepts; depression in the elderly', *The New England Journal of Medicine*, 19, 164–7.

Brodaty, H., L. Harris, K. Peters, K. Wilhelm, I. Hickie, P. Boyce, P. Mitchell, G. Parker & K. Eyers (1993), 'Prognosis of depression in the elderly', *British Journal of Psychiatry*, 163, 589–96.

Burvill, P.W., W.D. Hall, H.G. Stamper & J.P. Emmerson (1991), 'The prognosis of depression in old age', *British Journal of Psychiatry*, 158, 64–71.

Coleman, P.G. (1986), *Aging and Reminiscence Processes — Social and Clinical Implications*, New York: John Wiley & Sons.

Hanley, I. & E. Baikie (1984), 'Understanding and treating depression in the elderly' in I. Hanley & J. Hodge (eds), *Psychological Approaches to the Care of the Elderly*.

Hanley, I. & M. Gilhooly (1986), *Psychological Therapies for the Elderly*, London: Croom Helm.

Heal, D.J. & W.R. Buckett (1991), 'Development of anti-depressive drugs for the 90s: progress or procrastination', *International Journal of Geriatric Psychiatry*, 6 (6), 431–40.

Katona, C.L.E. (1993), 'Approaches in managing depression in the elderly' in *Depression in the Elderly*, Berlin Satellite Symposium, Abstracts, Smith, Kline, Beecham.

Knight, B. (1986), *Psychotherapy with Older Adults*, London: Sage Publications.

Morris, R.G. & L.W. (1991), 'Cognitive and behavioural approaches with the depressed elderly', *International Journal of Geriatric Psychiatry*, 6 (6), 407–14.

Murphy, E. (ed.) (1986), *Affective Disorders in the Elderly*, London: Churchill Livingstone.

Pitt, B. (1991), 'Depression in the general hospital setting', *International Journal of Geriatric Psychiatry*, 6 (6), 363–70.

Stoudemire, A., C.D. Hill, R. Morris & B.J. Levison (1993), *American Journal of Psychiatry*, 150 (10), 1539–40.

Thompson, L.W., D. Gallagher & J. Steinmetz-Breckenridge (1987), 'Comparative effectiveness of psychotherapies for depressed elders', *Journal of Consulting and Clinical Psychology*, 55 (3), 385–90.

Thorton, S. & J. Brothchie (1987), 'Reminiscence: a critical review of the empirical literature', *British Journal of Clinical Psychology*, 26, 93–111.

Wattis, J. & M. Church (1986), *Practical Psychiatry of Old Age*, London: Croom Helm.

Woods, R. & P. Britton (1985), *Clinical Psychology with the Elderly*, Kent: Croom Helm.

SUICIDE

Altergott, K. (1988), 'Qualities of daily life and suicide in old age: a comparative perspective', *Journal of Cross-cultural Gerontology*, 3, 361–76.

Blazer, D.G., J.R. Bachar & K.G. Manton (1986), 'Suicide in late life: review and commentary', *Journal of the American Geriatrics Society*, 34 (7), 519–25.

Cattell, H.R. (1988), 'Elderly suicide in London: an analysis of coroners' inquests', *International Journal of Geriatric Psychiatry*, 3, 251–61.

Lindesay, J. (1986), 'Suicide and attempted suicide in old age' in E. Murphy (ed.), *Affective Disorders in the Elderly*.

Lindesay, J. (1991), 'Suicide in the elderly', *International Journal of Geriatric Psychiatry*, 6, 355–61.

Moore, S.L. & B.L. Tanney (eds) (1991), *Suicide in Older Adults: Selected Readings*, Alberta, Canada: Suicide Information and Education Centre.

Osgood, N.J., B.A. Brant & A. Lipman (1991), *Suicide among the Elderly in Long-term Care Facilities*, New York: Greenwood Press.

Psychological Society of Ireland (1992), 'Suicide in Ireland', *The Irish Psychologist*, 18 (11), 118–21.

Zweig, R.A. & Hinrichsen (1993), 'Factors associated with suicide attempts by depressed older adults: a prospective study', *American Journal of Psychiatry*, 150 (ii), 1687–92.

ANXIETY, PHOBIAS AND HYPOCHONDRIASIS

Hersen, M. & V.B. Van Hasselt (1992), 'Behavioural assessment and treatment of anxiety in the elderly', *Clinical Psychology Review*, 12, 619–40.

Lindesay, J. (1991), 'Phobic disorders in the elderly', *British Journal of Psychiatry*, 159, 531–41.

MacDonald, M.L. & R.E. Schnur (1987), 'Anxieties and American elders: proposals for assessment and treatment' in L. Michelson and L.M. Ascher (eds), *Anxiety and Stress Disorders — Cognitive Behavioural Assessment and Treatment*, London: Guildford Press.

Michelson & Ascher (eds) (1987), *Anxiety and Stress Disorders*.

Twining, C. (1988), *Helping Older People, A Psychological Approach*, New York: John Wiley & Sons.

Wattis, J. & M. Church (1986), *Practical Psychiatry in Old Age*, Kent: Croom Helm.

ALCOHOL ABUSE
Albert, M.S. & M.B. Moss (eds) (1988), *Geriatric Neuropsychology.*

9 LOSS AND BEREAVEMENT
DYING AND DEATH
Bender, M., C. Lloyd & A. Cooper (1990), *The Quality of Dying,*
  Oxon: Winslow Press.
Kastenbaum, R. (1985), 'Dying and death: a life-span approach' in
  J.E. Birren & K.W. Schaie (eds), *Handbook of the Psychology of
  Aging.*

GRIEVING
Coping with Grief, *Helping the Bereaved* (see Voluntary and
  Statutory Services and Benefits).
Help the Aged, *Bereavement*, London.
Help the Aged/Cruse — Bereavement Care, *Bereavement — An
  Advice Leaflet about the Emotional and Practical Aspects of
  Dealing with Bereavement*, London: Help the Aged.
Lund, D.A. (ed.) (1989), *Older Bereaved Spouses*, London:
  Hemisphere Publishing Corporation.
Seale, C. (1990), 'Caring for people who die: the experience of
  family and friends', *Age and Society*, 10, 413–28.

10 YOU AS A CARER
Carers' Association (1992), *Carers Care Around the Clock*, Dublin.
Commission of the European Communities (1993), *Age and
  Attitudes—— Main Results from a Eurobarometer Survey.*
Coward, R.T. & J.W. Dwyer (1990), 'The association of gender,
  sibling network, composition and patterns of parent care by adult,
  adult children', *Research on Ageing*, 12 (2), 158–81.
Department of Health (1993), *Employer and Carers — BAPS*,
  England: Health Publications Unit.
Foy, M. (1993), 'Support available to carers of housebound infirm
  adults', *Milupa Education and Research Review*, 1 (16), 10–15.
Haffendden, S. (1991), *Getting it Right for Carers*, England: Dept of
  Health and Social Services, Inspectorate.
Joni Le Bris, H. (1993), *Family Care of Dependent Older People in
  the European Community*, Ireland: European Foundation for the
  Improvement of Living and Working Conditions.
Moane, G. (1993), 'Dependency and caring needs among the
  elderly', *Irish Journal of Psychology*, 14 (1), 189–203.

Morris, R.G., R.T. Woods, K.S. Davies & L.N. Morris (1991), 'Gender differences in carers of dementia sufferers', *British Journal of Psychiatry*, 158, 69–74.

National Council for the Elderly (1993), *Bearing Fruit, A Manual for Primary Schools*.

National Council for the Aged (1988), *Part I, A Study of Carers at Home and in the Community*, Government Publications Sales Office.

National Council for the Aged (1988), *Part II, The Caring Process: A Study of Carers in the Home*, Government Publications Sales Office.

O'Shea, E. (1993), *The Impact of Social & Economic Policies on Older People in Ireland*.

Ruddle, H. & J. O'Connor (1993), *Caring without Limits? Sufferers of Dementia/Alzheimer's Disease, A Study of Their Carers*, Policy Research Centre and the Alzheimer Society of Ireland.

Soroptimist International (1993), *Carers' Perception of Their Own Needs — Summary of Workshop Reports*, Ireland.

Springer, D. & T.H. Brubaker (1984), *Family Care-givers and Dependent Elderly*, London: Sage Publications.

11 ABUSE OF OLDER PEOPLE

Age Concern, *Abuse of Elderly People: Guidelines for Action*, England: Age Concern.

Brown, P. (1993), 'Elder abuse — fact or fiction?', *Clinical Psychology Forum*, 54, 17–19.

Coyne, A.C., W.E. Reichman & L.J. Berbig (1993), 'The relationship between dementia and elder abuse'.

Douglass, R.L. (1992), *Domestic Mistreatment of the Elderly — Towards Prevention*, American Association of Retired Persons.

Holt, M.G. (1994), 'Sexual abuse of older people: facing the reality', *Clinical Psychology Forum*, 67, May, 28–9.

Ogg, J. & C. Munn-Giddings (1993), 'Researching elder abuse', *Age and Society*, 13, 389–413.

Study Group on Violence against Elderly People (1992), *Violence against Elderly People*, Council of Europe Press.

12 CRIME AND THE FEAR OF CRIME

Breen, R. & D.B. Rottman (1985), *Crime Victimisation in the Republic of Ireland*, Report No. 121, The Economic and Social Research Institute.

Brillon, Y. (1988), *Victimization and Fear of Crime among the Elderly*, University of Montreal: International Centre for Comparative Criminology.

Irish Association for Victim Support, MRBI Poll (1986) carried out on behalf of the IAVS, *Reaction to Crime among the General Public.*

LaGrange, R.L. & K.F. Ferraro (1987), 'The elderly's fear of crime: a clinical examination of the research', *Research on Ageing*, 9 (3), 372–91.

Meade, A. (October 1992), address to 'Women and Safety', conference in Dublin Castle, Irish Association for Victim Support.

Midwinter, E. (1990), *The Old Order — Crime & Older People*, England: Centre for Policy on Ageing.

O'Neill, D., B. O'Shea, R. Lawlor, C. McGee, J.B. Walsh & D. Coakley (1989), 'Effects of burglary on the elderly', *British Medical Journal*, 298, 1618–19.

13 HOSPITAL

Department of Health (1992), *A Charter of Rights for Hospital Patients*, Dublin.

14 STAYING PUT OR MOVING

Bland, R. (1987), *Residential Care — Is It for Me?*, Edinburgh: Age Concern, HMSO.

Ebrahim, S., C. Wallis, S. Brittis, R. Harwood & N. Graham (1993), 'Long-term care for elderly people', *Quality in Health Care*, 2, 198–203.

Fried, S., D. Van Booven & C. Mc Quarrie (1993), *Older Adulthood — Learning Activities for Understanding Aging.*

National Council for the Aged (1989), *Sheltered Housing in Ireland: Its Role and Contribution in the Care of the Elderly*, Government Publications Sales Office.

Walker, A. et al. (1993), *Older People in Europe: Social and Economic Policies.*

Index

Glasnevin Crematorium, 188
glaucoma, 18
grandchildren, 62–3
grieving, 120–26
Grow, 188

Hard of Hearing Association, Irish, 193
Health and Social Security, British Department of, 181
Health Boards, 210–16
    services provided by, 213–16
health services,
    details of, 189
hearing-aids, 15–17
hearing loss, 13–17
heart attack,
    and sex, 34
high blood pressure,
    and sex, 34
Home Care Organisers, National Association of, 197
home help service, 215
Home Improvement Grant for Disabled Persons, 12
homosexuality, 37
hormone replacement therapy, 31, 32
Hospice Foundation, Irish, 193
hospital care programme, 212
hospital, 161–4
housing, 11–12
Housing Advisory and Research Service, National. *see* THRESHOLD
Housing Aid Scheme/Task Force, 216
humour, ageism in, 3–4
hypochondriasis, 106–7
hysterectomy, 36

Ileostomy and Colostomy Association of Southern Ireland, 189
illness. *see also* hospital
    and depression, 98, 100

leading to death, 111–13
incontinence, 74–8
    and dementia, 85
    help for, 77–8
Incorporated Law Society of Ireland, 189
information for carers, 140
intellectual abilities, 49–53
Invalidity Pension, 202
Irish Association for Counselling, 190
Irish Association for Victim Support, 190–91
Irish Association of Care Workers, 190
Irish Association of Chartered Physiotherapists, 190
Irish Association of Funeral Directors, 119, 190
Irish Association of Older People, 66, 190
Irish Association of Speech and Language Therapists, 190
Irish Association of Victim Support, 157
Irish Cancer Association, 112
Irish Cancer Society, 191
Irish Chiropodists' Association, 191
Irish Congress of Trade Unions, 51–2, 69, 70
Irish Countrywomen's Association (ICA), 66, 191
Irish Deaf Society, 191–2
Irish Diabetic Association, 192
Irish Epilepsy Association, 192
Irish Family Planning Association, 192
Irish Federation of Women's Clubs, 192–3
Irish Hard of Hearing Association, 193
Irish Hospice Foundation, 193
Irish Kidney Association, 193
Irish Motor Neurone Disease Association, 193
Irish Red Cross Society, 193